REAL KSAS -- KNOWLEDGE, SKILLS & ABILITIES -- FOR GOVERNMENT JOBS

...improve your chances of gaining federal employment by preparing top-notch KSAs

Anne McKinney, Editor

PREP PUBLISHING

FAYETTEVILLE, NC

PREP Publishing
1110 1/2 Hay Street
Fayetteville, NC 28305
(910) 483-6611

Library of Congress Cataloging-in-Publication Data

McKinney, Anne, 1948-
    Real KSAs : knowledge, skills & abilities for government jobs / Anne McKinney.
        p. cm. -- (Government job series)
    "Improve your chances of gaining federal employment by preparing top-notch KSAs."
    ISBN 1-885288-34-4
    1. Civil service positions--United States. 2. Applications for positions--United States.
    I. Title. II. Series.

    JK716.M35 2003
    352.6'3'02373--dc21   2003040541

Printed in the United States of America

By PREP Publishing

Business and Career Series:

RESUMES AND COVER LETTERS THAT HAVE WORKED

RESUMES AND COVER LETTERS THAT HAVE WORKED FOR MILITARY PROFESSIONALS

GOVERNMENT JOB APPLICATIONS AND FEDERAL RESUMES

COVER LETTERS THAT BLOW DOORS OPEN

LETTERS FOR SPECIAL SITUATIONS

RESUMES AND COVER LETTERS FOR MANAGERS

REAL-RESUMES FOR COMPUTER JOBS

REAL-RESUMES FOR MEDICAL JOBS

REAL-RESUMES FOR FINANCIAL JOBS

REAL-RESUMES FOR TEACHERS

REAL-RESUMES FOR STUDENTS

REAL-RESUMES FOR CAREER CHANGERS

REAL-RESUMES FOR SALES

REAL ESSAYS FOR COLLEGE & GRADUATE SCHOOL

REAL-RESUMES FOR AVIATION & TRAVEL JOBS

REAL-RESUMES FOR POLICE, LAW ENFORCEMENT & SECURITY JOBS

REAL-RESUMES FOR SOCIAL WORK & COUNSELING JOBS

REAL-RESUMES FOR CONSTRUCTION JOBS

REAL-RESUMES FOR MANUFACTURING JOBS

REAL-RESUMES FOR RESTAURANT, FOOD SERVICE & HOTEL JOBS

REAL-RESUMES FOR MEDIA, NEWSPAPER, BROADCASTING & PUBLIC AFFAIRS JOBS

REAL-RESUMES FOR RETAILING, MODELING, FASHION & BEAUTY JOBS

REAL-RESUMES FOR HUMAN RESOURCES & PERSONNEL JOBS

REAL-RESUMES FOR NURSING JOBS

REAL-RESUMES FOR AUTO INDUSTRY JOBS

REAL RESUMIX AND OTHER RESUMES FOR FEDERAL GOVERNMENT JOBS

REAL KSAS--KNOWLEDGE, SKILLS & ABILITIES--FOR GOVERNMENT JOBS

REAL BUSINESS PLANS AND MARKETING TOOLS

Judeo-Christian Ethics Series:

SECOND TIME AROUND

BACK IN TIME

WHAT THE BIBLE SAYS ABOUT...Words that can lead to success and happiness

A GENTLE BREEZE FROM GOSSAMER WINGS

BIBLE STORIES FROM THE OLD TESTAMENT

CONTENTS

REAL KSAS -- KNOWLEDGE, SKILLS & ABILITIES -- FOR GOVERNMENT JOBS

...improve your chances of gaining federal employment by preparing top-notch KSAs

Anne McKinney, Editor

Introduction To This Book

For many people, finding meaningful work and satisfying jobs is a key to overall satisfaction in life. Some people find satisfying work in the private sector. Others seek job satisfaction in non-profit organizations. Still others seek employment in federal, state, or local government. The purpose of this book is to provide a "competitive edge" to those individuals who seek to apply for jobs in the federal government, including the U.S. Postal Service.

Knowledge, Skills & Abilities (KSAs)

The theory behind this book is that **your best teacher is an excellent example**, and this book aims to provide you with dozens of clear and readable examples of the "KSAs" often needed to apply for government jobs. The samples you will see in this book are modeled on real documents used by real people to enter government service or gain promotion to a higher level. You are often asked to submit "supplementary narratives" in addition to the 171, 612, or Federal Resume describing your Knowledge, Skills, or Abilities (referred to as KSAs) in certain areas. This book is intended to help you prepare those important KSAs, and you will see outstanding examples of KSAs written to illustrate specific and required areas of knowledge, skills, or abilities.

If you follow the examples and advice in this book, you will maximize your chances of getting a federal government job.

Filling out your application for government positions

The way in which you fill out an application for a government job determines the "rating" you receive. On the application you turn in, you literally get a numerical rating up to 110% (scores above 100% can occur when, for example, a veteran of military service receives a 5% preference or a disabled veteran receives a 10% preference), so the better and more thorough your application, the higher your "score" will be. Your goal in submitting paperwork for a government job should be to receive the maximum rating or score you can get. The way to maximize your rating, which determines your eligibility or suitability for the job, is to submit applications which are well written, comprehensive, and persuasive.

The first step in applying for a government job is to locate Position Vacancy Announcements or Bulletins which provide the information pertaining to jobs the government is trying to fill. You can obtain these Position Vacancy Announcements from your local Civilian Personnel Office (CPO) or download them from the World Wide Web. Higher-level positions may be posted on the website OPM.gov and other websites are being created as this book is being created. Usually a Position Vacancy Announcement is about four or more pages long and tells you everything you need to know in order to apply for a specific job. Position Vacancy Announcements or Bulletins will tell you what kind of application to submit, what documents must accompany your application, and the date by which your application must be received or postmarked. A lengthy description of the job itself is provided on the Position Vacancy Announcement.

Finding Position Vacancy Announcements is often the hard part of federal employment, even to those already "in the system." If you are seeking your first position in federal government, your Job Opportunities Center is probably the best place to begin in your search for Position Vacancy Announcements. Most Position Vacancy Announcements announce that you should apply for a federal government job by submitting one of three documents: a Federal Form 171, the Optional Form 612, or a Federal Resume. This book provides outstanding examples of all three types of applications.

By now, you are probably realizing that applying for a federal government position requires some patience and persistence in order to complete rather tedious forms and get them in on time. Just when you thought you thought you thought you had achieved a satisfactory level of knowledge about the SF 171, OF 612, and Federal Resume, we need to make you aware of this sobering reality. The SF 171, OF 612, or Federal Resume may not be all you need to submit in order to apply for the federal position which interests you!

Many Position Vacancy Announcements or job bulletins for a specific job also tell you that, in order to be considered for the job you want, you must also demonstrate certain knowledge, skills, or abilities. In other words, you need to also submit written narrative statements, much like the Continuation Sheets you prepared for the SF 171 and OF 612, which microscopically focus on your particular knowledge, skill, or ability in a certain area. The next 130 pages are filled with examples of excellent KSAs (Knowledge, Skills, and Abilities) written to accompany a Federal Resume, SF 171, or OF 612.

Although you will be able to use the SF 171 or OF 612 or Federal Resume you prepare in order to apply for all sorts of jobs in the federal government, the KSAs you write are particular to a specific job and you may be able to use the KSAs you write only one time. If you get into the Civil Service system, however, you will discover that many KSAs tend to appear on lots of different job announcement bulletins. For example, "Ability to communicate orally and in writing" is a frequently requested KSA. This means that you would be able to use and re-use this KSA for any job bulletin which requests you to give evidence of your ability in this area.

> KSAs are supplementary statements which are required when applying for some jobs.

What does "Screen Out" mean? If you see that a KSA is requested and the words "Screen out" are mentioned beside the KSA, this means that this KSA is of vital importance in "getting you in the door." If the individuals who review your application feel that your screen-out KSA does not establish your strengths in this area, you will not be considered as a candidate for the job. You need to make sure that any screen-out KSA is especially well-written and comprehensive.

How long can a KSA be? A job vacancy announcement bulletin usually does not specify a length for a KSA, but each of your KSAs should probably be 1-2 pages long. Remember that the purpose of their requiring this KSA is to microscopically examine your level of competence in a particular area, so you need to be extremely detailed and comprehensive. Give examples and details wherever possible. Your written communication skills might appear more credible if you provide the details of the kinds of reports and paperwork you prepared. For example, an Accounting Technician might mention her work on STANFINS reports instead of just talking about financial reports.

In the pages which follow, you will see examples of KSAs used to apply for all kinds of jobs at all levels of federal service, ranging from entry-level Wage Grade (WG) positions such as Maintenance Technician, and entry-level General Schedule (GS) positions such as Clerk, to high-level Computer Scientist positions at the GS 14 and 15 level.

KSAs are extremely important in "getting you in the door" for a federal government job. If you are working under a tight deadline in preparing your paperwork for a federal government position, don't spend all your time preparing the SF 171, OF 612, or Federal Resume if you also have KSAs to do. Create "blockbuster" KSAs as well!

AIR OPERATIONS SUPERINTENDENT

JANICE DEANENE BRADY

SSN: 000-00-0000

AIR OPERATIONS SUPERINTENDENT, GS-11 ANNOUNCEMENT #XYZ123

KSA #1: Knowledge of all aspects of worldwide sensitive air support and employment mission requirements, including fixed wing, ground refueling, air refueling, navigation, and offensive/defensive employment operations.

I was recalled back to my current position due to several terrorist attacks within the U.S. and abroad. My country needed my expert knowledge of all aspects of worldwide sensitive air support and employment mission requirements. In my current position as an **AIR OPERATIONS SUPERINTENDENT, OPERATIONS CENTER,** I received a Joint Service Meritorious Medal for providing distinguished support for a classified, sensitive mission. I lead a section tasked as the U.S. Policy Administrators (USPA) focal point for all operational command and control (A6) issues impacting "must succeed" special access program missions supporting DOD's most elite forces. Lead teams implementing A6 policies and procedures to insert and extract clandestine forces and remove weapons of mass destruction from denied areas across the globe. Optimizes performance of four controllers to meet the demands of highly modified A6 procedures through classified training programs.

- Was evaluated in writing as a "Administration Ambassador!" Was praised in writing for "brilliantly revising group Status of Resources and Training Systems (SORTS) reporting procedures" and for "enterprisingly designing a communication-out recall system to ensure 98% verbal and physical contact with all assigned unit personnel."
- Was praised on a formal performance evaluation for "outstanding leadership" and was praised for saving a member from suicide through my "flawless deployment of a crisis response team."
- Single-handedly developed backup communication procedures for airborne assets, thereby ensuring 85 connectivity.
- Procured Over the Air Rekeying equipment from AFSOC to provide all airborne assets with COMSEC material in the event of emergency supersession. Designed procedures for subordinate unit to use Operation Center's alert crew data base.
- Increased aircrew combat readiness after researching, coordinating, and publishing procedures to test the readiness and response capability of the alert aircrews of three different classified aircraft.

Extensive experience in the following communication systems:
- Special Air Mission Andromedia System
- Global Decision Support System (GDSS)
- Command and Control Information Processing System (A6IPS)
- Secure Satellite Communication Radio (SATCOM)
- Ultra High Frequency Radio (UHF)/ Very High Frequency Radio (VHF)
- Defense Message System (DMS)
- Secure Telephone Unit III (STU-III)

In my previous job as **NCOIC, OPERATIONS CENTER,** I assisted in the development, coordination, and implementation of command and control (A6) policies and procedures for a selectively manned, classified organization performing U.S. Policy Administrators (USPA) tasked combat missions.

- Once saved an already-airborne asset threatened by an air refueling tanker ground alert by rapidly coordinating a divert location.

As **NCOIC, REPORTS BRANCH,** Sep 1996-Sep 2000, I maintained certification as a Special Air Mission (SAM) controller while developing and presenting training on SORTS requirements for 11 reporting commanders, their deputies, and 28 unit monitors. Provided leadership during an aircraft nose landing gear malfunction which led to the successful landing of the aircraft. Was recognized in writing for "superbly coordinating the launching of the entire SAM fleet" for a Memorial Day Tribute which involved the movement of 103 senators, congressmen, Joint Chiefs of Staff, and Air Force One and also orchestrated the launching of all SAM aircrafts.

As **NCOIC, QUALITY,** from June 1994-Sep 1996, I designed, implemented and managed the Quality Air Force (QAF) Program within the Objective Wing Command Post, and ensured that 40 people were properly trained and utilizing QAF principles. Facilitated evaluation processes and recommend improved courses of action. Assisted in the development of checklists and procedures for controlling and flight following all DOD fixed wing aircraft operations.

As **SPECIAL AIR MISSIONS CONTROLLER,** Apr 1992-June 1994, I provided direct command and control and worldwide flight following for Special Air Missions (SAM) aircraft carrying the President, Vice President, Cabinet members, members of Congress, and foreign heads of state. Coordinated several humanitarian relief missions.

As **COMMAND POST CONTROLLER,** Aug 1990-Apr 1992, I coordinated Presidential and Vice Presidential support missions as well as aeromedical evacuation channel missions.

As **EMERGENCY ACTIONS CONTROLLER,** Dec 1989-Aug 1990, I acted in an executive capacity for the wing commander in execution of emergency war orders (EWO) and plans for both US and NATO alliance combat forces. A formal performance evaluation said that my "error free actions and multi-position qualifications" were major reasons for being selected as Actions Controller of the Quarter. Performed emergency actions training for over 85 users located in 12 basewide work centers.

EDUCATION and TRAINING RELATED TO THIS KSA
Associate of Science degree in Applied Science in Information Systems Technology, Illinois Central College, East Peoria, IL, June 2001.
Senior Noncommissioned Officer, by correspondence, September 2001.
Air Force Trainer Course, 1999.
DOD Hostage Survival Training, January 1999.
DOD Information Security Orientation Course, October 1998.
Noncommissioned Officer Academy, 4 weeks, May 1998.
Introduction to Special Operations; Dynamics of International Terrorism May 1998.
Status of Resources and Training Systems Data Handlers Course, October 1992.
Noncommissioned Officer Leadership School, 6 weeks, February 1992.
Supervisor Development Course, March 1990.
Noncommissioned Officer Orientation Course August 1989.

AIR OPERATIONS SUPERINTENDENT

JANICE DEANENE BRADY

SSN: 000-00-0000

AIR OPERATIONS SUPERINTENDENT, GS-11 ANNOUNCEMENT #XYZ123

KSA #2: Knowledge of developing, implementing, and employing ground and airborne communication systems while conducting training and real world missions.

In my current position (March 2003-present) as **AIR OPERATIONS SUPERINTENDENT, OPERATIONS CENTER,** I lead a section tasked as U.S. Policy Administrators (USPA) focal point for all operational command and control (A6) issues impacting "must succeed" special access program missions supporting DOD's most elite forces.

- I was described in writing as "innovative" after designing a A6 process preventing aircraft interception by drug enforcement which was hailed as a "safety milestone."
- Single-handedly developed backup communication procedures for airborne assets, thereby ensuring 85 connectivity. Procured Over the Air Rekeying equipment from AFSOC to provide all airborne assets with COMSEC material in the event of emergency supersession. Designed procedures for subordinate unit to use Ops Center's alert crew data base.
- Was cited as a "key leader in major aircraft accident exercise" and a formal performance evaluation said that my security procedures protected sensitive mission details. Have expertly managed the operations center during multiple major exercises as well as numerous real world operations. During exercises and operations, managed crew alert posture and coordinated air refueling, air traffic control, deception, and ground support. On one occasion, increased aircrew combat readiness after researching, coordinating, and publishing procedures to test the readiness and response capability of the alert aircrews of three different classified aircraft.

Extensive experience in the following communication systems:
- Special Air Mission Andromedia System
- Global Decision Support System (GDSS)
- Command and Control Information Processing System (A6IPS)
- Secure Satellite Communication Radio (SATCOM)
- Ultra High Frequency Radio (UHF)/ Very High Frequency Radio (VHF)
- Defense Message System (DMS)
- Secure Telephone Unit III (STU-III)

In a previous position as **NCOIC, OPERATIONS CENTER,** I assisted in the development, coordination, and implementation of command and control (A6) policies and procedures for a selectively manned, classified organization performing U.S. Policy Administrators (USPA) tasked combat missions.

- Once saved an already-airborne asset threatened by an air refueling tanker ground alert during a critical mission.

From Sep 1996-Sep 2000, as **NCOIC, REPORTS BRANCH,** I maintained certification as a Special Air Mission (SAM) controller while developing and presenting training on SORTS requirements for 11 reporting commanders, their deputies, and 28 unit monitors. Provided clear, concise monthly briefings to the Wing Commander and senior wing leaders on all aspects of the SORTS program.

- Provided leadership during an aircraft nose landing gear malfunction which led to the successful landing of the aircraft. Was recognized in writing for "superbly coordinating the launching of the entire SAM fleet" for a Memorial Day Tribute which involved the movement of 103 senators, congressmen, Joint Chiefs of Staff, and Air Force One and orchestrated the launching of all SAM aircrafts.

As **NCOIC, QUALITY,** Jun 1994-Sep 1996, I designed, implemented and managed Quality Air Force (QAF) Program within the Objective Wing Command Post, and ensured that 40 people were properly trained and utilizing QAF principles. Facilitated evaluation processes and recommend improved courses of action. Designed new AMC airlift movement boards for daily and contingency use in primary and alternate command post. Assisted in development of checklists and procedures for controlling and flight following DOD fixed wing aircraft operations.

In a previous position as **SPECIAL AIR MISSIONS CONTROLLER,** Apr 1992-Jun 1994, I provided direct command and control and worldwide flight following for Special Air Missions (SAM) aircraft carrying the President, Vice President, Cabinet members, members of Congress, and foreign heads of state. Coordinated several humanitarian relief missions into Texas and Mexico in the aftermath of hurricane and tornado disasters. On numerous occasions, tracked and recovered lost aircraft parts.

From Aug 1990-Apr 1992, as a **COMMAND POST CONTROLLER,** coordinated several Presidential and Vice Presidential support missions and aeromedical evacuation channel missions.

As an **EMERGENCY ACTIONS CONTROLLER,** Dec 1989-Aug 1990, I acted in an executive capacity for the wing commander in execution of emergency war orders (EWO) and plans for both US and NATO alliance combat forces. A formal performance evaluation said that my "error free actions and multi-position qualifications" were major reasons for being selected as Air Controller of the Quarter. Performed emergency actions training for over 85 users located in 12 basewide work centers.

EDUCATION and TRAINING RELATED TO THIS KSA
Associate of Science degree in Applied Science in Information Systems Technology, Illinois Central College, East Peoria, IL, June 2001.
Senior Noncommissioned Officer, by correspondence, September 2001.
Air Force Trainer Course, 1999.
DOD Hostage Survival Training, January 1999.
DOD Information Security Orientation Course, October 1998.
Noncommissioned Officer Academy, 4 weeks, May 1998.
Introduction to Special Operations; Dynamics of International Terrorism, May 1998.
Status of Resources and Training Systems Data Handlers Course, October 1992.
Noncommissioned Officer Leadership School, 6 weeks, February 1992.
Supervisor Development Course, March 1990.
Noncommissioned Officer Orientation Course, August 1989.

AUDITOR

JODIE BLANKENSHIP
SSN: 000-00-0000
AUDITOR, GS-07 (TRAINEE GS-11) ANNOUNCEMENT #XYZ123

Auditor, GS-07 (Trainee GS-11) Announcement #XYZ123 KSA #1

KSA #1: Ability to conduct research, interpret results, and evaluate data.

My outstanding research and analytical skills were the key to my being offered my current position as a Medical Clerk with Reagan Army Medical Center (2002-present.) As an Intern with the Ambulatory Surgical Unit at Reagan Army Medical Center prior to accepting my current position, I applied my knowledge of audit techniques and analytical skills by developing a system for tracking nurse and staff time as well as patient flow, and I also developed a scheduling system for operating room and same-day-surgery patients. In addition, I also tracked the hours of nurses and other staff members in the Ambulatory Surgical Unit. In my current job, I am involved in numerous duties related to the internal review and audit compliance function with respect to the operations of this large medical facility. Because this facility must be accredited by the National Joint Hospital Accreditation Review Agency, I must perform a variety of audit assignments of low to medium complexity which require me to utilize conventional and advanced auditing techniques in gathering and evaluating pertinent data in order to assure that medical records and other operational areas are in conformance with the strict guidelines and policies of the reviewing authorities. In this job, I have applied my excellent accounting knowledge within a health care organization, and I have greatly refined my ability to conduct research, interpret results, and evaluate data based on computer generated records and database operations.

Notice this KSA seeks information about your ability. You may respond to such a KSA even if you don't have actual experience.

In my previous job as Accounting Technician with the Department of the Army (1999-02), my job required a basic knowledge of accounting terminology and codes necessary to process various transactions in an automated system as well as the ability to reconcile machine records generated by an automated system with hard copies of the source documents and an ability to detect and correct coding input errors. I continuously utilized my knowledge and understanding of accounting procedures involved in maintaining subsidiary ledgers in a general fund accounting system for administrative activities, and I was respected for my knowledge of the format, content, and use of various accounting documents such as obligations, invoices, and disbursements. I demonstrated my ability to conduct research, interpret results, and evaluate data while involved in a variety of accounting, auditing, and reconciliation activities. For example, I performed reconciliation and correction of errors on the following STANFINS reports:
- General Fund Analysis Exception Listing
- Activity Detail Cost Report
- Daily Preliminary Balance Report
- Non-Stock Fund Orders and Payable Report
- the Interfund portion on the "DELMAR" (Part I and II)
- the Aged Unclear Listing
- Interfund and GSA Edit and Balance Listing
- monthly Interfund Excepted Report
- the monthly Error Report

I maintained, reconciled, and adjusted one or more report files such as Outstanding Travel Allowances, TFO Voucher Suspense List, Daily TBO Balance List, Schedule, programming, preparation, and controls. I reviewed and organized various documents, including obligation and accrual transactions, to ensure accuracy of computations and completeness of data, validity of accounting classification, and determination of transaction necessary for the proper mechanical process. I determined if the obligation and/or accrual entries were required to properly update the accounts payable ledger or if only a disbursements transaction was required to properly update the disbursement ledger and liquidate the outstanding liability. While utilizing my analytical skills and ability to interpret results and analyze data, I verified accuracy of computer output for reporting data to command activities and higher headquarters. This included reconciling computer output with copy of input data, tracing errors, and making necessary adjustments.

On my own initiative, I have completed computer operations and database training:
- The Lotus Approach, DTCC, training period from 07/10/00 to 07/21/00: This was a continuing education class for somewhat experienced computer users who wanted to learn more about the Lotus Approach. Learned the concepts of a database and how to assess the need for a database in my working environment. Learned how to design and maintain a relational database, how to create and print reports from a database, and how to convert other types of databases into the Approach format.
- PC Classes for Windows, DTCC, training period from 08/25/00 to 09/13/00: Learned the capabilities of and how to properly use the standard software package used by RAMC in a networked environment. That package includes Windows 3.11, Harvard Graphics 3.0, Lotus 1-2-3, r5, Lotus Approach 3.01, cc:Mail 2.1, Lotus Organizer 1.0, and WordPerfect 6.0a networked by Novell NetWare 4.1.

Be very detailed about any education or training which is relevant.

Training and Education Related to this KSA:
I hold a Bachelor of Science in Business Administration from Baptist College which I received in 2000. I had completed this degree at nights and on weekends while excelling in my full-time job. With a concentration in Health Care Administration, my course work related to this KSA included:
- Principles of Accounting I
- Cost Accounting I
- Statistics for Business/Economics
- Principles of Microeconomics
- Money and Banking
- Computer Business Applications

I also hold an Associate of Applied Science in Banking and Finance which I earned from Dickinson Technical Community College in 1997. Highlights of my course work in this degree program related to this KSA were:
- Business Math and Business Math Applications
- Business Law I and II
- Principles of Banking Operations
- Money and Banking
- Analysis of Financial Systems
- Management Accounting

AUDITOR

JODIE BLANKENSHIP

SSN: 000-00-0000

AUDITOR, GS-07 (TRAINEE GS-11) ANNOUNCEMENT #XYZ123

Auditor, GS-07 (Trainee GS-11) Announcement #XYZ123 KSA #2

KSA #2: Ability to use a wide range of audit techniques, to include interviews, automation databases, questionnaires, and statistical analysis practices.

In my current job as Medical Clerk with Reagan Army Medical Center (2002-present), part of my job is to computerize the 24-hour-a-day utilization reports of nurse and staff requirements daily while scheduling surgical appointments for 35 physicians. I have received two awards for excellence in work performance which were based in large part on my outstanding performance in utilizing audit techniques including interviews, automation databases, and statistical analysis practices to improve daily operations. As an Intern with the Ambulatory Surgical Unit at Reagan Army Medical Center prior to accepting my current position, I applied my knowledge of audit techniques and analytical skills by developing a system for tracking nurse and staff time as well as patient flow, and I also developed a scheduling system for operating room and same-day-surgery patients. In addition, I also tracked the hours of nurses and other staff members in the Ambulatory Surgical Unit. While in my current job, I have pursued extensive continuing education related to automation databases including a course at DTCC entitled the Lotus Approach which refined my ability to create databases and trained me to convert other types of databases into the Approach format. I am entrusted with vast responsibility related to maintaining medical paperwork in top-notch condition for purposes of compliance with the policies and procedures of a wide range of regulatory bodies including the National Joint Hospital Accreditation Review Agency. I must perform a variety of audit assignments of low to medium complexity which require me to utilize conventional and advanced auditing techniques in gathering and evaluating pertinent data in order to assure that medical records and other operational areas are in conformance with the strict guidelines and policies of the reviewing authorities. I routinely utilize interviews, questionnaires, and statistical analysis methods in order to assure the perfect accuracy and accountability of medical records for which I am responsible related to matters which include patient care, pharmaceutical control, and other areas.

In my previous job as Accounting Technician with the Department of the Army (1999-02), I became skilled in utilizing a wide range of audit techniques including interviews, automation databases, questionnaires, and statistical analysis practices. Part of my job involved using my knowledge of accounting terminology and codes necessary to process various transactions in an automated system as well as the ability to reconcile machine records generated by an automated system with hard copies of the source documents and an ability to detect and correct coding input errors. I continuously utilized my knowledge and understanding of accounting procedures involved in maintaining subsidiary ledgers in a general fund accounting system for administrative activities, and I was respected for my knowledge of the format, content, and use of various accounting documents such as obligations, invoices, and disbursements. I demonstrated my ability to conduct research, interpret results, and evaluate data while involved in a variety of accounting, auditing, and reconciliation activities. For example, I performed reconciliation and correction of errors on the following STANFINS reports:

Often a KSA begins with your current job and proceeds job-by-job through your career demonstrating your ability.

- General Fund Analysis Exception Listing
- Activity Detail Cost Report
- Daily Preliminary Balance Report
- Non-Stock Fund Orders and Payable Report
- the Interfund portion on the "DELMAR" (Part I and II)
- the Aged Unclear Listing
- Interfund and GSA Edit and Balance Listing
- monthly Interfund Excepted Report
- the monthly Error Report

I maintained, reconciled, and adjusted one or more report files such as Outstanding Travel Allowances, TFO Voucher Suspense List, Daily TBO Balance List, Schedule, programming, preparation, and controls. I reviewed and organized various documents, including obligation and accrual transactions, to ensure completeness of data, validity of accounting classification, and determination of transaction necessary for the proper mechanical process. I determined if the obligation and/or accrual entries were required to properly update the accounts payable ledger or if only disbursements transaction was required to properly update the disbursement ledger and liquidate the outstanding liability.

Remember you are "selling" your experience as well as your potential.

Training and Education Related to this KSA:
I hold a Bachelor of Science in Business Administration from Baptist College which I received in 2000. I had completed this degree at nights and on weekends while excelling in my full-time job. My course work related to this KSA included:

Principles of Accounting I	Cost Accounting I
Statistics for Business/Economics	Principles of Microeconomics
Money and Banking	Computer Business Applications

I also hold an Associate of Applied Science in Banking and Finance. Highlights of my course work in this degree program related to this KSA were:

Business Math and Business Math Applications	Business Law I and II
Principles of Banking Operations	Money and Banking
Analysis of Financial Systems	Management Accounting

Training programs which I have also completed include these:
- The Lotus Approach, DTCC, from 07/10/00 to 07/21/00: the Approach format.
- PC Classes for Windows, DTCC, training period from 06/23/99 to 07/11/99: Learned the capabilities of and how to properly use the standard software package used by RAMC in a networked environment. That package includes Windows 3.11, Harvard Graphics 3.0, Lotus 1-2-3, r5, Lotus Approach 3.01, cc:Mail 2.1, Lotus Organizer 1.0, and WordPerfect 6.0a networked by Novell NetWare 4.1.

AUTOMOTIVE WORKER

GEORGE ROBERT ADAMS

SSN: 000-00-0000

AUTOMOTIVE WORKER, WG-08/10 ANNOUNCEMENT #XYZ123

**Automotive Worker,
WG-08/10
Announcement #XYZ123
KSA #1**

KSA #1: Ability to perform the duties of an automotive worker without more than normal supervision.

Overview of knowledge in this KSA:

Over a period of 22 years in assignments with the U.S. Army, I have held responsible positions relating directly to automotive maintenance activities. I am thoroughly familiar with company-level maintenance on diesel powered vehicles and throughout my military career used a hands-on approach during troubleshooting and parts replacement actions.

Experience related to this KSA:

From 1998-03, I was assigned as a Manager and Supervisor for the 7th Medical Group at Ft. Myer, VA, where I made the decisions based on my own judgment of what parts needed to be replaced and prioritized automotive work on three major types of diesel vehicles: the HMMMWV, 2 1/2-ton, and 5-ton trucks as well as occasionally working on forklifts. My knowledge of automotive work resulted in my selection as the person entrusted with several hundred thousand dollars worth of vehicles and equipment while transporting this equipment over a distance of several thousand miles in both military and civilian-leased vehicles.

This KSA asks for evidence that someone can work with minimal supervision.

From 1992-98, as an Instructor in a military training school at Ft. Leonard Wood, MO, I applied my knowledge of automotive work while teaching classes of up to 60 students and ensuring students were properly trained in the maintenance of transportation vehicles and equipment.

From 1988-92, I was a Maintenance Technician and Supervisor. In my first assignments in Germany I was a Maintenance Technician and learned to work independently while replacing parts in military diesel powered vehicles. My next assignment was at Ft. Bragg, NC, where I was soon selected to be a Maintenance Supervisor and became skilled in overseeing automotive workers while still continuing to gain hands-on experience. Additional experience in Korea gave me the opportunity to make decisions and do automotive work on diesel vehicles with no supervision.

Education and training related to this KSA:

Courses which helped me acquire or refine my knowledge of automotive work include the following:

- diploma — light wheel vehicle/power generator mechanic basic technical course
- training the instructor
- basic oxygen and acetylene welding
- mechanic supervision
- technical publications and logistics
- recovery vehicle operations
- operator and organizational maintenance
- automatic transmissions

KSA #2: Knowledge of automotive components and assemblies to include use of tools and test equipment.

Overview of knowledge in this KSA:

Over a period of 22 years in assignments with the U.S. Army, I have held responsible positions relating directly to automotive maintenance activities in which I have become thoroughly familiar with company-level maintenance on diesel powered vehicles. Throughout my military career I used a hands-on approach while troubleshooting and making determinations on which parts to replace while using basic tools including wrenches and screwdrivers and my own knowledge.

Experience related to this KSA:

From 1998-03, I was assigned as a Manager and Supervisor for the 7th Medical Group at Ft. Myer, VA, where I have used my knowledge of diesel powered vehicles along with the proper tools and equipment for each stage of the repair process. Through my many years of experience I am highly skilled in using my judgment to determine what parts needed to be replaced and prioritized automotive work on three major types of diesel vehicles: the HMMMWV, 2 1/2-ton, and 5-ton trucks as well as occasionally working on forklifts.

From 1992-98, as an Instructor in a military training school at Ft. Leonard Wood, MO, I applied my knowledge of automotive components, assemblies, and equipment while teaching classes of up to 60 students and ensuring students were properly trained in the maintenance of transportation vehicles and equipment.

From 1988-92, I was a Maintenance Technician and Supervisor. In my first assignments in Germany I was a Maintenance Technician and learned to work independently while replacing parts in military diesel powered vehicles. My next assignment was at Ft. Bragg, NC, where I was soon selected to be a Maintenance Supervisor and became skilled in overseeing automotive workers while still continuing to gain hands-on experience. Additional experience in Korea gave me the opportunity to make decisions and do automotive work on diesel vehicles with no supervision.

Education and training related to this KSA:

Courses which helped me acquire or refine my knowledge of automotive components, tools, and test equipment include the following:

    diploma — light wheel vehicle/power generation mechanic basic technical course
    training the instructor
    basic oxygen and acetylene welding
    mechanic supervision
    technical publications and logistics
    recovery vehicle operations
    operator and organizational maintenance
    automatic transmissions

Automotive Worker, WG-08/10 Announcement #XYZ123 KSA #2

An "overview" of your knowledge may be a useful way to highlight an extensive background.

AUTOMOTIVE WORKER

GEORGE ROBERT ADAMS

SSN: 000-00-0000

AUTOMOTIVE WORKER, WG-08/10 ANNOUNCEMENT #XYZ123

KSA #3: Ability to interpret instructions, specifications, reference manuals, and other regulatory guidance.

Overview of knowledge in this KSA:

During my 22 years with the U.S. Army, I have held responsible positions relating directly to automotive maintenance activities where the ability to use and understand parts manuals and other reference materials is an important factor while troubleshooting and repairing diesel powered vehicles.

Experience related to this KSA:

From 1998-03, as a Manager and Supervisor for the 7th Medical Group at Ft. Myer, VA, where I routinely used parts manuals and reference material while checking on the proper replacement parts to be used after making determinations on how to repair vehicles. In this unit I oversaw mechanics working on three major types of diesel vehicles: the HMMMWV, 2 1/2-ton, and 5-ton trucks as well as occasionally working on forklifts. As the military makes changes in its inventory of vehicles I have been required to keep up with the latest changes and aware of where to find the most up-to-date information. The varied types of technical publications I have had to interpret applied to such areas as inspections, troubleshooting, maintenance, repairs, modifications, calibration, and testing of vehicular equipment.

Being detailed is important in this KSA.

From 1992-98, as an Instructor in a military training school at Ft. Leonard Wood, MO, I applied my knowledge of automotive work while teaching classes of up to 60 students and ensuring students were properly trained in the maintenance of transportation vehicles and equipment.

From 1988-92, I was a Maintenance Technician and Supervisor. In my first assignments in Germany I was a Maintenance Technician and became familiar with using parts manuals and other technical reference material as I was learning to do parts replacements on military vehicles. My next assignment was at Ft. Bragg, NC, where I was soon selected to be a Maintenance Supervisor and became skilled in overseeing automotive workers while still continuing to gain hands-on experience. Additional experience in Korea gave me the opportunity to make decisions and do automotive work on diesel vehicles while constantly being aware of keeping informed of changes to the military's inventory of vehicles.

Education and training related to this KSA:

Courses which helped me acquire or refine my knowledge of how to interpret instructions, specifications, reference manuals and other regulatory guidance included the following:

    diploma — light wheel vehicle/power generation mechanic basic technical course
    mechanic supervision
    technical publications and logistics
    operator and organizational maintenance

GEORGE ROBERT ADAMS

SSN: 000-00-0000

AUTOMOTIVE WORKER, WG-08/10 ANNOUNCEMENT #XYZ123

KSA #4: Ability to troubleshoot.

Overview of knowledge in this KSA:

Over a period of 22 years in assignments with the U.S. Army, I have held responsible positions relating directly to automotive maintenance activities where the ability to troubleshoot was a major element of my responsibilities. I am thoroughly familiar with company-level maintenance on diesel powered vehicles and throughout my military career used a hands-on approach during troubleshooting and parts replacement actions.

Experience related to this KSA:

From 1998-03, as a Manager and Supervisor for the 7th Medical Group at Ft. Myer, VA, I was the person in charge of making decisions and carrying out troubleshooting activities in order to diagnose problems and decide what parts needed to be replaced and prioritized automotive work on three major types of diesel vehicles: the HMMMWV, 2 1/2-ton, and 5-ton trucks as well as occasionally working on forklifts.

From 1992-98, as an Instructor in a military training school at Ft. Leonard Wood, MO, I applied my knowledge of automotive work while teaching classes of up to 60 students and ensuring students were properly trained in the maintenance of transportation vehicles and equipment. One of the most important aspects of this training was to teach the students the basics of the mechanics of the vehicles they would be working on so that they could troubleshoot problems on their.

From 1988-92, I was a Maintenance Technician and Supervisor. In my first assignments in Germany I was a Maintenance Technician and learned to work independently while replacing parts in military diesel powered vehicles. This was the time period when I refined my troubleshooting skills so that in my next assignment at Ft. Bragg, NC, where I was soon selected to be a Maintenance Supervisor. In supervisory positions I still made it a point to maintain my hands-on experience. Additional experience in Korea gave me the opportunity to make decisions and do automotive work on diesel vehicles with no supervision.

Education and training related to this KSA:

Courses which helped me acquire or refine my knowledge of automotive work and become skilled in troubleshooting include the following:

> diploma — light wheel vehicle/power generator mechanic basic technical course
> training the instructor
> basic oxygen and acetylene welding
> mechanic supervision
> technical publications and logistics
> operator and organizational maintenance
> automatic transmissions

Automotive Worker, WG-08/10 Announcement #XYZ123 KSA #4

Don't let a vague KSA throw you; provide details.

BUDGET ANALYST

PATRICIA E. HAMMOND

SSN: 000-00-0000

BUDGET ANALYST, GS-08 ANNOUNCEMENT #XYZ123

KSA #1: Knowledge of budget programming, preparation, and controls.

In my current job as Assistant Financial Officer for the U.S. Department of Treasury (DOT) (2003-present), I am involved in all aspects of budget programming, preparation, and controls while developing, monitoring, and reviewing financial reports, payroll, accounts payable, internal review follow-up, and banking data. I served as the point of contact for all matters dealing with the accounting function, and I compute, analyze, and interpret ratio analyses of various aspects of operations in order to identify problem areas or unfavorable conditions which may have developed. I monitor the establishment and collection of accounts receivable, review all purchase orders for services provided on a reimbursable basis confirming accuracy of information and data, and verify accuracy and timely submission of all financial documents prior to forwarding to DOT Financial Services. While routinely applying my knowledge of software functions to produce a wide range of financial documents often requiring complex formats, I certify funds available for all expenditures for the Billing Fund and guest houses. I advise the DOT Chief and Assistant Chief of Billing about proposed budget programming, preparation, and controls while monitoring the Capital Purchase and Minor Construction (CPMC) program. I gather, verify, and consolidate a variety of narrative and statistical data used in the formulation of budget requirements, and I prepare detailed operational and budget variance reports to include budget estimates, fact sheets, briefing papers, trend situations, and current program/activity status reports.

In both my current job and the one below, I have been involved with a wide range of personnel issues including typing up Incentive Awards, inputting employee time, distributing payroll, and calculating a wide range of payroll costs and benefits. Using the data which I compiled along with data provided by other sources, I have produced Attendance Reports for numerous projects.

In my previous job with the Department of Defense, Finance and Accounting Department (2000-03), I was promoted from Lead Accounting Technician to Accounts Payable Manager because of my knowledge of budget programming, preparation, and controls. Within six months of my arrival, I was promoted to a supervisory position and was in charge of overseeing payments in excess of $23.2 million while personally serving the organization's three largest vendors. While managing and evaluating 8 technicians, I planned, organized, scheduled, and directed their activities in consolidating, reconciling, and journalizing accounts payable data to effect timely payments. During my tenure in this job I displayed my exceptional initiative and leadership while playing a major role in two major projects within the department. One project concerned a delay in processing vendor invoices for merchandise purchased for sale in Mexico and the second project concerned the $1.1 million value of open items in dispute for both Mexican and Asian accounts. I led my staff in researching internal documentation related to the distribution system for Mexico bookstores, and we brought invoices up to date while restoring goodwill with many vendors. Through my leadership, we were able to see the value of dollar items in dispute shift from $1.1 million to $.02 million.

In my previous job with the Armament Research, Development and Engineering Center (ARDEC) at Lexington, KY, I demonstrated my knowledge of budget programming, preparation, and controls while excelling as Operations Clerk from 1998-00. I compiled budget estimates for each department monthly for establishing the budget in the fiscal year, and I ensured timely submission of the required budget estimates so that consolidation of budget data could be submitted to higher headquarters within the given suspenses. I also maintained resource control ledgers to show status of funds allocated and posted adjustments required, and I prepared and submitted official documents to the higher headquarters of ARDEC. Furthermore, I assisted in the formulation and revision of the annual budget estimate for the operation of the facility, and I developed monthly budgetary guidance based upon yearly expense forecasts for management.

In my job as Accountant with the Sodexho Food Services from 1997-98, I displayed my knowledge of budget programming and operations, my excellent analytical communication and analytical skills, as well as my ability to interpret guidelines and regulations. I verified budget data, read and interpreted error listings, and initiated corrective action while also verifying, computing, and disbursing funds to authorized vendors. I reviewed preliminary and final reports for accuracy of input, verified total dollar amount of batch transactions, and I researched and settled discrepancies. I demonstrated my knowledge of automated information systems in the process of requesting all computer run executions necessary to maintain files, and I updated computerized programs. I constantly implemented changes and tried to improve the accounting system in cooperation with management and budget guidelines.

Education and Training related to this KSA:
Received B.S. degree with a concentration in Business Management and a minor in Accounting from University of Kentucky, Lexington, KY, 1995.
Completed Advanced Budgeting Training in Memphis, TN, September 1998.
Completed training programs sponsored by the Department of Defense related to these and other areas:
- Equal Employment Opportunity
- Workshops on Harvard Graphics, WordPerfect, Lotus 1-2-3, Microsoft Office (Word, Excel, and PowerPoint) and dBase III
- Currently completing computer class on Microsoft Office, ACCESS

BUDGET ANALYST

PATRICIA E. HAMMOND

SSN: 000-00-0000

BUDGET ANALYST, GS-08 ANNOUNCEMENT #XYZ123

KSA #2: Analytical Skills.

In my current job as Assistant Financial Officer for the U.S. Department of Treasury (DOT) (2003-present), I utilized my analytical skills on a daily basis while developing, monitoring, and reviewing financial reports, payroll, accounts payable, internal review follow-up, and banking data. My analytical skills are required as I compute, analyze, and interpret ratio analyses of various aspects of operations in order to identify problem areas or unfavorable conditions which may have developed. I monitor the establishment and collection of accounts receivable, review all purchase orders for services provided on a reimbursable basis confirming accuracy of information and data, and verify accuracy and timely submission of all financial documents prior to forwarding to DOT Financial Services. While routinely applying my knowledge of software functions to produce a wide range of financial documents often requiring complex formats, I certify funds available for all expenditures for the Billing Fund and guest houses. I advise the DOT Chief and Assistant Chief of Billing about proposed budget programming, preparation, and controls while monitoring the Capital Purchase and Minor Construction (CPMC) program. I gather, verify, and consolidate a variety of narrative and statistical data used in the formulation of budget requirements, and I prepare detailed operational and budget variance reports to include budget estimates, fact sheets, briefing papers, trend situations, and current program/activity status reports.

In both my current job and the one below, I have been involved with a wide range of personnel issues including typing up Incentive Awards, inputting employee time, distributing payroll, and calculating a wide range of payroll costs and benefits. Using the data which I compiled along with data provided by other sources, I have produced Attendance Reports for numerous projects.

In my previous job with the Department of Defense, Finance and Accounting Department (2000-03), I was promoted from Lead Accounting Technician to Accounts Payable Manager within six months of my arrival. I won widespread praise for my outstanding analytical skills after I was promoted to a supervisory position and was in charge of overseeing payments in excess of $23.2 million while personally serving the organization's three largest vendors. While managing and evaluating 8 technicians, I planned, organized, scheduled, and directed their activities in consolidating, reconciling, and journalizing accounts payable data to effect timely payments. During my tenure in this job I displayed my exceptional analytical skills while playing a major role in two major projects within the department. One project concerned a delay in processing vendor invoices for merchandise purchased for sale in Mexico and the second project concerned the $1.1 million value of open items in dispute for both Mexican and Asian accounts. I led my staff in researching internal documentation related to the distribution system for Mexico bookstores, and we brought invoices up to date while restoring goodwill with many vendors. Through the application of my strong analytical skills, we were able to see the value of dollar items in dispute shift from $1.1 million to $.02 million.

In my previous job with the Armament Research, Development and Engineering Center (ARDEC) at Lexington, KY, I was extensively involved in analyzing budget information while excelling as Operations Clerk from 1998-00. I audited daily cash and credit sales for accuracy and completeness, and I verified and reconciled record of sales against actual monies received and resolved discrepancies. I recommended solutions and new procedures for handling problems related to errors in existing accounts. I also constantly reviewed and researched directives and budget related manuals to assure correct reporting and proper evaluation of attendance requirements within the ARDEC structure. In the process of receiving supplies and reviewing invoices for accuracy, I conducted surveys for non-ARDEC for cost comparisons and, after extensive analysis, I developed prices for merchandise to reflect the determined discount. Furthermore, I identified attendance requirements, developed work schedules, and process payroll while also auditing monthly balances and reconciling information. I compiled budget estimates for each department monthly for establishing the budget in the fiscal year, and I ensured timely submission of the required budget estimates so that consolidation of budget data could be submitted to higher headquarters within the given suspenses. I also maintained resource control ledgers to show status of funds allocated and posted adjustments required, and I prepared and submitted official documents to the higher headquarters of ARDEC. Furthermore, I assisted in the formulation and revision of the annual budget estimate for the operation of the facility, and I developed monthly budgetary guidance based upon yearly expense forecasts for management.

In my job as Accountant with Sodexho Food Services from 1997-98, I displayed my knowledge of budget programming and operations, my excellent analytical communication and analytical skills, as well as my ability to interpret guidelines and regulations. I verified budget data, read and interpreted error listings, and initiated corrective action while also verifying, computing, and disbursing funds to authorized vendors. I reviewed preliminary and final reports for accuracy of input, verified total dollar amount of batch transactions, and I researched and settled discrepancies. I demonstrated my knowledge of automated information systems in the process of requesting all computer run executions necessary to maintain files, and I updated computerized programs. I constantly implemented changes and tried to improve the accounting system in cooperation with management and budget guidelines.

Education and Training related to this KSA:
Received B.S. degree with a concentration in Business Management and a minor in Accounting from University of Kentucky, Lexington, KY, 1995.
Completed Advanced Budgeting Training in Memphis, TN, September 1998.
Completed training programs sponsored by the Department of Defense related to these and other areas:
- Equal Employment Opportunity
- Workshops on Harvard Graphics, WordPerfect, Lotus 1-2-3, Microsoft Office (Word, Excel, and PowerPoint) and dBase III
- Currently completing computer class on Microsoft Office, ACCESS

BUILDING MANAGER

SEAN V. TIMMONS

SSN: 000-00-0000

BUILDING MANAGER, GS-07 ANNOUNCEMENT #XYZ123

**Building Manager,
GS-07
Announcement #XYZ123
KSA #1**

KSA #1: Knowledge of government building practices, regulations, and policies.

Through my military career, which I began as an enlisted soldier and finished as a CW4, I have been placed in charge of multimillion-dollar assets and in charge of government buildings.

From 2001-02, while serving as an Instructor Pilot and Property Manager at Ft. Bragg, handled a wide range of responsibilities in addition to my job as an instructor pilot. *Property Management and Maintenance Management Responsibilities:*

- Played a key role in determining maintenance needs of the fifteen UH-60A helicopters in this organization's fleet.
- Was responsible for the development and implementation of an annual and long-range maintenance program with emphasis on preventive maintenance. Coordinated and scheduled for critical repairs and maintenance/cleaning and conducted installation or cleaning in the facility and grounds. Monitored all maintenance and equipment installation projects for timeliness, correctness, and completion. Oversaw replacement and/or repair of fixtures and devices of buildings which housed the organization's aviation fleet. Exercised control and responsibility over the facility ensuring that all necessary maintenance, repair, alternations or modifications were accomplished.

This KSA relates to a Property Management position.

From 1998-01 as Property Officer for the 419th Special Operations Aviation Detachment (Airborne) at Yuma Proving Ground was in charge of $70 million in equipment including four buildings and a hangar. In that same job I also functioned as Executive Officer so it was my responsibility to oversee the management of maintenance building, dining facilities, medical facility barracks, and administrative buildings. Since this organization was in a "start-up" phase, it was my responsibility to establish the organization's first annual and long-range maintenance program with emphasis on preventive maintenance. Coordinated schedules for critical repairs and maintenance/cleaning and conducted installation or cleaning in the facility and grounds. Since it was my responsibility to purchase all equipment and fixtures within the structures which I managed, I exercised control of the equipment installation projects for timeliness and correctness. Exercised control and responsibility over devices of the building.

My training and education related to this KSA includes:
Basic Noncommissioned Officer Course, 1996; Advanced NCO Course, 1997
Warrant Officer Basic Course, 2000; Warrant Officer Advanced Course, 2002
My formal education has helped me acquire knowledge of effective property management techniques. I hold a B.S. in Professional Aeronautics with a Minor in Safety. I am completing a Master of Science in Aerospace Technology and hold an A.S. in Criminal Justice.

SEAN V. TIMMONS

SSN: 000-00-0000

BUILDING MANAGER, GS-07 ANNOUNCEMENT #XYZ123

KSA #2: Ability to communicate effectively, both orally and in writing.

I believe my outstanding communication skills, both oral and written, have been the key to my highly successful military career which began as an enlisted soldier, progressed rapidly into the NCO ranks, and then into the warrant officer career field. In all of my jobs since 2001, I have worn the hat of Instructor Pilot and/or Flight Examiner, which put me in the position of training, evaluating, and communicating with other pilots. In the formal performance evaluation for my most recent job during the period 2002-03, was cited as the "key element in the successful formation and train-up of Mike Company." Trained 10 pilots from RL3 to RL1 status in day, night, and night vision goggles in a three-month period in a new organization recently formed under the Aviation Restructuring Initiative. Was described in writing as "a spectacular role model for all the young warrant officers in the company" and was praised for leading by example and making myself available at all times to provide advice or guidance. Cited as "an unequaled source of learning for aviators of all experience levels" and "a trainer who radiates self confidence and enthusiasm that is infectious to all."

Also proved my ability to communicate effectively, orally and in writing, in activities other than pilot training and evaluation. For example, I was DA-selected and personally requested by the commanding officer of a newly started organization in 1998-01 at Yuma Proving Ground, AZ. It was my responsibility to act as Property Officer and Information Management Officer for this special operations aviation unit. As one of my first management actions, I literally got on the phone and secured $300,000 in funds which allowed me to get the organization into a mission-ready posture. While managing the organization's $1.4 million budget and making all purchasing decisions related to equipment and property needed by this organization, I communicated extensively with vendors to obtain assets.

My communication skills were evident in my career as an enlisted soldier, too. For example, as Senior Drill Sergeant from 1997-98, I trained and supervised six other drill sergeants at a correctional facility which received up to 60 new soldiers every nine weeks who had committed criminal offenses of some type. Earned widespread respect for my communication skills and was praised in a formal enlisted evaluation report:
- "Has developed innovative motivational training which instilled a high degree of team work among the trainee personnel."
- "His efforts have constantly resulted in higher motivated teams with superior personal standards and a higher degree of morale than other teams in the Activity."

My training and education related to this KSA includes:
Basic Noncommissioned Officer Course, 1996; Advanced NCO Course, 1997
Warrant Officer Basic Course, 2000; Warrant Officer Advanced Course, 2002
B.S. in Professional Aeronautics with a Minor in Safety

You'll see the communication KSAs very frequently!

CLERK

LYDIA MICHELLE HINDEMITH
SSN: 000-00-0000
CLERK (TYPING), GS-05 ANNOUNCEMENT #XYZ123

**Clerk (Typing),
GS-05
Announcement #XYZ123
KSA #1**

KSA #1: Knowledge of grammar, spelling, capitalization, and punctuation.

In my current position as Office Manager, I work essentially without supervision and therefore must rely on my own excellent knowledge of grammar, spelling, capitalization and punctuation. I type correspondence, reports, and memoranda in final form and without supervision. As Office Manager, I control all documents for the office, assuring that all deadlines are met. I take great pride in the fact that my knowledge of grammar, spelling, capitalization and punctuation allow us to present a very polished and professional look in all written communication.

In my job as Personnel Administrative Specialist, I was selected to serve as Rear Detachment S-1 NCOIC as a Specialist E-4, even though this position usually was reserved for an individual at the rank of SFC (E-7). This special selection was partially in recognition of my superior knowledge of grammar, spelling, capitalization and punctuation which I continually used to type correspondence, reports, and memoranda in final. I was extremely knowledgeable of the written forms, documents, and paperwork used in the personnel administration field as I typed personnel evaluations such as NCOERs, prepared finance documents related to employee payroll, and proofread documents, reports, and other written communication. I prepared written communication for the signature of executives.

You'll see this KSA required for many office administration jobs.

In my job as Personnel Administration Specialist and Unit Clerk from 1999-02, I received respected awards in recognition of my excellent knowledge of spelling, punctuation, capitalization, and grammar as I prepared reports, correspondence, and memoranda. As Unit Clerk, I received the Army Achievement Medal for my efforts in reducing critical data blanks on the SIDPERS System, which allowed my organization to become one of the first units within 2d Army to reach the goal of "zero backlog" of personnel documents. This accomplishment was due in large part to my excellent spelling and grammar as well as my command of the rules of punctuation and capitalization while accurately and quickly completing reports, memoranda, and correspondence.

In my jobs from 1995-99 as Administration Specialist, I prepared both military and nonmilitary correspondence in final form while also handling a variety of complex office management duties. I became known for excellent spelling, capitalization, grammar, and punctuation.

Education and Training related to this KSA:
More than two years of college-level training related to this KSA:
USAR Unit Administration Basic Course, three weeks, 2002
Administrative Specialist Course, 33 credit hours, 2001
Primary Leadership Development Course, two weeks, 2000
Battalion Training Management Course, two days, 2000
Maintenance Management Course, two days, 1998
Clerk-Typist Course, eight weeks, 1996

KSA #2: Knowledge of format and clerical procedures used in typing a variety of materials.

In my current position as Office Manager, I am the resident expert on the knowledge of format and clerical procedures used in typing a variety of materials for a company which provides services to commercial, industrial, and residential customers. I type correspondence, reports, and memoranda in final form and without supervision. I maintain files such as chronological, time and attendance, personnel, and other files, and I apply my knowledge of format and clerical procedures in ordering materials using a variety of written communication forms. I work usually without supervision in my current job, and I must continually rely on my resourcefulness and analytical skills as a constantly add to my knowledge of specialized terminology used in this business. As Office Manager, I control all documents for the office, assuring that all deadlines are met.

In my job as Personnel Administrative Specialist, I was selected to serve as Rear Detachment S-1 NCOIC as a Specialist E-4, even though this position usually was reserved for an individual at the rank of SFC (E-7). This special selection was due to my demonstrated knowledge of format and clerical procedures used in typing a variety of materials including correspondence, reports, and memoranda. I was extremely knowledgeable of the format and clerical procedures used in the personnel administration field as I typed personnel evaluations such as NCOERs, prepared finance documents related to employee payroll, and proofread documents, reports, and other written communication.

In my job as Personnel Administration Specialist and Unit Clerk from 1999-02, I received respected awards in recognition of my excellent knowledge of the format and clerical procedures involved in preparing reports, correspondence, and memoranda. As Unit Clerk, I received the Army Achievement Medal for my efforts in reducing critical data blanks on the SIDPERS System, which allowed my organization to become the one of the first units within 2d Army to reach the goal of "zero backlog" of personnel documents. This accomplishment was due in large part to my knowledge of the format and clerical procedures used in order to quickly and accurately complete reports, memoranda, and correspondence in final form. In my jobs from 1995-99 as Administration Specialist, I prepared both military and non-military correspondence in final form.

Education and Training related to this KSA:
USAR Unit Administration Basic Course, three weeks, 2002
Administrative Specialist Course, 33 credit hours, 2001
Primary Leadership Development Course, two weeks, 2000
Battalion Training Management Course, two days, 2000
Maintenance Management Course, two days, 1998
Clerk-Typist Course, eight weeks, 1996

Clerk (Typing), GS-05 Announcement #XYZ123 KSA #2

Focus on the precise procedures you are knowledgeable of in this type of KSA.

COMPUTER SCIENTIST

JOSEPH B. BLOOM

SSN: 000-00-0000

COMPUTER SCIENTIST, GS-12 ANNOUNCEMENT #XYZ123

KSA #1: Knowledge of hardware/software evaluation and procurement.

While working as a FORTRAN programmer at Columbia University and cowriting a related paper that was later published, I evaluated the comparative strengths of different programming languages (FORTRAN 77, Unix C-shell, etc.) which could be used separately or in combination to add new modules to the program (MOLDYN) that I was upgrading for the Columbia University chemistry department. Applied the principles learned in my undergraduate course-work (which included a course on High-Level Languages and Data Structures) as well as a working knowledge of the hardware platform on which the program in my project was to be used.

During the course of this project, and frequently during my tenure at the Columbia University NMR-lab as an undergraduate, I learned from professional systems administrators about the problems associated with upgrading the lab's hardware so as to maximize its effectiveness under severe budgetary constraints.

As a hardware technician for the chemistry department at Columbia University, I demonstrated my ability to inspect, repair, and maintain computers and computer systems while performing troubleshooting to the component level. Gained experience in inspecting, repairing, and maintaining hardware including tape drives, line printers, card readers, digital circuitry, multiplexers, terminals, disk memory, keyboards, and display stations. Implemented diagnostic programs and used testing equipment for troubleshooting, tracing logic and schematics, and wiring diagrams.

*A Computer Scientist may
encounter this KSA*

While a graduate student at Princeton University, I learned to conduct routine operational analysis and formulate system concept architectural designs, functional specifications, software development, system integration and documentation aspects of computer systems. Worked with senior academics, scientists, and engineers on computer operating systems and language processors to determine status of various reliability, performance, and quality characteristics of systems.

Education and training related to this KSA:
- Master of Science degree, Computer Science, Princeton University (2003).
- Bachelor of Science degree, Computer Science, Columbia University, graduated Magna Cum Laude (1998).

KSA #2: Ability to analyze, understand, and apply data processing principles for computer applications.

Computer Scientist, GS-12 Announcement #XYZ123 KSA #2

While working as a FORTRAN programmer at Columbia University and cowriting a related paper that was later published, I evaluated the comparative strengths of different programming languages (FORTRAN 77, Unix C-shell, etc.) which could be used separately or in combination to add new modules to the program (MOLDYN) that I was upgrading for the Columbia University chemistry department. Applied the principles learned in my undergraduate course-work (which included a course on High-Level Languages and Data Structures) as well as a working knowledge of the hardware platform on which the program in my project was to be used.

I extensively modified a large multimodular program in FORTRAN 77 that calculated characteristics of the internal motions of molecules on the basis of input measurements derived from NMR spectrometers.

Be sure to mention achievements!

- Worked closely with the users of this program while developing and implementing their applications.
- Performed a wide range of technical actions including planning and coordinating for hardware and software maintenance, developing and implementing database management as well as backup and archival procedures, troubleshooting problems, and designing specifications related to the upgrade of the this program in the future.

The program modifications I implemented in this project were made to achieve two ends:
1. The automatic reading of large data files into a program that formerly required each datum to be manually entered on a screen.
2. The automatic generation of large simulated data sets based on small sets of actual measurements.

Demonstrated my ability to research, plan, and implement a sophisticated project requiring the application of advanced data processing principles and mathematical statistical theory. Planned and conducted project-related studies which included preparing specifications and developing new procedures as well as modifying existing procedures. Analyzed and evaluated the accuracy and validity of data. Developed and applied measures/models to resolve problems. Documented results. While utilizing the high-programming language FORTRAN 77, demonstrated my ability to creatively and resourcefully apply my programming knowledge while combining it with my knowledge of statistical software. Routinely performed duties including but not limited to: sampling, collecting, computing, and analyzing statistical data.

Education and training related to this KSA:
- Master of Science degree, Computer Science, Princeton University (2003).
- Bachelor of Science degree, Computer Science, Columbia University, graduated Magna Cum Laude (1998).

COMPUTER SCIENTIST

JOSEPH B. BLOOM

SSN: 000-00-0000

COMPUTER SCIENTIST, GS-12 ANNOUNCEMENT #XYZ123

Computer Scientist, GS-12 Announcement #XYZ123 KSA #3

KSA #3: Ability to analyze work processes and apply knowledge of data processing principles.

While working as a Programmer and Mathematical Statistician for the Department of Chemistry at Princeton University, I extensively modified a large multimodular program in FORTRAN 77 that calculated characteristics of the internal motions of molecules on the basis of input measurements derived from NMR spectrometers.

- Worked closely with the users of this program while developing and implementing their applications.
- Performed a wide range of technical actions including planning and coordinating for hardware and software maintenance, developing and implementing database management as well as backup and archival procedures, troubleshooting problems, and designing specifications related to the upgrade of the this program in the future.

The program modifications I implemented in this project were made to achieve two ends:

1. The automatic reading of large data files into a program that formerly required each datum to be manually entered on a screen.
2. The automatic generation of large simulated data sets based on small sets of actual measurements.

This young scientist is mostly "selling" his graduate education.

Demonstrated my ability to research, plan, and implement a sophisticated project requiring the application of mathematical statistical theory. Planned and conducted project-related studies which included preparing specifications and developing new procedures as well as modifying existing procedures. Analyzed and evaluated the accuracy and validity of data. Developed and applied measures/models to resolve problems. Documented results. While utilizing the high-programming language FORTRAN 77, demonstrated my ability to creatively and resourcefully apply my programming knowledge while combining it with my knowledge of statistical software. Routinely performed:

- Sampling
- Collecting, computing, and analyzing statistical data

To upgrade the program mentioned above, I had a number of detailed discussions with the program's users in which I assessed their needs and analyzed their work processes in order to determine and design the kinds of changes in the program that they needed. I had to learn a lot about how the program would be used in practice, and apply my knowledge of data processing principles to implement modifications that would save its users time.

Education and training related to this KSA:

- Master of Science degree, Computer Science, Princeton University (2003).
- Bachelor of Science degree, Computer Science, Columbia University, graduated Magna Cum Laude (1998).

KSA #4: Knowledge of conceptual design of computer systems.

As a graduate student at the Princeton University, I learned to conduct routine operational analysis and formulate system concept architectural designs, functional specifications, software development, system integration and documentation aspects of computer systems. Worked with senior academics, scientists, and engineers on computer operating systems and language processors to determine status of various reliability, performance, and quality characteristics of systems.

In my undergraduate coursework on assembly-language programming and computer organization, I mastered a good deal of material on the internal components of individual computers. In other courses, both on the undergraduate and the graduate level, I learned about the conceptual design of both parallel and distributed computer systems.

Finally, as a Hardware Technician for the Department of Chemistry at Columbia University, I demonstrated my ability to inspect, repair and maintain computers and computer systems while performing troubleshooting to the component level. Gained experience in inspecting, repairing and maintaining hardware, including tape drives, line printers, card readers, digital circuitry, multiplexers, terminals, disk memory, keyboards, and display stations. Implemented diagnostic programs and used testing equipment for troubleshooting, tracing logic and schematics, and wiring diagrams.

Education and training related to this KSA:
- Master of Science degree, Computer Science, Princeton University (2003).
- Bachelor of Science degree, Computer Science, Columbia University, graduated Magna Cum Laude (1998).

Computer Scientist, GS-12 Announcement #XYZ123 KSA #4

COMPUTER SPECIALIST

REYNALDO T. DOMINGUEZ

SSN: 000-00-0000

COMPUTER SPECIALIST, GS-10 ANNOUNCEMENT #XYZ123

KSA #1: Ability to communicate effectively.

In my present role as a Computer Scientist at the FAA Technical Center at the O'Hare International Airport from May 2003-present, my effective communication skills have been of vital importance especially in my capacity of contract administrator which includes preparing all documentation, negotiating with vendors, budgeting, supervising the performance of contractors, and providing the day-to-day management oversight. During a period of severe understaffing, assumed additional responsibility as Acting Branch Manager for Information Systems Engineering Branch and was cited as being the key staff member who kept operations on schedule. Represented the FAA for the Local Area Network (LAN) support services contract by overseeing all facets of LAN management and end-user support in order to ensure all contract terms and conditions were carried out; worked closely with personnel from the GSA, MTI, and other agencies and vendors to negotiate terms and verify performance. Utilized my communication skills and subject matter knowledge as coordinator and instructor for OATS technical refresher courses. Developed, implemented, and then published the technical center's software standards for use with microcomputers. Developed curriculum for, and instructed classes in Local Area Networking and Basic Unix while participating in the Technical Center's In-House Training Program.

As a Computer Specialist at the Los Angeles Naval Shipyard (CA) from August 1998-June 2003, filled supervisory and managerial responsibilities as the senior specialist in a four-person team in the Zone Technology Division of the Planning Department: directed the day-to-day performance of the team as well as planning and coordinating the implementation of computer-based projects for two computer networks. Communicated on a regular basis with customers while coordinating support services and developed an ADP training program in which I provided instruction in computer operations, programming, and systems analysis.

From January 1995 to August 1998 as a System Manager/Mathematician at the Los Angeles Naval Shipyard (Los Angeles, CA), I provided technical administrative support for a large CAD (Computer-Aided Design) network system.

As a Mathematician and Programmer at the Los Angeles Naval Shipyard from December 1992-January 1995, I provided customer relations support with managers and engineers while working with them in close cooperation to establish design and implementation criteria. From November 1988 to October 1990 served in the U.S. Navy at Newport News, VA. Advanced to supervisory roles and provided training for subordinate personnel. Applied my communications skills while serving in the U.S. Naval Reserve (1991-present) in roles such as career counselor, Leading Petty Officer, and instructor.

Education and training related to this KSA:
Hold B.S. degree in Engineering with a minor in Mathematics in 1992.

KSA #2: Ability to apply Equal Employment Opportunity (EEO) and Human Relations skills to the work environment.

From May 2003-present, as a Computer Scientist for the FAA Technical Center at O'Hare International Airport, I have applied my ability to apply EEO and Human Relations skills in my capacity as the senior software specialist. Because of my involvement in numerous highly technical projects, I have been called on to ensure compliance with EEO guidelines and provide leadership while dealing with customers, co-workers, and subordinates. During a period of severe understaffing, assumed additional responsibility as Acting Branch Manager for Information Systems Engineering Branch and was cited as being the key staff member who kept operations on schedule. Allocated work assignments, ensured high quality customer relations, resolved conflicts as they arose and before they could escalate, and negotiated with upper level management to resolve sensitive situations.

Represented the FAA for the LAN support services contract by overseeing all facets of LAN management and end-user support in order to ensure all contract terms and conditions were carried out; worked closely with personnel from the GSA, MTI, and other agencies and vendors to negotiate terms and verify performance. While LAN Lead, one of my most important contributions to ensuring compliance with EEO guidelines was when I was recognized for my diplomatic and discreet handling of a politically sensitive situation regarding EEO violations which resulted in the dismissal of the site manager for the LAN support contract: as the LAN Team Leader from March-November 2001, was active in overseeing EEO and human relations activities while coordinating the activities of 20 support contractors.

From August 1998-June 2003 as a Computer Specialist at the Los Angeles (CA) Naval Shipyard, fulfilled supervisory and managerial responsibilities as the senior specialist in a four-person team in the Zone Technology Division of the Planning Department: directed the day-to-day performance of the team as well as planning and coordinating the implementation of computer-based projects for two computer networks. My skills in human relations management was also demonstrated while training personnel in computer operations, programming, and systems analysis as well as in the routine daily supervision of skilled technical personnel.

Training and experience related to this KSA:
- Attended college full-time after three years of service in the Navy and earned a B.S. in Engineering with a minor in Mathematics.
- Completed extensive training which included:
  Performance-based Statements of Work, Management Concepts, Inc., FAA Technical Center, Chicago, IL, 2001, 24 hours
- Thinking Outside the Box, National Seminars Group, FAA Technical Center, Chicago, IL, 2000, 8 hours

CONTRACT ADMINISTRATOR
GWENDOLYN McLEOD

SSN: 000-00-0000
CONTRACT ADMINISTRATOR, GS-09 ANNOUNCEMENT #XYZ123

KSA #1: Ability to communicate orally and in writing.

Overview of experience and knowledge related to this KSA:
Experience from 2000-03 related to this KSA:
As a contract specialist, prepared virtually every type of written product associated with the contracting field. Communicated both orally and in writing to contractors, buying commands, Congressional or higher echelon personnel on a variety of topics by preparing correspondence or detailed reports on negotiations or modifications. Because of my contracting knowledge, as well as my excellent communication skills, became a trusted advisor and respected colleague and was frequently contacted to give technical advice regarding all aspects of contracting. In the absence of the chief, was frequently called on to be the acting chief and supervise five purchasing agents and one procurement clerk. Began with a level 1 Contacting Officer Warrant and then completed training which permitted me to receive a warrant to manage contracts up to $100,000 (level 2).

Was the contract specialist who processed the more difficult purchase orders, most of which related to ADP hardware, software, and maintenance services. Was responsible for all aspects of contracting transactions from initiation through award and administration of the contract once awarded. Served as the technical expert for other purchasing agents and provided functional guidance, assistance, and on-the-job training as necessary to new contract specialists. Handled the acquisition of complex technical equipment, supplies, and services through the use of invitations for bids and requests for proposals. Demonstrated my knowledge of and ability to analyze Federal Acquisition Regulations, FIRMR, Treasury Procurement Regulations, Federal Property Management Regulations, GSA Regulations, and IRS Manual and Interoffice Issuances. Proceeded step-by-step through he contracting process beginning with the review of assigned requisitions and the determination of the appropriate method of procurement – sealed bidding or negotiation.

This KSA was written for a Contract Administrator seeking a job in a different region.

Analyzed ADP, telecommunications, and similar complex requisitions in order to make determinations on whether purchasing, leasing with an option to purchase, or renting would be in the best interest of the government. Considered and selected the best type of maintenance for such requisitions. Established procurement strategies by reviewing specifications as well as manuals, catalogs, and technical brochures and resolving issues with manufacturing representatives and requisitions. After my analysis, completed a synopsis of procurements and then developed/issued solicitation documents. Selected the appropriate clauses which clearly stated all specification requirements and responded to all inquiries on assigned procurements. Selected the appropriate contract type and performed cost/price analysis of contractor bids and proposals received. On contracts, negotiated prices, specifications and requirements, and delivery dates with contractors. Performed detailed analysis of offers which included such information as a review of past bids and awards. Prepared the final contracts including specifications, packing and shipping requirements, system acceptability testing requirements, and appropriate standard clauses. Prepared and issued delivery routes against nationally negotiated contracts. Clarified issues such as billing procedures, and provided guidance to contractors concerning obligations to perform within contractual terms. Because of my thorough knowledge of the contracting business, advanced to handle the most complex transactions and contracts within this office. Received all requisitions over $25,000 and reviewed the packages for completeness and accuracy as well as obtaining local approval. Prepared the orders up to the point of award (up to $100,000) and forwarded them to the National Office to be completed. Tracked all requisitions and prepared a monthly report of the status of the requisitions at the National Office.

Communicating in writing and orally in my job as a Purchasing Agent 1997-00: As a purchasing agent, expertly prepared a wide variety of written products related to purchasing and contracting. Handled all details of purchasing from the receipt of the purchase request to the finalization of the purchase order or Imprest Fund purchase. Bought base procurement items such as lumber for repairing houses and concrete to use in construction and repairs. Also bought ceramic materials which were extensively used in this region of the country for roofing and other purposes. Was responsible for purchasing items as diverse as nails and tools to sporting equipment and nearly any type of item used in the hospital. Reviewed assigned requisitions and determined appropriate method of procurement. After synopsizing procurements and developing and issuing solicitation documents, selected contract type and then performed cost/price analysis of contractor bids and proposals received. Prepared final contracts, including specifications, packing and shipping requirements, system acceptability testing requirements, and appropriate standard clauses. Acquired knowledge and the ability to analyze Armed Services Procurement Regulations, Department of Defense Regulations, Department of the Army Regulations, and Federal Property Management Regulations.

Do a two-page KSA if you need to.

Highlights of education and training related to this KSA: Hold a B.S. degree from the University of Tennessee. Have taken advantage of every opportunity to increase my knowledge of contracting through formal courses, seminars, and workshops including these:
- Management Analysis and Review (2001)
- Government Contract Law (2000)
- Defense Small Purchases Basic Course (2000)
- Techniques of Contracting (1999)
- Contracting Officer Technical Representative/Quality Assurance Evaluator (1999)
- Competition Advocate's Training – Competition in Contracting (1998)
- Justification for Other than Full and Open Competition (1998)

CONTRACT ADMINISTRATOR

GWENDOLYN McLEOD

SSN: 000-00-0000

CONTRACT ADMINISTRATOR, GS-09 ANNOUNCEMENT #XYZ123

KSA #2: Ability to meet and deal effectively with others.

In my most recent job as a contract specialist from 2/15/03 to present, excelled in administering the contract with Konica for 32 copiers and was the author of the training manual used to teach local personnel to use this new equipment. In this capacity I met regularly with and dealt effectively with a wide variety of people including civilian vendors. I was the point of contact in charge of arranging for these vendors to teach classes in which local personnel learned to use the copiers correctly. I also dealt with others while involved in most aspects of contract administration which included making recommendations during contract disputes, small purchase actions, and contract termination actions as well as during the negotiation of rates and charges, modifications, small purchase actions, and the issuance of contract modifications and change orders. Applied my ability to deal with others effectively while conducing complex negotiations in order to acquire equipment and services for the computing center. While using my purchasing expertise and research skills to reduce contract costs, was the point of contact for maintenance and repair calls as well as for checking the machines, escorting the service technician and explaining the problem, monitoring their work on the machines, handling the paperwork for payment, and tracking funds. In general, was counted on to solve many problems in the contracting area and streamlined the renewal process.

Applied my effective "people" skills during a functional reorganization from resources management to support services and personally underwent a radical redefinition of my responsibilities and program areas. One of my major new responsibilities was in the area of helping coach and train new analysts who assumed my old responsibilities. Trained and provided mentoring and guidance in the areas of procedures for running the copy center, processing print requests, administering a cost-per-copy program, and monitoring contract renewals for FY 03. Displayed my time management skills and willingness to assist other employees while working continuously under a heavy workload and extremely tight deadlines. Refined the ability to prioritize simultaneous high-priority jobs and worked closely in cooperation with my supervisor to ensure needs and expectations were met. Was cited for my availability to other workers and willingness to help them meet their goals during peak periods.

From 2/00 to 3/03 as a contract specialist, became a trusted advisor to higher level management personnel and a respected colleague who was often called on by others to provide technical advice regarding all aspects of contracting. In the capacity of technical advisor to other purchasing agents and new contracting specialists, provided on-the-job training, dealt with personnel from outside the organization while acting as point of contact for the acquisition of complex technical equipment, supplies, and services through the use of invitations for bids and requests for proposals. As the bid opening officer, conducted contract negotiations and managed the procurement process for specialized ADP equipment as well as for accompanying maintenance, repair, and technical services. Demonstrated the ability to communicate clearly, tactfully, and effectively and deal with a wide range of people from employees, to vendors, to managers, to HTB representatives. Became recognized as the chief problem solver for any type of contract administration problems and became the individual in charge of training new employees in the proper procedures for contract preparation and administration. These skills were also applied during dispute resolution activities when I worked with contractors and government personnel to handle disputes and was the one who issued the final decision. Processed protests to the agency, FGP, or FTCDB according to applicable regulations. Stayed aware and anticipated possible problems so disputes could be avoided.

From 11/97 to 2/00 as a purchasing agent with the Internal Revenue Service, applied my skills in dealing with others in an effective manner while providing guidance to contractors, reviewing and analyzing any problems which occurred, investigating problems, and processing disputes. Was sought out for my positive attitude, cheerful manner, and reputation as a fast worker and asked to help out in the administrative area during an extremely busy period with a heavy backlog of work.

From 8/96 to 11/97 as a homemaker and mother, applied my ability to deal with others effectively in numerous community volunteer roles and held leadership roles in numerous organizations. Volunteered more than 150 hours in an elementary school reading and remediation program and more than 216 hours as a kindergarten instructor and classroom assistant. Was elected to the executive board of a PTA and served on numerous scholarship and arts committees.

From 7/94 to 8/96 as a purchasing agent, demonstrated strong analytical skills and a record of excellent performance and was selected to receive special training in construction contract administration. In this job I was required to deal with people effectively while developing and refining skills in negotiating terms and prices with contractors. Was often called on to clarify issues such as billing procedures and equipment and material substitutions.

Education and training related to this KSA
Hold a Bachelor of Science Degree in Political Science from the Seattle Pacific University. In addition to my extensive hands-on, on-the-job education and training in every aspect of the contracting process, have taken advantage of every opportunity to increase my knowledge of contracting through formal courses, seminars, and workshops including:
- Analysis Review of Management (4/03)
- Law and Government Contracts (11/03)
- Defense Purchases Training (9/02)
- Techniques of Contracting (6/02)
- Technical Officer/Contract Representative (TOCR)/Quallity Assurance Evaluator (QAE) Competition Advocate's Training - Competition in Contracting (3/01)
- Justification for Other than Full and Open Competition (10/01)
- Preparing Statements of Work and Purchasing Descriptions (5/00)
- ADP Contracting (4/00)
- Procurement Techniques (1/00)
- Contracting by Negotiations (12/00)
- Contracting by Sealed Bid (8/99)
- Small Purchase/Scheduled Contracts (8/99)
- Cost/Price Analysis and Negotiation Techniques (11/99)
- Contract Administration (2/98)
- Defense Procurement Management Course (6/97)
- Defense Small Purchases (3/97)

CONTRACT ADMINISTRATOR

GWENDOLYN MCLEOD

SSN: 000-00-0000

CONTRACT ADMINISTRATOR, GS-09 ANNOUNCEMENT #XYZ123

KSA #3: Ability to Interpret and Apply Regulations.

I have demonstrated my ability to interpret and apply regulations throughout my career in various civil service positions in medical and clerical environments. I have become respected for my strong personal initiative in performing self-study on my own time to familiarize myself with appropriate regulations so that I can perform my job in an expert fashion. In the highly regulated field which the medical field is, it is vital that I remain abreast of constantly changing regulations so that I can resourcefully and correctly interpret and apply them.

In my current position as a **Patient Administration Clerk** (2003-present), I ensure that the establishment, maintenance, and disposition of medical records for the patients of Brooke Army Medical Center is performed according to strict regulations and procedures. The main focus of my job is updating and maintaining outpatient medical records and registering patients into the Composite Health Care System (CHCS). It is my responsibility to follow interpret and apply regulations as I verify patient's eligibility for service under DEERS and provide information regarding DEERS eligibility to patients. Prepare medical record folders for new admissions and update information in patient records, as requested; ensure that patient's name, social security number, and unit address are accurately documented in their medical records. Generate patient identification labels for each folder and code medical records according to the established filing system. Pull individual medical records for physicians, for use in studies, appointments at specialty clinics, quality assurance audits, etc, to include conducting searches to find lost records. Document follow-up actions initiated to locate the records. Receive, process, and file treatment records, consultations, and diagnostic tests, as well as laboratory and diagnostic results.

In an earlier job as a **File Clerk** for the Internal Revenue Service, I received several respected awards which were largely based on my personal initiative as well as my ability to interpret and apply regulations. It was my responsibility to demonstrate knowledge of the preparation of tax returns and documents and all of the regulations which pertained to their filing, retention, and processing. While at the Internal Revenue Service, I became accustomed to working in an environment in which there was "no room for error" and in which attention to detail and adherence to strict regulations was required at all times.

As a **Secretary** at Brooke Army Medical Center (2004), I obtained patient charts, X-ray films, and other medical records as requested by health care providers to ensure patient care. Prepared lab slips as needed for health care providers; obtained signature upon completion and directed patients to appropriate clinics or services for follow-up care. Received and screened visitors and took telephone calls. Personally provided nontechnical information to callers or visitors; referred those whose questions I could not answer to appropriate staff members. Coordinated with personnel assigned to other medical or diagnostic services within the medical center to facilitate patient care. Interviewed patients or family members to obtain factual information and explained unit services, policies, procedures, and regulations, as well as complaint procedures to patients and family members. Ensured that all medical treatment forms were readily available for use by nurses and physicians to document patient care services. Prepared admission packets, trauma packets, and lab packets to expedite the medical care treatment process for patients reporting to the emergency room. Relieved other advice line care providers and medical clerks who worked in the front office for breaks and lunches.

In a previous position as a **Medical Clerk** at Brooke, I interviewed patients being admitted to the hospital and determined eligibility for treatment. Set up clinical record file folders and prepared related materials. Prepared admission packets, including completion of Absent Sick patients. Obtained information on injury cases and serious jump injuries; provided information to MEDCEN Information Office for release to XVIII Airborne Corps HQS. Answered personal and telephonic inquiries concerning patients and MEDCEN services and facilities. Furnished information, referring callers to proper agencies for more detailed information. Operated the hospital's paging system, emergency 9-code system, and emergency response systems. Performed data entry, entering patient information into the Automated Quality of Care Evaluation System (AQCESS). Corrected, edited, and verified the reentry of corrected data into the IAS system; keyed updated diagnoses into the system as directed by physicians. Distributed IAS output reports to MEDCEN staff as required and coordinated with the Medical Statistical Section to ensure accuracy of occupied bed counts and overall patient accountability.

As a **Clerk and Typist** with the Patient Administration Division/Civilian Medical Claims at Brooke Army Medical Center, I developed and performed investigative research of medical claims. Received medical bills from civilian hospitals, physicians, and ambulance companies. Screened medical bills for correct medical terminology and insured proper medical justification to support the claim. Requested detailed narratives from civilian hospitals or physicians who had admitted or treated a military member. Upon receipt of a claim, carefully screened requests to ensure that procedures listed matched the medical procedures actually performed. Utilized various ARs, directives, pamphlets, MEDCEN policies, and established office procedures, which dictate proper procedures for processing medical claims. Counseled active duty personnel regarding their civilian medical and dental entitlements while in various duty statuses.

Education and Training Related to This KSA:
Completed training in Medical Terminology, May 2002.
Earned a certificate in Basic Medical Field Terminology, May 2002.
Completed training related to Records Maintenance and the Information/Privacy Act, 2000.
• Earned a certificate in Records Maintenance/Information/Privacy Act, November 2000.
Completed Customer Service Training, 1999.
Completed Production and Efficiency Training sponsored by the IRS, 1998.
Completed Proofreading Training, 1996.
Completed Computer Course, 1996.

COOK SUPERVISOR

MARK DAVIS FLYNN

SSN: 000-00-0000

COOK SUPERVISOR, WG-10 ANNOUNCEMENT #XYZ123

KSA #1: Ability to lead or supervise.

Throughout my military career (1996-1999 and 2002-2003) and in two civilian jobs, one as the Director of Food Service Operation with Keebler (2000-2002), and as the Assistant Cafeteria Director at the University of Miami (1999-2000), have refined and perfected leadership and supervisory skills while hiring, training, and supervising 16 employees.

In my most recent job as a Food Service Supervisor, Consolidated Dining Facility, Ft. Monmouth, NJ (2003-present), supervise food service personnel capable of feeding 1,000 soldiers per meal. Was officially described in a formal evaluation as "always sets the example with appearance," "superior ability to influence soldiers to perform," and "enforces standards for mission accomplishment." Was recognized for my ability to guide tasks from conception to completion. Coached subordinates to win 18th Airborne Corps "Culinary Specialist of the Year" award.

As a Food Service Supervisor with the Consolidated Dining Facility in Germany (1995-96), personally trained a soldier who went on to be selected for "Brigade Cook of the Quarter." Became known for my willingness to share time and "considerable knowledge" with others. Was officially described as have "strong leadership attributes and a strong desire to excel."

This is a management KSA.

As a Food Service Sergeant with a rapid deployment engineer company (1994-95), Ft. McCoy, WI, supervised the night baking shift of four noncommissioned officers and three specialists for a consolidated dining facility feeding 700 soldiers per meal. Supervised three supervisors and two specialists on the Army Field Feeding System.

As a Food Service Sergeant (Shift Leader) with a medical battalion, supervised operation of unit food service activity in field or garrison; provided technical guidance to four personnel in proper food preparation, temperatures, and time periods and ensured that all tasks were accomplished in accordance with food service operations. Was recognized for my emphasis on teamwork and cohesion within the section.

While at Keebler Bakery, Miami, FL, as the Director of Food Service Operations (2000-2002), stepped into a situation where the company was experiencing a long period of nonprofit mostly due to poor hiring practices and immediately turned profits largely by "weeding through" unskilled and unprofessional employees, training those remaining employees, and hiring skilled professionals within a very tight budget. Created training programs and practically "rewrote" the training guidelines.

Education and training related to this skill:

- Excelled in military-sponsored leadership and development training programs designed to mold the military's top supervisory personnel.
- Learned supervisory skills and effective leadership techniques while earning an associate's degree in Food Service Management.

KSA #2: Knowledge of Technical Practices.

Throughout my food service career as a Cook, Food Service Supervisor, and a Dining Facility Manager, my experience combined with formal training programs has developed my ability to perform the theoretical, artistic, and precise work involved in food service and has developed my knowledge of cooking ingredients and my ability to judge products by odor, taste, color, consistency, and temperature.

For example I know from my experience:

Details give credibility.

- **how to identify spices:** garlic powder, poultry seasoning, thyme, oregano, chicken and beef bastes, etc. I have excellent taste buds, and specialize in preparing tasty sauces and gravies.
- **how to cook poultry and dressing** until internal temperatures reach 165 degrees F.
- **how to cook pork** to internal temperatures of 150 degrees F or until the meat is white.
- **how to use bayonet-type thermometers** to evaluate doneness.
- **how to use proper cooking methods** for many different types of ingredients: e.g., both tomato and milk products, because of their acidity, will burn or scorch very quickly. The solution is to use a double-broiler.
- **how to substitute ingredients:** e.g., I have often substituted ketchup for tomato paste, sage for poultry seasoning, etc. As a cook, wherever dietary restraints or lack of supplies presented a problem, my knowledge of substitution of ingredients has helped me often.
- **how to determine correct ingredient measurements:** As a cook, I weighed ingredients using a very accurate scale. This gave me excellent experience in seeing exactly what correct ingredient measurement looked like, to the point now where I am an excellent judge by sight as well.
- **how to use proper, safe, and sanitary methods to store food:** e.g., putting foods in shallow containers (flat pans) and marking the date and time of refrigeration; after initial chilling, refrigerating foods at temperatures at or below 45 degrees F; etc.

My knowledge of cooking ingredients has also come from sections of food preparation courses I have taken, specifically:
- Food Handling Course, Ft. Monmouth, NJ, 1998
- Food Management Course, Ft. McCoy, WI, 1995
- Food Service Course, Ft. Stewart, GA, 1995
- Food Service Course, Ft. Polk, LA, 1994
- Successfully completed 30 credits towards an Associate of Arts degree in Hospitality Management, International Correspondence School, 1998
- A.A., Food Service Management, Miami Technical Community College, Miami, FL, 1999

COOK SUPERVISOR

MARK DAVIS FLYNN

SSN: 000-00-0000

COOK SUPERVISOR, WG-10 ANNOUNCEMENT #XYZ123

KSA #3: Ability to interpret instructions, specifications, etc. (other than blueprints).

Throughout my military career (2002-2003 and 1996-1999), I have been required to strictly follow Army Regulation 30-1 which is a comprehensive manual governing all operations involving military food service functions as well as follow Army Regulation 30-21 which is a comprehensive manual governing the food program specifically for the Army Field Feeding System.

These regulations layout specific guidelines covering:

Requisitioning	Receiving
Issue procedures	Turn-in procedures
Inventories	Accounting
Return of residuals	Reports
Medical feeding standards	Inpatient census
Inpatient accounting	

In addition, follow recipe cards and written menu instructions which includes:
Reviewing portions
Checking to ensure correct number of servings
Confirming preparation time of all items
Properly cutting, weighing, and measuring of portions
Cooking procedures including roasting, baking, boiling, stewing, steaming, and frying
Regulating cooking temperatures and pressures during cooking
Operating manuals for crimp machines, buffalo choppers, meat tenderizers, microwave ovens, special roast beef cookers, mixers, grinders, slicers, steam kettles, electric coffee urns, stoves, convection ovens, grills, tilt grills, potato peelers, dishwashers, refrigerators, freezers, steam tables, and other specialized food preparation and service equipment, both powered and mechanical, and all in accordance with written safety regulations
Portioning and serving of all food and beverage items including salads and desserts
Properly preserving all leftovers for future use

KSA #4: Ability to use and maintain tools and equipment.

From March 1996 to the present, as a Cook, Food Service Supervisor, Director of Food Service Operations, and Assistant Cafeteria Director, I have developed my skills in using and maintaining kitchen tools and equipment.

Specifically, since June 2003, in my current job as a Supervisor, Consolidated Dining Facilities, Ft. Monmouth, NJ, I have safely operated the following powered and mechanical kitchen equipment and utensils:

- **mixers:** for mixing dough, potatoes, pudding, etc.
- **grinders/slicers:** for meat and vegetables (e.g. for meat loaf, grind onions with meat)
- **steam kettles:** for steaming vegetables (put a little water in, add vegetables, and steam)
- **electric coffee urns:** for brewing fresh coffee
- **stoves:** for cooking gravies, stews, etc.
- **convection ovens:** for baking bread and cakes, roasting and broiling meats, etc.
- **grills, tilt grills:** for frying eggs, pancakes, French toast, etc.
- **peelers:** to peel potatoes and carrots
- **steam tables:** for keeping prepared items hot
- **dishwashers, refrigerators and freezers:** for cleaning and storing
- **knives, cutting boards, spatulas, etc.**
- **crimp machines:** to compress pie dough
- **buffalo chopper:** to grind and shred vegetables
- **meat tenderizers:** to tenderize meat
- **roast beef cookers:** for cooking roast beef in a special, tender way.

Also as a Supervisor with Keebler Bakery Cafeteria, Miami, FL (2000-02), I continually, on a daily basis, instructed the 30 people in my cafeteria in the safe use of all the above mentioned equipment.

The following courses included training in the safe operation of kitchen tools and equipment:
- Food Handling Course, Ft. Monmouth, NJ, 1998
- Food Management Course, Ft. McCoy, WI, 1995
- Food Service Course, Ft. Stewart, GA, 1995
- Food Service Course, Ft. Polk, LA, 1994
- Successfully completed 30 credits towards an Associate of Arts degree in Hospitality Management, International Correspondence School, 1998
- A.A., Food Service Management, Miami Technical Community College, Miami, FL, 1999

Criminal Investigator (Ranking Factor)

ROSS A. CHELSEA

SSN: 000-00-0000

CRIMINAL INVESTIGATOR, GS-09/13 ANNOUNCEMENT #XYZ123

Ranking Factor (A): Knowledge of physical security concepts, principles, and practices to include the functional application of electronic security methods to mitigate risks and enhance facility security.

In my current position as a Criminal Investigator for the Las Cruces Police Department, Protective Services Division, GS-09/13 (2002-present), I clearly demonstrate knowledge of physical security concepts principles, and practices while monitoring the physical security at the main Federal Building in Las Cruces.

At the main Federal Building, I monitor physical security to ensure that an adequate number of surveillance cameras are in place, that all surveillance cameras are installed in the most efficient locations, and that they are functioning properly. Oversee, control, and assure the adequate placement and proper functioning of electronic card access systems which use a magnetic strip to disengage the door lock, and monitor the issuing of key cards for the system. Work closely with the Property Manager to ensure that adequate controls are in place over the physical keys to the building and that sufficient and adequate locks are installed to secure the premises.

As the resident expert on physical security matters, I provide training to all contract guards assigned to National Security Agency (NSA)-protected buildings for the entire state of New Mexico. Instruct these contract security personnel in all aspects of Federal building security policies, practices, and procedures, to include the operations of the X-ray and magnetometer. Train contract personnel on building rules and regulations, NSA policies on the use of force, and all other matters related to physical security as implemented by the NSA on Federal property under our protection.

Consulted with tenant agencies, assisting them in the implementation of self-protection plans to cope with emergency situations. Provided advice and guidance on ways to improve physical security to victims of crime and participated in crime prevention seminars, instructing classes of office managers and other personnel on common physical security practices and the importance of following these practices to ensure the safety of their employees.

After the bombing of several Federal buildings and bomb threats, I was instrumental in assessing and enhancing the physical security at the main Federal buildings in Portales and Las Cruces, New Mexico. Oversaw the placement and installation of X-ray machines and magnetometers in both buildings, as well as assigning and directing the number and placement of contract security forces throughout both buildings.

Enhanced security at the Albuquerque, NM Congressional Offices, replacing outdated security panels and installing duress alarms in the offices of two Senators and one Congressman.

Conduct security assessments and monitor physical security at Las Cruces Police Department location, checking to ensure that the fencing and lighting around outdoor play areas is adequate to provide clear visibility and security. Ensure that there are clear lines of sight to all play areas, so that no intruders could be hiding inside the fences, concealed behind shrubbery, landscaping, or play equipment. Inspect locking mechanisms on all doors to verify that they provide substantial protection to the children and personnel within the building, and could not be easily compromised due to problems with locks of inferior quality. While conducting security assessments of the LCPD, I recommended the implementation of a video surveillance system for the facilities; this recommendation has been tentatively approved and will be implemented once the necessary funds have been appropriated.

Education and Training Related to the KSA:

Bachelor of Science in Criminal Justice, with concentrations in Sociology and Correctional Administration, minor in International Studies, New Mexico State University, Las Cruces, NM, 1999.

Completed numerous additional training and development courses at the New Mexico Police Academy in Albuquerque, NM, which included:

- Advanced Physical Security Training Course, 80 hours, 2001
- Data Recovery and Analysis Training Course, 40 hours, 2001
- Financial Investigations Practical Skills Training Course, 40 hours, 2000
- Criminal Intelligence Analyst Training Course, 80 hours, 1999
- Personnel Security Adjudication Training Course, 40 hours, 1999
- Basic Criminal Investigation Course, 320 hours, 1998
- Basic Police Course, 320 hours, 1998

Completed supervisory training courses sponsored by the Las Cruces Police Department, Las Cruces, NM, including:

- Supervising: A Guide for All Levels, 8 hours, 2000
- Constructive Discipline for Supervisors, 6 hours, 2000
- Basic Supervision Course, 6 hours, 2000

Criminal Investigator (Ranking Factor)

ROSS A. CHELSEA

SSN: 000-00-0000

CRIMINAL INVESTIGATOR, GS-09/13 ANNOUNCEMENT #XYZ123

Ranking Factor (B): Knowledge of law enforcement concepts, principles, and practices.

In my current position as a Criminal Investigator for the Las Cruces Police Department, Protective Services Division, GS-09/13 (2002-present), my knowledge of law enforcement concepts, principles, and practices is exhibited while planning, organizing, and conducting criminal and noncriminal investigations, and performing mobile and stationary surveillance to observe the activities of individuals involved in the investigation. When sufficient evidence is obtained to justify such action, I prepare requests for and obtain search warrants. Process crime scenes to obtain such physical evidence as latent fingerprints, hair and skin samples, fibers, etc. Operate concealed cameras, audio and videocassette recorders, directional microphones, and other technical investigative aids. Conduct and document interviews with victims, witnesses, and suspects, using learned interrogative techniques to obtain corroborative statements to support the physical evidence.

Most recently, I was assigned to an internal investigation with the Washington Headquarters Services. The position involved investigating fraudulent or inappropriate use of government property by federal employees. Under the auspices of the Washington Headquarters Services, I conducted a week-long surveillance of the suspect, during which time I observed him misusing his government vehicle on numerous occasions, to include allowing non-government personnel the use of the vehicle. In addition, there was some evidence involving contracting fraud, specifically fraudulent payments to government officials by another government employee. This aspect of the investigation is still ongoing.

In April of 2002, a case involving theft of government property involving a number of Hispanic artifacts was turned over to the National Security Agency for investigation. The thefts had occurred in 1998, at which time the International Affairs Division reported the matter to the Las Cruces Police Department. The LCPD took no action, as the case involved Federal government property, and thus was under the jurisdiction of the LCPD. Because the value of the stolen property was only $10,500, the case was assigned a low priority by the LCPD. As a result, almost no action had been taken until the case was turned over to the National Security Agency and assigned to me. The investigation called for a detailed internal audit of the museum's accounting and inventory records. After careful examination of the NSA's invoices, bills of lading, shipping manifests, and payment records, I was able to positively identify the 10 pieces that had been stolen and confirm the dates that they were received. Despite the four-year time lag between the commission of the crime and the start of the investigation, my efforts resulted in recovery of all the stolen artifacts and the identification and apprehension of a suspect, who was charged with felony theft of government property.

I also conducted an internal investigation in a 2000 case involving suspicious payments to a long-term government contractor that was deferred to the NSA by the LCPD Investigator, who had no investigator on-site. I was assigned to the case, which involved performing a comprehensive and detailed audit of accounting files for the office of the

Representative Department. I reviewed all LCPD contracts, invoices, work orders, payment requests, and authorizations, reconciling all figures to ensure that actual payment amounts matched the figures agreed to in the contract, and that all work which had been paid for was actually performed. As a result of this investigation, it was determined that there were no irregularities in LCPD payments to the contractor. No charges were brought in the matter.

In 2001, I was assigned to an investigation for the Washington Headquarters Services office related to possible fraudulent acquisition of surplus government property. The investigation centered on recent transfers of government surplus communications equipment and vehicles, including dump trucks, heavy construction equipment, boats, light trucks, etc. by the Department of Transportation. After conducting a thorough audit of all accounting paperwork for both agencies, I was able to prepare a complete list of items received from government surplus in order to determine whether or not these items had been obtained under false pretenses. These items were supposedly requisitioned for use by the requesting agencies, but on investigation, I determined that the property was being sold, given to, or used improperly for the benefit of private individuals or companies. As a result of my audit, one investigation was closed and the property in question was seized by the government. Due to the extent of the property fraudulently obtained, other related investigations are still ongoing.

Earlier as Lead Detective/ Police Officer (1995-1997), I supervised four or more Investigative Police Officers per assigned shift, overseeing their performance in the full range of law enforcement duties, including but not limited to conducting initial and follow-up investigations, processing crime scenes to obtain physical evidence, and processing search and arrest warrants. Served as a uniformed Police Officer and leader/ trainer in the Protective Services Division, ensuring the safety and protecting the civil rights of individuals while they were on controlled property that was owned or under the control of one of its tenant agencies. Maintained order, preserved the peace, and protected all controlled property. Conducted initial and follow-up investigations of reported thefts, burglaries, assaults, and threats, as well as instances of vandalism and narcotics violations. Interviewed victims, witnesses, and suspects during the investigative process.

Education and Training Related to the KSA:

Bachelor of Science in Criminal Justice, with concentrations in Sociology and Correctional Administration, minor in International Studies, New Mexico State University, Las Cruces, NM, 1999.

Completed numerous additional training and development courses at the New Mexico Police Academy in Albuquerque, NM, which included:

- Advanced Physical Security Training Course, 80 hours, 2001
- Data Recovery and Analysis Training Course, 40 hours, 2001
- Financial Investigations Practical Skills Training Course, 40 hours, 2000
- Criminal Intelligence Analyst Training Course, 80 hours, 1999
- Personnel Security Adjudication Training Course, 40 hours, 1999
- Basic Criminal Investigation Course, 320 hours, 1998
- Basic Police Course, 320 hours, 1998

Criminal Investigator (Ranking Factor)

ROSS A. CHELSEA

SSN: 000-00-0000

CRIMINAL INVESTIGATOR, GS-09/13 ANNOUNCEMENT #XYZ123

Criminal Investigator, GS-09/13 Announcement #XYZ123 Ranking Factor C

Ranking Factor (C): Skill in practicing good customer service.

In my present position as a Criminal Investigator for the Las Cruces Police Department (2002-present), I demonstrate my skill in practicing good customer service while interacting daily with employees of various tenant agencies and other customers on a variety of subjects. Receive and resolve customer complaints related to parking enforcement and violations, malfunctioning electronic key cards, and both complaints and compliments regarding the behavior and demeanor of contract security and LCPD personnel interacting with customers.

Participate in the LCPD's Security Committees, representing the department before meetings to discuss security concerns at the Federal buildings. In this capacity, I recommend the physical security specialist crime prevention seminars and classes that we offer, and interact with customers in order to address and alleviate any worries they might have related to the physical security of the premises. In these meetings, I also present information regarding electronic and video security and surveillance systems that could improve the security stance of the building.

Attended a number of lectures and seminars at the Washington DC's National and Regional Headquarters providing better customer service to clients, customer-oriented policing, and other service-related topics.

In earlier positions as a Lead Detective/Police Officer (1995-1997), I provided exceptional customer service while responding to a variety of complaints. While conducting initial and follow-up investigations of reported crimes, dealt with victims and witnesses in a polite and courteous manner. Effectively interacted with individuals who were often distressed in a calming, persuasive manner in order to secure eyewitness testimony and other information necessary to resolving the case.

Education and Training Related to the KSA:

Bachelor of Science in Criminal Justice, with concentrations in Sociology and Correctional Administration, minor in International Studies, New Mexico State University, Las Cruces, NM, 1999.

Completed numerous additional training and development courses at the New Mexico Police Academy in Albuquerque, NM, which included:

- Advanced Physical Security Training Course, 80 hours, 2001
- Data Recovery and Analysis Training Course, 40 hours, 2001
- Financial Investigations Practical Skills Training Course, 40 hours, 2000
- Criminal Intelligence Analyst Training Course, 80 hours, 1999
- Personnel Security Adjudication Training Course, 40 hours, 1999
- Basic Criminal Investigation Course, 320 hours, 1998
- Basic Police Course, 320 hours, 1998

Completed supervisory training courses sponsored by the Las Cruces Police Department, Las Cruces, NM.

ROSS A. CHELSEA

SSN: 000-00-0000

CRIMINAL INVESTIGATOR, GS-09/13 ANNOUNCEMENT #XYZ123

Ranking Factor (D): Ability to supervise.

In my current position as a Criminal Investigator, GS-09/13, for the Las Cruces Police Department (2002-present), I demonstrate my ability to supervise and to coordinate the work of others in a variety of ways.

As the resident expert on physical security matters, I provide training to all contract guards assigned to NSA-protected buildings for the entire state of New Mexico. Instruct these contract security personnel in all aspects of Federal building security policies, practices, and procedures, to include the operations of the X-ray and magnetometer. Train contract personnel on building rules and regulations, NSA policies on the use of force, and all other matters related to physical security as implemented by the NSA on Federal property that is under our protection. I assume the leadership role in NSA meetings, participate in the Portales, New Mexico conferences, and hold responsibility for the reporting and oversight of NSA Repair and Alteration projects. I also provide advice and status for all physical security reassessments.

In an earlier position as Lead Detective/Police Officer in Silver City, NM (1993-1995), I supervised for or more Police Officers per assigned shift, overseeing their performance of the full range of law enforcement duties, including but not limited to conducting initial and follow-up investigations, processing crime scenes to obtain physical evidence, and processing search and arrest warrants. Served as a leader and trainer in the Protective Services Division, instructing junior officers and other personnel in NSA practices, policies, and procedures as well as in the performance of their daily duties as Police Officers. Previously, while serving as a uniformed Police Officer for the Sierra County Police Department (1989-1991), I was frequently called on to serve as Senior Officer, directing the work of as many as four junior uniformed officers. Monitored the performance of new officers responding to calls, checking on the officer and advising them as necessary to ensure that they were following appropriate procedures so that any arrests or other official actions were documented properly in order to allow the case to be prosecuted.

While serving my country as a Noncommissioned officer in the U.S. Army, I managed as many as nine personnel while leading and providing supervisory oversight and training to a nuclear weapons team. Oversaw training schedules for all personnel under my supervision, in addition to personally teaching some training courses.

Education and Training Related to the KSA:

Bachelor of Science in Criminal Justice, with concentrations in Sociology and Correctional Administration, minor in International Studies, New Mexico State University, Las Cruces, NM, 1999.

Completed numerous additional training and development courses at the New Mexico Police Academy in Albuquerque, NM, which included:

- Advanced Physical Security Training Course, 80 hours, 2001
- Data Recovery and Analysis Training Course, 40 hours, 2001

Criminal Investigator (Ranking Factor)

ROSS A. CHELSEA

SSN: 000-00-0000

CRIMINAL INVESTIGATOR, GS-09/13 ANNOUNCEMENT #XYZ123

Ranking Factor (E): Ability to work independently for extended periods.

In my current position as a Special Agent, GS-09/13, for the Criminal Investigation Section of the Las Cruces Police Department, Protective Services Division (2002-present), I have clearly demonstrated my ability to work independently while single-handedly completing a number of complex investigations.

Most recently, I was assigned to an internal investigation involving fraudulent or inappropriate use of government property by a Federal employee. Under the auspices of the Washington Headquarters Services, I single-handedly conducted a week-long surveillance of the suspect, during which time I observed him misusing his government vehicle on numerous occasions, to include allowing non-government personnel to use the vehicle. In addition, there was some evidence involving contracting fraud, specifically fraudulent payments to government officials by another government employee. This aspect of the investigation is still ongoing.

In April of 2002, I worked independently for a more extended time on a case involving theft of government property, specifically a number of Hispanic artifacts. I was assigned to investigate after the case was turned over to the National Security Agency for investigation. The thefts had occurred in 1998, at which time the International Affairs Division reported the matter to the Las Cruces Police Department. The Las Cruces police took no action, as the case involved Federal government property, and thus was under the jurisdiction of the LCPD. Because the value of the stolen property was only $10,500, the case was assigned a low priority by the LCPD. As a result, almost no action was taken until the case was turned over to the National Security Agency and assigned to me.

Working the investigation on my own, I conducted a detailed internal audit of the museum's accounting and inventory records. After careful examination of the invoices, bills of lading, shipping manifests, and payment records, I was able to positively identify the 10 pieces that had been stolen and confirm the dates that they were received. My efforts were solely responsible for the recovery of all the stolen artifacts and the identification and apprehension of a suspect, in spite of a four-year time lag between the commission of the crime and the start of my investigation. The suspect was subsequently arrested and charged with felony theft of government property.

I also independently conducted an internal investigation in a 2000 case involving suspicious payments to a long-term government contractor that was deferred to the NSA by the LCPD Investigator, who had no investigator on-site. I was assigned to the case, and immediately undertook the arduous task of meticulously poring over all financial accounts, records, and transaction for the office of the NSA Customer Representative Department. I reviewed all contracts, invoices, work orders, payment requests, and authorizations, reconciling all figures to ensure that actual payment amounts matched the figures agreed to in the contract, and that all work which had been paid for was actually performed. As a result of my three-week investigation, it was determined that there were no irregularities in the payments to this contractor, and no charges were brought in the matter.

In 2001, I was assigned to complete an investigation for the Washington Headquarters Services related to possible fraudulent acquisition of surplus government property. The investigation centered on recent transfers of government surplus communications equipment and vehicles, including dump trucks, heavy construction equipment, boats and light trucks by the Department of Transportation. After conducting a thorough audit of all accounting paperwork for both agencies, I was able to prepare a complete list of items received from government surplus in order to determine whether or not these items had been obtained under false pretenses. These items were supposedly requisitioned for use by the requesting agencies, but on investigation, I determined that the property was being sold, given to, or used improperly for the benefit of private individuals or companies. As a result of my audit, one investigation was closed and the property in question was seized by the government. Due to the extent of the property fraudulently obtained, other related investigations are still ongoing.

Education and Training Related to the KSA:
Bachelor of Science in Criminal Justice, with concentrations in Sociology and Correctional Administration, minor in International Studies, New Mexico State University, Las Cruces, NM, 1999.

Completed numerous additional training and development courses at the New Mexico Police Academy in Albuquerque, NM, which included:
- Advanced Physical Security Training Course, 80 hours, 2001
- Data Recovery and Analysis Training Course, 40 hours, 2001
- Financial Investigations Practical Skills Training Course, 40 hours, 2000
- Criminal Intelligence Analyst Training Course, 80 hours, 1999
- Personnel Security Adjudication Training Course, 40 hours, 1999
- Basic Criminal Investigation Course, 320 hours, 1998
- Basic Police Course, 320 hours, 1998

CUSTOMS OFFICER

LAURA C. ROBERTS

SSN: 000-00-0000

CUSTOMS OFFICER, GS-07/09 ANNOUNCEMENT #XYZ123

KSA #1: Knowledge of range of processing functions related to importation of merchandise, i.e., formal entry, warehouse, TIB, protest, claims, liquidations, collections, etc. (Understanding a wide range of functions associated with the importation of merchandise.)

In my capacity as a Customs Inspector, I have acquired expert knowledge of a wide range of functions associated with the importation of merchandise and I expertly perform the full range of inspection, enforcement, and examination work relating to the enforcement of Customs and other agency laws and regulations. It is my job to regulate the import/export of merchandise, cargo, and articles accompanying travelers into and out of the U.S. at designated places of entry, and arrival and departure of vessels, aircraft, and vehicles engaged in such transport. I must also exclude terrorists, drugs, and other contraband from the U.S., and enforce of quotas and marketing agreements. Furthermore, I must collect and protect revenues due the U.S.

With regard to cargo processing in particular, I physically examine and inspect articles being imported or exported to verify merchandise is correctly invoiced and can be entered into commerce of the U.S. or is cleared to be exported. As Reviewing Officer, I analyze entries to determine examination required using automated systems such as National Information and Research Center of Seattle, Selective Commercial System, Treasury Enforcement Communications System, National Telecommunications and Legal Services System, Cargo Regulator, and others. Using this information and drawing on my own expertise, I make decisions related to determining whether cargo-mail-baggage requires more intensive examination and I advise the examining officer of the type of exams required. As Examining Officer, I perform inspection based on reviewing officers' advice, performing document review, intensive examination, and other methods. I sometimes override the recommendation from the computer system or reviewing officer upon my discovery of information indicating appropriate action.

- It is my job to examine cargo and documents relative to purchase and shipment to detect merchandise imported-exported contrary to law. I examine merchandise to determine if it meets conditions necessary for import-export, and I deny permits unless requirements are met. I oversee unloading of cargo or in-bond shipments, and I am responsible for proper placement of cargo for expeditious weighing, gauging, measuring, or sampling. I also make decisions to release cargo under proper entry-delivery permits.
- Am responsible for enforcing laws and regulations governing compliance of bonded warehouses and foreign trade zones (FTZs). By conducting on-site inspections, as well as through review and analysis of all accounts and records of transactions, I insure that all merchandise is entered, manipulated, manufactured, or removed properly. I conduct cargo security of FTZs, container stations, and other locations where merchandise is stored, and I compare results with Customs security standards and regulatory requirements.
- I prepare informal entries covering commercial importations up to allowable values, and I retain goods not supported by permits or licenses in bonded premises for further processing. I classify and determine value of goods, and I release free and dutiable

goods while handling the responsibility for control and accounting for monies and instruments received when collecting duties and taxes.
- I must utilize my knowledge of processing functions related to importation of merchandise as I visually and physically inspect cargo, baggage, and mail; search suspected violators of laws and seize prohibited or smuggled articles; search conveyances; inspect records and documents; seize contraband, equipment, and vehicles; and make arrests.

My knowledge of the full range of processing functions is also in evidence as I perform as an Examining Officer, Reviewing Officer, and member of a special team. In that capacity, I demonstrate my knowledge in this area as I inspect travelers, conveyances, and accompanying baggage and other articles to quickly identify subjects for additional attention and to facilitate processing for legitimate international travelers. I must demonstrate my knowledge in this area as I make on-the-spot decisions and take actions on situations that may provide evidence of smuggling, fraud, terrorism, or other violations. My communication skills are fully applied as I inspect and search private vehicles, aircraft, boats, etc. accompanying arriving persons. I have greatly refined my knowledge of processing functions related to the importation of merchandise as I coordinate with a wide variety of people in the process of inspecting, classifying, and assessing and/or collecting duties and taxes on baggage and articles imported.

Frequently designated as an Immigration Inspector, I apply my knowledge related to the processing of merchandise for importation as I perform dual-inspection duties which include enforcing assigned laws and regulations concerning import-export of baggage, cargo, and freight, and the movement of passengers and vehicles through the facility. I demonstrate my knowledge of processing functions related to the importation of merchandise as I visually and physically inspect cargo, baggage, and mail; search suspected violators of laws and seize prohibited or smuggled articles. I also demonstrate my knowledge of the processing functions related to the importation of merchandise as I search conveyances, inspect records and documents, seize contraband, equipment, and vehicles, and make arrests.

Training related to my knowledge of processing functions:
Training: In addition to extensive on-the-job training as a Customs Officer, I have completed training in the following areas which helped me acquire related knowledge and skills:
- U.S. Department of Immigration Orientation & Training, 2001
- Training in Microsoft Word and Excel 2000; Windows NT, 2001
- Passenger Interview Vehicle Inspection Training, 2001
- CPR, 2000
- U.S. Department of Immigration Canine Enforcement Officer Course, 1999
- U.S. Department of Immigration Basic Inspector Course, 1998
- U.S. Department of Immigration Basic Training Classes, 1998-99
- Quarterly Hands-on Firearms/Weapons and Class Training, 1998-present
- Agriculture/ U.S. Department of Immigration Cross Training, 1998
- Correctional Officer Associated Courses, 1997
- Patrol Dog Handler Drug Detection Course, 1997
- Patrol Dog Handler, 1996
- Military Police School, 1996

CUSTOMS OFFICER

LAURA C. ROBERTS

SSN: 000-00-0000

CUSTOMS OFFICER, GS-07/09 ANNOUNCEMENT #XYZ123

KSA #2: Knowledge of tariff and other import-related laws, regulations, policies, procedures, and precedents. (This element includes the application of laws, rules, regulations, etc., in order to apply requirements for importation of merchandise to a specific situation and to make determinations of compliance.)

In my current job as a Customs Officer, I routinely demonstrate my knowledge of tariff and other import-related laws, regulations, procedures, and precedents while conducting tariff classification and performing appraisals to assess the customs duties owed on commercially imported merchandise. I apply Federal laws, rules, regulations, etc., while scrutinizing items imported commercially, ensuring compliance with a wide range of government requirements. Perform the full range of inspection, enforcement, and examination work relating to the enforcement of Customs and other agency laws and regulations concerning the following functional areas:

- Import/export of merchandise, cargo, and articles accompanying travelers into and out of the U.S. at designated places of entry, and arrival and departure of vessels, aircraft, and vehicles engaged in such transport;
- Excluding terrorists, drugs, and other contraband from the U.S., as well as enforcing quotas and marketing agreements;
- Collecting and protecting revenues due the U.S.

I demonstrated my knowledge of import-related laws and regulations while handling the responsibility for 8 significant seizures totaling 240 pounds of illegal narcotics valued at $967,000 and ensuring that the evidence was stored and catalogued appropriately.

In addition, I analyze incoming entry documents packages to prioritize handling as required by the established line of merchandise, prior to conducting a more intensive review for final classification, appraisement, and related action. Verify documents to ensure pertinence of entries to their assigned line of merchandise, the applicability of quotas or other import restrictions, and the presence, completeness, accuracy, and consistency of all required import-related statistical information and required forms. Liquidate entries not requiring additional documentation, consideration of superseded tariff provisions, or lengthy arithmetic computations. Compute final amount of duty and any tax owed by or to be refunded to the importer.

I demonstrate my knowledge of tariff and other import-related laws and regulations as I visually and physically inspect cargo, baggage, and mail; search suspected violators of laws and seize prohibited or smuggled articles; search conveyances; inspect records and documents; seize contraband, equipment, and vehicles; and make arrests. Since my duties frequently expose me to some personal risk, I must make prudent decisions as I exhibit my ability to analyze, assess facts and data, determine the appropriate action and solution according to the situation, and make determinations on compliance issues.

As an Examining Officer, Reviewing Officer, and member of a special team, I inspect travelers, conveyances, and accompanying baggage and other articles to quickly identify subjects for additional attention and to facilitate processing for legitimate international travelers. I must always analyze a situation quickly in order to make on-the-spot decisions and take actions on situations that may provide evidence of smuggling, fraud, terrorism, or other violations. My knowledge of tariff and other import-related laws, regulations, procedures, and precedents, is applied as I inspect and search private vehicles, aircraft, boats, etc. accompanying arriving persons. I have greatly refined my analytical skills in the process of inspecting, classifying, and assessing and/or collecting duties and taxes on baggage and articles imported.

Frequently designated as an Immigration Inspector, I also exhibit my knowledge of tariff and other import-related laws, regulations, etc. as I perform duties to legally determine admissibility of all persons attempting entry to the U.S., including primary inspection activities which require obtaining a legal declaration; verifying immigration status; making appropriate referral decisions; and any other cross designation duties appropriate, such as issuing documents. I also apply my analytical skills while carrying out other dual-inspection duties which including enforcing assigned laws and regulations concerning import-export of baggage, cargo, and freight, and the movement of passengers and vehicles through the facility.

Education and training related to this ability:
College: My analytical, communication, decision-making, and problem-solving skills were refined in the process of pursuing my Associate degree in Accounting and Economics from Seattle Central Community College, Seattle, WA.
Training: In addition to extensive on-the-job training as a Customs Officer, I have completed training in the following areas which helped me acquire related knowledge and skills:
- U.S. Department of Immigration Orientation & Training, 2001
- Training in Microsoft Word and Excel 2000; Windows NT, 2001
- Passenger Interview Vehicle Inspection Training, 2001
- CPR, 2000
- U.S. Department of Immigration Canine Enforcement Officer Course, 1999
- U.S. Department of Immigration Basic Inspector Course, 1998
- U.S. Department of Immigration Basic Training Classes, 1998-99
- Quarterly Hands-on Firearms/Weapons and Class Training, 1998-present
- Agriculture/ U.S. Department of Immigration Cross Training, 1998
- Correctional Officer Associated Courses, 1997
- Patrol Dog Handler Drug Detection Course, 1997
- Patrol Dog Handler, 1996
- Military Police School, 1996

CUSTOMS OFFICER

LAURA C. ROBERTS

SSN: 000-00-0000

CUSTOMS OFFICER, GS-07/09 ANNOUNCEMENT #XYZ123

KSA #3: Knowledge of identifying characteristics and trade practices related to imported merchandise. (This element includes general knowledge of the technical and physical characteristics, commercial uses, methods of determining value, production, marketing, and distribution practices associated with imported merchandise and requirements for admissibility.)

In my capacity as a Customs Inspector, I have acquired expert knowledge of identifying characteristics and trade practices involving a wide range of functions associated with the importation of merchandise. I demonstrate this knowledge while expertly performing the full range of inspection, enforcement, and examination work relating to the enforcement of Customs and other agency laws and regulations. I regularly appraise imported articles or products falling within designated commodity areas as well as interpreting and applying tariff schedules and value law on an ongoing basis. In cases when documentation does not provide a sufficient basis to correctly apply laws and regulations, I physically examine samples of the imported merchandise, interview importers, and consult with persons knowledgeable about the physical characteristics or trade practices associated with particular kinds of imported merchandise.

It is also my job to regulate the import/export of merchandise, cargo, and articles accompanying travelers into and out of the U.S. at designated places of entry, and arrival and departure of vessels, aircraft, and vehicles engaged in such transport. Demonstrate a thorough working knowledge of commonly applied Customs regulations, import requirements of other agencies, tariff classification principles, and bases of value under the applicable Trade Agreement Acts, as well as sources of factual and interpretive information. I must also exclude terrorists, drugs, and other contraband from the U.S., and ensure the enforcement of quotas and marketing agreements. In addition to the above duties, I collect and protect revenues due the U.S.

With regard to cargo processing in particular, I physically examine and inspect articles being imported or exported to verify merchandise is correctly invoiced and can be entered into commerce of the U.S. or is cleared to be exported. As Reviewing Officer, I analyze entries to determine examination required using automated systems such as National Information and Research Center of Seattle, Selective Commercial System, Immigration Enforcement and Communications System, National Telecommunications and Legal Services System, U.S. Cargo Regulator System and others. Using this information and also drawing on my own expertise, I make decisions related to determining whether cargo-mail-baggage requires more intensive examination and I advise the examining officer of the type of exams required. As Examining Officer, I perform inspection based on reviewing officers' advice, performing document review, intensive examination, and other methods. I sometimes override the recommendation from the computer system or reviewing officer upon my discovery of information indicating that another action is appropriate.

- It is my job to examine cargo and documents relative to purchase and shipment to detect merchandise imported-exported contrary to law. I examine merchandise to determine if it meets conditions necessary for import-export, and I deny permits unless requirements are met. I oversee unloading of cargo or in-bond shipments, and I am responsible for proper placement of cargo for expeditious weighing, gauging, measuring, or sampling. I also make decisions to release cargo under proper entry-delivery permits.

- Am responsible for enforcing laws and regulations governing compliance of bonded warehouses and foreign trade zones. By conducting on-site inspections, as well as through review and analysis of all accounts and records of transactions, I insure that all merchandise is entered, manipulated, manufactured, or removed properly. I conduct cargo security, container stations, and other locations where merchandise is stored, and I compare results with Customs security standards and regulatory requirements.
- I prepare informal entries covering commercial importation up to allowable values, and I retain goods not supported by permits or licenses in bonded premises for further processing. I classify and determine value of goods, and I release free and dutiable goods while handling the responsibility for control and accounting for monies and instruments received when collecting duties and taxes.

I must utilize my knowledge of identifying characteristics and trade practices related to imported merchandise while visually and physically inspecting cargo, baggage, and mail; searching suspected violators of laws and seize prohibited or smuggled articles; searching conveyances; inspecting records and documents; seize contraband, equipment, and vehicles; and making arrests.

Previous jobs which refined my knowledge of identifying characteristics and trade practices related to imported merchandise:
- In my job as Canine Enforcement Officer from 07/99-11/01, I gained expert knowledge of trade practices and identifying characteristics related to imported merchandise as I utilized a drug detector dog to interdict narcotics/contraband arriving in the U.S. I learned to prepare a variety of written documents related to inspection of conveyances, cargo, baggage, freight, open areas, and building searches utilizing the detector dog.
- In my job as a Customs Inspector from 05/97-07/99, I gained knowledge related to the laws governing imports and exports.
- As an Immigration Inspector from 03/96-05/97, I refined my knowledge of identifying characteristics and trade practices related to imported merchandise while screening applicants for admission into the U.S.

Training related to my knowledge of processing functions:
Training: In addition to extensive on-the-job training as a Customs Officer, I have completed training in the following areas which helped me acquire related knowledge and skills:
- U.S. Department of Immigration Orientation & Training, 2001
- Training in Microsoft Word and Excel 2000; Windows NT, 2001
- Passenger Interview Vehicle Inspection Training, 2001
- CPR, 2000
- U.S. Department of Immigration Canine Enforcement Officer Course, 1999
- U.S. Department of Immigration Basic Inspector Course, 1998
- U.S. Department of Immigration Basic Training Classes, 1998-99
- Quarterly Hands-on Firearms/Weapons and Class Training, 1998-present

CUSTOMS OFFICER

LAURA C. ROBERTS

SSN: 000-00-0000

CUSTOMS OFFICER, GS-07/09 ANNOUNCEMENT #XYZ123

KSA #4: Ability to interpret and apply Federal laws, rules, regulations, precedents, etc. (This element includes the application of laws, rules, regulations, procedures, etc., to a specific situation or problem and making determinations on compliance.)

In my current job as Customs Officer, I routinely demonstrate my ability to interpret and apply Federal laws, rules, regulations, precedents, etc., while performing the full range of inspection, enforcement, and examination work relating to the enforcement of Customs and other agency laws and regulations concerning the following functional areas:

- Import/export of merchandise, cargo, and articles accompanying travelers into and out of the U.S. at designated places of entry, and arrival and departure of vessels, aircraft, and vehicles engaged in such transport;
- Excluding terrorists, drugs, and other contraband from the U.S., and enforcement of quotas and marketing agreements;
- Collecting and protecting revenues due the U.S.

I analyze via the Department of Immigration regulations. I applied my ability to interpret and apply Federal laws and regulations while handling the responsibility for 8 significant seizures totaling 240 pounds of illegal narcotics valued at $967,000.

I demonstrate my ability to analyze, interpret, and apply laws and regulations as I visually and physically inspect cargo, baggage, and mail; search suspected violators of laws and seize prohibited or smuggled articles; search conveyances; inspect records and documents; seize contraband, equipment, and vehicles; and make arrests. Since my duties frequently expose me to some personal risk, I must make prudent decisions as I exhibit my ability to analyze, assess facts and data, determine the appropriate action and solution according to the situation, and make determinations on compliance issues.

As an Examining Officer, Reviewing Officer, and member of a special team, I inspect travelers, conveyances, and accompanying baggage and other articles to quickly identify subjects for additional attention and to facilitate processing for legitimate international travelers. I must always analyze a situation quickly in order to make on-the-spot decisions and take actions on situations that may provide evidence of smuggling, fraud, terrorism, or other violations. My knowledge of Federal laws, rules, regulations, precedents, etc., is applied as I inspect and search private vehicles, aircraft, boats, etc. accompanying arriving persons. I have greatly refined my analytical skills in the process of inspecting, classifying, and assessing and/or collecting duties and taxes on baggage and articles imported.

Frequently designated as an Immigration Inspector, I also exhibit my ability to interpret and apply rules, etc. as I perform duties to legally determine admissibility of all persons attempting entry to the U.S., including primary inspection activities which require obtaining a legal declaration; verifying immigration status; making appropriate referral decisions; and any other cross designation duties appropriate, such as issuing documents.

I also apply my analytical skills while carrying out other dual-inspection duties which include enforcing assigned laws and regulations concerning import-export of baggage, cargo, and freight, and the movement of passengers and vehicles throughout the facility.

Previous jobs which refined my ability to interpret and apply Federal laws, rules, regulations, precedents, etc.:

- In my job as Canine Enforcement Officer from 07/99-11/01, I extensively utilized my ability to interpret and apply rules as I used a drug detector dog to interdict narcotics/contraband arriving in the U.S. I refined my analytical skills in the process of the inspection of conveyances, cargo, baggage, freight, open areas, and building searches utilizing the detector dog.
- In my job as a Customs Inspector from 05/97-07/99, I refined my knowledge of the laws governing imports and exports.
- As an Immigration Inspector from 03/96-05/97, I refined my skill in interpretation of laws and rules while conducting preliminary screenings of applicants for admission into the U.S.
- In my prior job as a Correctional Officer from 10/94-03/96, I polished my ability to interpret and apply regulations as I dealt with incarcerated persons. Since security and safety concerns were always present, I learned to assess situations quickly and make prudent decisions rapidly. Learned to quickly assess a volatile matter and take swift and appropriate action to prevent situations between inmates from escalating until they were out of hand.
- In my job as a Military Police Patrol/Drug Dog Handler from 01/92-10/94, I used my skills as I completed a wide variety of law enforcement paperwork. I took statements from victims, suspects, and criminals in accordance with military law and regulations, and I wrote incidental reports as needed. I displayed my knowledge as I authored written documents and reports praised for their clarity, logic, and attention to detail.

Education and training related to this ability:

College: My analytical, communication, decision-making, and problem-solving skills were refined in the process of pursuing my Associate degree in Accounting and Economics from Seattle Central Community College, Seattle, WA.

Training: In addition to extensive on-the-job training as a Customs Officer, I have completed training in the following areas which helped me acquire related knowledge and skills:

- U.S. Department of Immigration Orientation & Training, 2001
- Training in Microsoft Word and Excel 2000; Windows NT, 2001
- Passenger Interview Vehicle Inspection Training, 2001
- CPR, 2000
- U.S. Department of Immigration Canine Enforcement Officer Course, 1999
- U.S. Department of Immigration Basic Inspector Course, 1998
- U.S. Department of Immigration Basic Training Classes, 1998-99
- Quarterly Hands-on Firearms/Weapons and Class Training, 1998-present
- Agriculture/ U.S. Department of Immigration Cross Training, 1998
- Correctional Officer Associated Courses, 1997
- Patrol Dog Handler Drug Detection Course, 1997
- Patrol Dog Handler, 1996

DENTAL LAB TECHNICIAN

FAITH M. JOHNSTON

SSN: 000-00-0000

DENTAL LAB TECHNICIAN, GS-05/07 ANNOUNCEMENT #XYZ123

KSA #1: Knowledge of instruments, chemical, materials, and devices used in all phases of dental laboratory technology (e.g., plasters, stones, impression materials, metals, alloys, waxes, resin, light-cured resins, tin-foil substitutes, fuel, flux, monomer, solvents, polishing agents, wetting agents, acids, investments).

In my jobs as Chairside Dental Assistant with Dr. Sweeney from 2001-03 and with Dr. Francis from 2000-01, assisted doctors in chairside duties and was also responsible in opening and closing the office, order office equipment and supplies, as well as developing treatment plans and presenting them to patients. Demonstrated my skill in taking impressions while also controlling inventory and maintaining a current log and MSDS (Material Safety Data Sheets). Conducted training for new personnel on office equipment and material including B10 Hazardous Materials Shipment. Assisted in all phases of general dentistry including prosthodontics, surgical removal of impacted third molars, pediatrics, and amalgam and composite fillings. Charted and maintained patient records. Exposed and developed dental radiographs. Also assisted in endodontics, prosthodontics, and utilization of nitrous oxygen, and application of sealants. Prepared new patient documentation and evaluations of diet, dental habits, and vital signs. Assisted in crown and bridge work, prosthetics, nonsurgical periodontal therapy, and restorative and cosmetic dentistry.

Demonstrated my knowledge of hydrocolloid impression materials, mixing, measuring cleaning and safety precautions as well as knowledge of reversible hydrocelloids such as agar impression materials. Also demonstrated knowledge of irreversible hydrocolloids such as alginates. Became knowledgeable of the different temperatures at which agar impression materials become a solid and a liquid. Was skilled in setting times for normal set and fast set alginate. Demonstrated my knowledge of thermoplastic, impression compound, stick compound, and tray compound. Demonstrated familiarity with zinc oxide impression pastes, bit registration pastes, surgical pastes. Also demonstrated knowledge in elastomeric impression materials (rubber based impression materials) such as polysulfide, silicone, polysiloxane, polyethers, gypsum products and visible light-care impression materials. Worked with different classification of gypsum products, mixing ratio of gypsum products (water/powder ratio), setting time of gypsum products. Demonstrated familiarity with different alloys: base-metal, porcelain bonding, noble metal alloy as well as with soldering and welding.

KSA #2: Knowledge of the requirements to successfully fabricate fixed and removable dental appliances (e.g., knowledge of the anatomy of the head, face, oral structures to include the physiology of muscle functions as it relates to the movement of the jaw).

Dental Lab Technician, GS-05/07 Announcement #XYZ123 KSA #2

In my jobs as Chairside Dental Assistant with Dr. Sweeney from 2001-03 and with Dr. Francis from 2000-01, assisted doctors in chairside duties and was also responsible in opening and closing the office, order office equipment and supplies, as well as developing treatment plans and presenting them to patients. Demonstrated my skill in taking impressions while also controlling inventory and maintaining a current log and MSDS (Material Safety Data Sheets). Conducted training for new personnel on office equipment and material including B10 Hazardous Materials Shipment. Assisted in all phases of general dentistry including prosthodontics, surgical removal of impacted third molars, pediatrics, and amalgam and composite fillings. Charted and maintained patient records. Exposed and developed dental radiographs. Also assisted in endodontics, prosthodontics, and utilization of nitrous oxide, and application of sealants. Prepared new patient documentation and evaluations of diet, dental habits, and vital signs. Assisted in crown and bridge work, prosthetics, non-surgical periodontal therapy, and restorative and cosmetic dentistry.

As a Chairside Dental Assistant, maintained knowledge of the technical and precise margins needed to fabricate a properly fitting bridge or crown. Gained familiarity with the polyether materials, polyvinal solixane materials, alginate materials used to take impression for partials, dentures, and crown and bridge work. Demonstrated skill in handling and disinfecting rubber base materials and different impression materials. With certificate in Dental Radiology, took and mounted X rays. Maintained knowledge of anatomic landmarks of the head, jaws, tongue, etc. Became proficient in bite-wings, penapicals, panorex and caphalomatic X rays. Became familiar with anatomic landmarks and bones of the skull. Became familiar with bones and landmarks of the head palate and anatomic landmarks of the mandible. Also demonstrated familiarity with muscles of mastication and facial expression.

As a high school student, majored in Dental Lab Technology and was trained to fabricate full acrylic dentures and partial acrylic denture as well as partial cast dentures. Worked closely with dentist and patient.

EDITORIAL ASSISTANT

MELANIE T. EUBANKS

SSN: 000-00-0000

EDITORIAL ASSISTANT, GS-09 ANNOUNCEMENT #XYZ123

KSA #1: Ability to edit written material.

In my most recent position as a Field Office Assistant for the Department of Defense, I composed and prepared initial drafts of all correspondence for the office. Carefully proofread and edited this initial draft, making necessary changes to ensure precision of language, correct grammatical usage, and compliance with the appropriate format under the rules and regulations of correspondence. Also prepared all personnel actions for the office, to include editing, proofreading, and preparing final drafts of performance appraisals and incentive awards. Used style manuals, technical and non-technical dictionaries, and other references to ensure correctness of grammar and usage as well as precision of language. This position involved writing, editing, proofreading, and final printing of a large volume of letters, memos, reports, and other correspondence, as I posted transactions for over 35 contractors and more than 150 subcontractors. Was known for my sound judgment, exceptional communication and organizational abilities, and attention to detail.

In earlier positions as the Secretary and stenographer to the Chiefs of the Plans and Operations Division and Logistics Communication, I edited and proofread all office correspondence, including letters, memos, reports, and personnel actions, using style manuals, technical and non-technical dictionaries, and other reference materials to ensure correctness of grammar and usage, precision of language, and adherence to proper formats according to the rules and regulations of correspondence. I composed and prepared initial drafts of all correspondence, proofread and edited the initial draft, made necessary changes and prepared the final documents. As I worked closely with a senior rater, this position involved editing, proofreading, and final preparation of a heavy volume of personnel actions, including OERs, EPRs, recommendations for military awards, and civilian employee appraisals (DA-7223). Performed stenography duties, recording minutes of weekly staff meeting and other information which I then compiled, edited, and modified for use in memos, reports, letters, and other correspondence.

Education and Training related to this KSA:
- Correspondence English Usage, Kessler AFB, Mississippi
- Programmed English Usage, Kessler AFB, Mississippi
- United States Message Text Formats (MTF), Andrews AFB, Maryland
- Building a Professional Image, Andrews AFB, Maryland

Education and Training Related to This KSA:
In addition to the Certificates I received from Central Florida Community College and the Bethune-Cookman College, the following courses have been helpful in refining my skills in this area:
- Correspondence English Usage, Kessler AFB, Mississipppi
- Programmed English Usage, Kessler AFB, Mississipppi
- United States Message Text Formats (MTF), Andrews AFB, Maryland
- Building a Professional Image, Andrews AFB, Maryland

MELANIE T. EUBANKS

EDITORIAL ASSISTANT, GS-09 ANNOUNCEMENT #XYZ123

KSA #2: Skill in interpersonal relations.

In my most recent position as Field Office Assistant to the Department of Defense, I demonstrated my skill in interpersonal relations on a daily basis while interacting on a personal and professional level with military and civilian personnel of diverse ranks and backgrounds. Dealt with a heavy volume of office traffic, tactfully and diplomatically fielding questions and complaints from contractors, subcontractors, military personnel, and office visitors both in person and over the telephone and radio. Referred civilian contractors to Lockheed Martin, and provided contractors with information regarding the location of supplies ordered for their job sites. Performed liaison between civilian contractors, engineers, and warehouse personnel, relaying important information or taking messages if I could not resolve a problem or answer an inquiry. Frequently received calls from contractors who were angry or upset due to supply problems or other delays; handled these calls expertly, using tact and diplomacy to defuse the situation, then presenting the contractors concerns to the appropriate person in order to efficiently resolve the conflict. Answered multi-line phones in a courteous and professional manner, routing incoming calls to the appropriate person, taking telephone messages, and providing callers with information over the phone.

In earlier positions as Secretary to the Chiefs of the Plans and Operations Division and of the Logistics Communication Division, I interacted daily with a large number of people, both on the phone and in person. I recorded telephone messages and answered multi-line phones, effectively communicating with callers in order to ascertain the purpose of their call. Responded to caller inquiries, furnishing information and resolving their problems when possible and directing calls to the supervisor or appropriate personnel when I was unable to assist them. Maintained lines of communication and developed strong working relationships with higher, lateral, and subordinate counterparts at military headquarters in order to facilitate the exchange of information concerning each division's affairs.

Education and Training Related to This KSA:
In addition to the Certificates I received from Central Florida Community College and the Bethune-Cookman College, the following courses have been helpful in refining my skills in this area:
- Correspondence English Usage, Kessler AFB, Mississipppi
- Programmed English Usage, Kessler AFB, Mississipppi
- United States Message Text Formats (MTF), Andrews AFB, Maryland
- Building a Professional Image, Andrews AFB, Maryland

ENGINEERING EQUIPMENT OPERATOR

JOHNNY L. SIMMS

SSN: 000-00-0000

ENGINEERING EQUIPMENT OPERATOR, WG-09 ANNOUNCEMENT #XYZ123

Engineering Equipment Operator, WG-09 Announcement #XYZ123 KSA #1

KSA #1: Ability to do the work of an engineering equipment operator without more than normal supervision (screen out).

Although my current job is not in the engineering equipment operation field, as a Correctional Officer I am entrusted with the responsibility of working in an environment where I often work without supervision while overseeing inmates in an 850-person inmate facility. In the U.S. Army I became accustomed to working without supervision while operating various equipment and trucks in the Army engineer field as well as when I became promoted to General Engineering Supervisor and Construction Engineer Supervisor. I operated and maintained heavy and light engineering equipment in locations that included Vietnam, Germany, Korea, Wisconsin, Florida, Kentucky, Georgia, salt flats in Utah, deserts of California, Oklahoma, Arkansas, Virginia, Panama, Honduras, Saudi Arabia, and Iraq.

In my previous job as a Highway Maintenance Worker/Equipment Operator in 2001, I worked frequently without supervision while utilizing my expertise in operating chain saws, laying bricks, using bush axes, mixing mortar and concrete, and working in the Asphalt Section. In this job with the Department of Transportation, I utilized my background in operating many types of heavy and light equipment used to excavate, backfill, or grade earth. I performed heavy, physical work often in rugged outdoor conditions, and I was known for my total adherence to the strictest safety standards.

These KSAs helped a Correctional Officer "get out of prison" and back into the engineering and construction field.

As a Truck Driver/Equipment Operator from 2000-01, I worked virtually without supervision while operating heavy equipment including driving an 18-wheeler with a roll-off trailer in order to deliver scrap metals from industries and to haul materials for recycling. I also operated a forklift, scoop loaders, and a car crusher in environments which required my strict attention to safety standards while I worked with little or no supervision.

As a Truck Driver/Equipment Operator from 1998-00, I worked frequently with little to no supervision while operating equipment including bulldozers, scrapers, and trash compactors in the landfill in Salt Lake City, UT. I also operated a 10,000-pound forklift to load and unload materials, and I drove a 10-wheel roll-off truck while transporting containers from five convenience centers in the Salt Lake City area. While using the bulldozer, usually in situations in which I worked without supervision, I operated in a variety of situations on rocky, soft and uneven ground, graded curves and shoulders, hills, steep slopes, and other surfaces.

In 1998, as an Equipment Operator, I worked routinely without supervision while operating various types of heavy and light equipment used in small construction jobs. Equipment I utilized included track loader, 15-ton tandem dump trucks, and bulldozers as well as vibratory roller and motor grader.

From 1997-98, as an Operations Sergeant, I managed 10 individuals for an engineer brigade combat airborne organization, and I trained and supervised engineering equipment operators.

As a Construction Inspector from 1995-97, I managed 10 individuals specializing in survey, drafting, and soil analysis. Projects I managed required that I provide oversight for construction equipment operators using light and heavy equipment to excavate, backfill, or grade earth.

As a Platoon Sergeant for engineering organizations from 1993-95, I supervised the utilization and maintenance of over 40 items of heavy equipment including bulldozers, graders, scrapers, compactors, and various trucks, and I frequently trained equipment operators in performing the work of engineering equipment operators. While training and supervising engineering equipment operators, I received numerous safety awards.

As a Construction Equipment Supervisor from 1990-93, I received four Commendation Medals and two Certificates of Achievement for my outstanding work in managing a heavy equipment platoon and for managing a light equipment platoon. I provided extensive hands-on equipment training to engineering equipment operators involved in projects which including construction of a 4200 foot flight landing strip at White Sands Missile Range, NM and numerous other major construction projects including a road in Palmerola, Honduras, and a flight landing strip at Ft. Sill, OK. I also supervised equipment operators in the earth moving operations which led to the successful completion of over two miles of improved roadway, with limited materials and resources, over unsuitable and previously unpassable terrain.

From 1985-90, I excelled in jobs as a Heavy Equipment Platoon Sergeant and I routinely operated and supervised others in operating heavy construction equipment and machinery on major projects. Throughout my military career, I received numerous awards recognizing my outstanding achievements in operating equipment safely.

My training and education related to this KSA includes:
I have attended numerous schools and training programs which have equipped me with the skills and knowledge necessary to operate engineering equipment.
- Brick Masonry, 2001
- Carpentry, 1994, 2001
- Supervisory Maintenance Course, 1990
- NCO Academy, 1998
- Maintenance Management Operations Course, 1996
- Roads and Airfield Course, 1995
- First Sergeant Administration Course, 1997
- Engineer NCO Advance Course, U.S. Army Engineer School, 2000
- Air Movement Operations Course, 1995
- Airlift Planners Course, 1995
- In addition to my regular drivers license, I hold a Commercial Drivers License (CDL) and am an expert forklift operator.

ENGINEERING EQUIPMENT OPERATOR

JOHNNY L. SIMMS

SSN: 000-00-0000

ENGINEERING EQUIPMENT OPERATOR, WG-09 ANNOUNCEMENT #XYZ123

Engineering Equipment Operator, WG-09 Announcement #XYZ123 KSA #2

KSA #2: Ability to operate engineering equipment safely.

I offer more than 20 years of experience in safely operating engineering equipment, and I have received numerous safety awards and honors based on my achievements in the areas of safety. In addition, I have trained numerous equipment operators in the safe operation of most types of construction and engineering equipment. While serving my country in the U.S. Army, I worked primarily as a General Engineering Supervisor and Construction Engineer Supervisor, and I operated and trained others to operate engineering equipment safely. I have operated engineering equipment safely in locations that included Vietnam, Germany, Korea, Wisconsin, Florida, Kentucky, Georgia, salt flats in Utah, deserts of California, Oklahoma, Arkansas, Virginia, Panama, Honduras, Saudi Arabia, and Iraq.

In my job as a Highway Maintenance Worker/Equipment Operator in 2001, I became known for my observance of the highest safety standards while utilizing my expertise in operating chain saws, laying bricks, using bush axes, and mixing mortar and concrete. In this job with the Department of Transportation, I utilized my background in operating many types of heavy and light equipment used to excavate, backfill, or grade earth. I performed heavy, physical work often in rugged outdoor conditions, and I was known for my total adherence to the strictest safety standards.

This is a safety KSA.

As a Truck Driver/Equipment Operator from 2000-01, I maintained an unblemished safety record while operating heavy equipment including driving an 18-wheeler with a roll-off trailer in order to deliver containers of scrap metals from industries and to haul materials for recycling. I also operated a forklift, scoop loaders, and a car crusher in environments which required my strict attention to safety standards while I worked with little or no supervision.

With a perfect safety record as a Truck Driver/Equipment Operator from 1998-00, I operated equipment including bulldozers, scrapers, and trash compactors in the landfill in Salt Lake City, UT. I also operated a 10,000-pound forklift to load and unload materials, and I drove a 10-wheel roll-off truck while transporting containers from five convenience centers in the Salt Lake City area. While using the bulldozer and scraper, usually in situations in which I worked without supervision, I performed a variety of functions on soft and uneven ground, graded curves and shoulders, hills, steep slopes, and other surfaces.

In 1998, as an Equipment Operator, I maintained an outstanding safety record operating various types of heavy and light equipment used in small construction jobs. Equipment I utilized included track loader and bulldozers as well as a vibratory roller.

As a Construction Inspector from 1997-98, I developed safety programs and instilled absolute commitment to the highest safety practices while managing 10 individuals specializing in survey, drafting, and soil analysis, and projects I managed often required that I provide oversight for construction equipment operators using light and heavy equipment to excavate, backfill, or grade earth.

As a Platoon Sergeant for engineering organizations from 1993-95, I continuously monitored safety procedures while supervising the operation/utilization and maintenance of over 40 items of heavy equipment including bulldozers, graders, scrapers, compactors, and various trucks, and I frequently trained equipment operators in performing the work of engineering equipment operators. While training and supervising engineering equipment operators, I received numerous safety awards. As a Construction Equipment Supervisor from 1990-95, I received four Commendation Medals and two Certificates of Achievement for my outstanding work in safely managing a heavy equipment platoon and for managing a light equipment platoon. I provided extensive hands-on equipment training to engineering equipment operators involved in projects which including construction of a 4200 foot flight landing strip at White Sands Missile Range, NM and numerous other major construction projects including a road in Palmerola, Honduras, and a flight landing strip at Ft. Sill, OK. I also supervised equipment operators in the earth moving operations which led to the successful completion of over two miles of improved roadway, with limited materials and resources, over unsuitable and previously unpassable terrain.

From 1985-90, I acquired excellent safety practices while excelling in jobs as a Heavy Equipment Platoon Sergeant and I routinely operated and supervised others in operating heavy construction equipment and machinery on major projects. I operated and maintained 20-ton dump trucks, 10-ton tractors with lowboy trailers, 2 ½ truck, 1 ½ ton trailer, and ¼ ton jeep. In prior jobs, I operated engineering equipment safely and often with little to no supervision as a Loader Operator and as a Quarry Machine Operator.

My training and education related to this KSA includes:
Numerous schools and training programs I have attended, including the following, had component parts which emphasized safety practices and procedures as well as quality control and quality assurance:
- Brick Masonry, 2001
- Carpentry, 1994, 2001
- Supervisory Maintenance Course, 1990
- Maintenance Management Operations Course, 1996
- Roads and Airfield Course, 1995
- Engineer NCO Advance Course, U.S. Army Engineer School, 2000
- Air Movement Operations Course, 1995
- Airlift Planners Course, 1995
- In addition to my regular drivers license, I hold a Commercial Drivers License (CDL) and am an expert forklift operator.

ENGINEERING EQUIPMENT OPERATOR

JOHNNY L. SIMMS

SSN: 000-00-0000

ENGINEERING EQUIPMENT OPERATOR, WG-09 ANNOUNCEMENT #XYZ123

Engineering Equipment Operator, WG-09 Announcement #XYZ123 KSA #3

KSA #3: Ability to interpret instructions, specifications, etc., related to engineering equipment operator work.

Throughout my 20-plus years of construction industry and engineering operations experience, I refined my ability to interpret instructions, work orders, and specifications to enhance quality assurance, time constraints, and profitability. I have demonstrated in ability to interpret instructions, work orders, and specifications during projects in locations that included Vietnam, Germany, Korea, Wisconsin, Florida, Kentucky, Georgia, salt flats in Utah, deserts of California, Oklahoma, Arkansas, Virginia, Panama, Honduras, Saudi Arabia, and Iraq.

In my current job as a Corrections Officer, it is literally a matter of life or death that I correctly interpret instructions and work orders in the 850-inmate facility in which I work.

As a **Highway Maintenance Worker/Equipment Operator** in 2001, I exercised diligence in interpreting instructions, work orders, drawings, blueprints, and specifications as I properly operated trucks and equipment including chain saws as well as laid bricks, used bush axes, and mixed mortar and concrete.

As a **Truck Driver/Equipment Operator** from 2000-01, I daily interpreted instructions, work orders, and specifications while operating heavy equipment including driving an 18-wheeler with a roll-off trailer in order to deliver scrap metals form industries and to haul materials for recycling. I also interpreted work orders while operating a forklift, scoop loaders, and a car crusher. As a **Truck Driver/Equipment Operator** from 1998-00, I interpreted instructions, work orders, and specifications while operating equipment including bulldozers, scrapers, and trash compactors in the landfill in Salt Lake City, UT. I also interpreted work orders in the process of operating a 10,000-pound forklift to load and unload materials and in driving a 10-wheel roll-off truck to transport containers from five convenience centers in the Salt Lake City area. As an **Equipment Operator** in 1998, I interpreted instructions, work orders, and specifications while operating various types of heavy and light equipment used in small construction jobs. Equipment included track loader and bulldozers as well as a vibratory roller.

As a **Construction Inspector** from 1995-97, I trained and managed 10 individuals to interpret instructions, work orders, and specification the functional areas of survey, drafting, and soil analysis. A routine part of that interpretation involved reading and interpreting sketches, drawings, blueprints, and narrative specifications pertaining to the job to be accomplished.

As a **Construction Equipment Supervisor** from 1990-95, I routinely read and interpreted sketches, drawings, blueprints, and narrative specifications pertaining to the job to be accomplished while supervising the operation/utilization and maintenance of over 40 items of heavy equipment including bulldozers, graders, scrapers, compactors, and various trucks. Part of this job also involved reading and interpreting maintenance manuals and repair specifications.

As a **Construction Equipment Supervisor** managing a heavy equipment platoon and a light equipment platoon, I trained equipment operators to read and interpret sketches, drawings, blueprints, and narrative specifications while involved in projects which including construction of a 4200 foot flight landing strip, other major construction projects including a road in Honduras, and a flight landing strip in Oklahoma. I also supervised equipment operators in interpreting work orders, instructions, and specifications while involved in earth moving operations.

From 1975-82, as a **Heavy Equipment Platoon Sergeant**, I routinely interpreted work orders, instructions, and specifications while operating and supervising others in operating heavy construction equipment and machinery on major projects safely and often with little to no supervision.

My training and education related to this KSA includes:
Numerous schools and training programs have helped me refine my ability to interpret instructions, work orders, and specifications:
- Brick Masonry, 2001
- Carpentry, 1994, 2001
- First Sergeant Administration Course, 1997
- Battalion Training Management Course, 1998
- Roads and Airfield Course, 1995
- Engineer NCO Advance Course, U.S. Army Engineer School, 2000
- Air Movement Operations Course, 1995
- Airlift Planners Course, 1995
- Supervisory Maintenance Course, 1990
- Maintenance Management Operations Course, 1996
- First Corps Command Leadership School, 1990

EQUAL OPPORTUNITY ADVISOR

ADAM C. ELLIS

SSN: 000-00-0000

EQUAL OPPORTUNITY ADVISOR, GS-11 ANNOUNCEMENT #XYZ123

KSA #1: Skill in oral and written communications in order to deal effectively with a variety of individuals; prepare and present findings and recommend specific action; provide advice to managers, supervisors, and employees; and provide program training.

As an Equal Opportunity Advisor for the Department of Veterans Affairs (1999-04), I demonstrated my skill in oral and written communications while designing, planning, and establishing "from scratch" the Equal Opportunity program and office for my organization. I authored a 70-page organizational-level Affirmative Action Plan (AAP) that was later adopted for use by higher headquarters, in addition to developing written training materials and writing lesson plans for a Facilitator Instruction Program which produced more than 55 trained facilitators throughout the organization. Utilized my strong verbal communication skills while providing classroom and on-the-job training to and certifying all 28 general managers and supervisors within the organization and more than 175 unit-level facilitators. Methods of instruction included oral lectures, question-and-answer sessions, multimedia presentations, and providing additional assistance outside of the classroom to individuals having difficulty with the course materials. Certified as an Equal Opportunity Advisor and Instructor, I personally instructed and produced three Senior Advisors and managing and counseling more than 375 personnel while implementing the organization's "Regard for All" training sessions.

I demonstrated my written communication skills as well as my knowledge of current technology when I designed, authored the written content for, and constructed the organization's Equal Opportunity Web page. Including a 24-hour automated hotline facilitated easier access to information and services for personnel with Equal Opportunity issues. I demonstrated my oral communication and listening skills while regularly executing sensing sessions and human relations surveys to determine areas where the Equal Opportunity program needed to improve, gauging prevalent attitudes towards Equal Opportunity Employment issues and contributing to personal growth throughout the organization. Reviewed and analyzed existing EO policies, procedures, and practices, presenting recommendations for change both verbally and in writing to prevent discrimination and sexual harassment. Conducted quarterly installation-level Affirmative Action meetings, preparing materials for verbal presentation as well as interpreting, explaining, and presenting policies concerning Equal Opportunity to personnel throughout the installation.

In earlier positions as an Equal Employment Specialist and EO Advisor (1997-99), I demonstrated my strong communication skills while assisting in the design, planning, and implementation of Equal Opportunity Programs at the installation level, as well as planning and conducting special emphasis programs. Conducted formal classroom and on-the-job training of newly assigned Equal Opportunity Advisors on installation and equal opportunity policies and procedures. Delivered instructional materials effectively through verbal presentations, role-playing, and preparation of written course materials.

I reviewed and analyzed existing policies, procedures, and practices, recommending modifications where necessary to prevent discrimination and sexual harassment.

Conducted quarterly installation-level Affirmative Action meetings as well as interpreting, explaining, and presenting policies concerning Equal Opportunity to personnel throughout the installation.

Authored and developed an exhaustive training program on extremist groups, consisting of extensive written classroom materials, that was adopted for use at the higher headquarters level. Provided formal classroom instruction and on-the-job training in the knowledge and skills required of an Equal Opportunity leader to 35 personnel; mentored 85 Equal Opportunity leaders throughout the installation. An articulate communicator, was selected from other Equal Opportunity officers to serve as guest lecturer at the Advanced Management Course for enlisted supervisors.

Education and Training Related to this KSA:
Completed numerous military training and development courses, which included:
- Master Core Advisor Course, 2002; Army Equal Opportunity Counselor Training Course, 2001; Defense Equal Opportunity Management Institute Equal Opportunity Staff Advisor Course, 10 weeks, 1998.
- First Sergeant's Course, 2 weeks, 1998; Advanced Management Course for enlisted supervisors, 10 weeks, 1996; Basic Management Course for enlisted supervisors, 2 weeks, 1999; Primary Leadership and Development Course, 3 weeks, 1998.
- Small Unit Instructor Training Course, 1 week, 1996; Platoon Training Workshop, 3 weeks, 1996.
- Am proficient with Windows ME & XE as well as Microsoft Word, Excel, and PowerPoint.

EQUAL OPPORTUNITY ADVISOR

ADAM C. ELLIS

SSN: 000-00-0000

EQUAL OPPORTUNITY ADVISOR, GS-11 ANNOUNCEMENT #XYZ123

KSA #2: Skill in applying both conventional and innovative fact finding, analytical, and problem-solving methods and techniques to analyze facts, identify problems, report findings, and make conclusions, to include what corrective or appropriate action was taken.

During my tenure as an Equal Opportunity Advisor for the Department of Veterans Affairs (1999-04), I exhibited my skill in fact finding and analysis while designing, planning, and establishing "from scratch" the creation of the Equal Opportunity program and office for my organization. Researched the current status of the organization's Equal Opportunity program, policies, and procedures, and conducted interviews with senior officials, managers, supervisors, and personnel throughout the organization in order to determine the specific Equal Opportunity needs of the organization. After identifying the need for more effective written guidelines, I authored an 70-page organizational-level Affirmative Action Plan (AAP) that was later adopted for use by higher headquarters.

In earlier positions as an Equal Employment Specialist and EO Advisor (1997-99), I demonstrated my analytical and problem-solving skills while assisting in designing, planning, and implementation of Equal Opportunity Programs at the installation level, as well as planning and conducting special emphasis observances. Assisted in managing special emphasis programs, to include planning, organization, and execution. Trained newly assigned Equal Opportunity personnel on installation and equal opportunity policies and procedures. Processed, determined the validity of, and initiated appropriate action on individual Equal Opportunity complaints. Reviewed and analyzed existing policies, procedures, and practices, recommending modifications where necessary to prevent discrimination and sexual harassment. Conducted installation-level Affirmative Action meetings as well as interpreting, explaining, and presenting policies concerning Equal Opportunity to personnel throughout the installation.

Successfully orchestrated the Department of Veterans Affairs Sexual Harassment seminar, involving over 850 personnel as well as developing and implementing instructional programs at the installation level designed to prevent sexual harassment. Enhanced and refined the installation's Equal Employment Counselors Course. Was credited in an official evaluation with "flawlessly developing the Commanding General's quarterly Equal Employment Opportunity presentation," and "masterfully constructing a slide show briefing on the Special Emphasis Program for the Chief of Staff." Personally initiated action that resulted in the revision of Standard Operating Procedures (SOPs) and equal opportunity policies already in place on the installation.

Developed an exhaustive training program on extremist groups that was adopted at the higher headquarters level. Provided instruction in the knowledge and skills required of an Equal Opportunity leader to 35 personnel; mentored 85 Equal Opportunity leaders throughout the installation. An articulate communicator, was selected from other Equal Opportunity officers to serve as guest lecturer at the Advanced Management Course for enlisted Supervisors.

Education and Training Related to this KSA:

Completed numerous military training and development courses, which included:

- Master Core Advisor Course, 2002; Army Equal Opportunity Counselor Training Course, 2001; Defense Equal Opportunity Management Institute Equal Opportunity Staff Advisor Course, 10 weeks, 1998.
- First Sergeant's Course, 2 weeks, 1998; Advanced Management Course for enlisted supervisors, 10 weeks, 1996; Basic Management Course for enlisted supervisors, 2 weeks, 1999; Primary Leadership and Development Course, 3 weeks, 1998.
- Small Unit Instructor Training Course, 1 week, 1996; Platoon Training Workshop, 3 weeks, 1996.
- Am proficient with Windows ME & XE as well as Microsoft Word, Excel, and PowerPoint.

EQUAL OPPORTUNITY ADVISOR

ADAM C. ELLIS

SSN: 000-00-0000

EQUAL OPPORTUNITY ADVISOR, GS-11 ANNOUNCEMENT #XYZ123

KSA #3: Knowledge of federal employment programs pertaining to affirmative employment, special emphasis programs, and equal employment opportunity programs.

As an Equal Employment Specialist for the Department of Veterans Affairs (1999-04) performed duties that included the development, administration, and evaluation of the Command's Equal Employment Opportunity Program, and served as an Equal Employment Opportunity Specialist, Counselor, and Instructor. I provided guidance on EO inquiries into pre-complaints of discrimination, giving advice on EEO federal guidelines and procedures as well as suggested possible means of resolving the pre-complaint. Designed and implemented Equal Employment Opportunity programs of instruction, providing training on EO principles, policies, and procedures to approximately 4550 personnel throughout the installation. Personally managed, monitored and made recommendations on annual Special Emphasis Programs, overseeing the planning organization, and coordination of special observances. Developed short term and long range EO goals for the installation, based on analysis of work force statistical data revealing areas where under-representation existed. Developed and implemented unique methods of informing managers and supervisors of the objectives of the special emphasis programs. Advised the Commanding General of practices affecting equal employment of women and minorities and recommended appropriate corrective action to eliminate unfair practices.

Gathered empirical and objectively verifiable data relating to the employment of 925 women and minority groups throughout the work force. Prepared charts and graphs depicting work force profiles, broken down by individual groups and organizations. Assisted in developing the quarterly and annual review of the organization's affirmative action goals based on projected vacancies and the number of positions required to correct under-representation. Analyzed EO trends evidenced in the statistical data gathered and made recommendations for the organization's Affirmative Employment Plan that fulfilled management's equal opportunity responsibilities.

Coordinated EEO special emphasis program activities with appropriate staff members of the African American Employment Program Managers, Office of Civilian Personnel, Federal Women's Program Managers, Asian Employment Program Manager, and the Equal Opportunity Officer. Assisted special employment program coordinators in their efforts to locate and place handicapped persons and disabled veterans. Prepared yearly reports for the internal program by requesting data and gathering information from Equal Opportunity Specialists concerning each specific special emphasis program area. Analyzed and consolidated the information into a report assessing the overall effectiveness of the program.

Counseled individuals with potential complaints, including federal employees and applicants for employment who believed they may have had grounds for filing an EEO complaint. Listening to the individual's description of the problem, drawing out relevant facts and related issues in order to determine the validity of the pre-complaint helped to determined whether or not their situation constituted a matter that could be pursued through EEO channels. Explained the EEO complaint process to individual, describing what constitutes grounds for a complaint and the rights of the complainant. Resolved complaints in an informal manner by obtaining facts to define and clarify the issues presented. Conducted fact-finding and research, meeting with and interviewing managers and coworkers of complainants, and reviewing pertinent records, files, and documents in order to develop a thorough knowledge of the particulars of the complaint. Drafted final reports ensuring that all issues were presented and resolved.

Prepared and processed paperwork for individual complaints of discrimination, ensured requirements and time limits for each phase of EEO complaint processing was met (pre-complaint through formal appeal process). Processed informal and formal complaints in accordance with established regulations, guidelines, policies, and procedures. Reviewed complex cases to determine applicable guidelines. Coordinated requirements for formal complaints of discrimination. Forwarded certified letters to complainants acknowledging receipt of their formal complaints. Reviewed alleged complaints for adherence to regulatory requirements, coordinated paperwork/attachments, and prepared acceptance letters, and provided fund cites.

Education and Training Related to this KSA:
Completed numerous military training and development courses, which included:
- Master Core Advisor Course, 2002; Army Equal Opportunity Counselor Training Course, 2001; Defense Equal Opportunity Management Institute Equal Opportunity Staff Advisor Course, 10 weeks, 1998.
- First Sergeant's Course, 2 weeks, 1998; Advanced Management Course for enlisted supervisors, 10 weeks, 1996; Basic Management Course for enlisted supervisors, 2 weeks, 1999; Primary Leadership and Development Course, 3 weeks, 1998.
- Small Unit Instructor Training Course, 1 week, 1996; Platoon Training Workshop, 3 weeks, 1996.
- Am proficient with Windows ME & XE as well as Microsoft Word, Excel, and PowerPoint.
- First Sergeant's Course, 2 weeks, 1998; Advanced Management Course for enlisted supervisors, 10 weeks, 1996; Basic Management Course for enlisted supervisors, 2 weeks, 1999; Primary Leadership and Development Course, 3 weeks, 1998.
- Small Unit Instructor Training Course, 1 week, 1996; Platoon Training Workshop, 3 weeks, 1996.
- Am proficient with Windows ME & XE as well as Microsoft Word, Excel, and PowerPoint.

FABRIC WORKER

RICHARD S. WAUGH

SSN: 000-00-0000

FABRIC WORKER, WG-07 ANNOUNCEMENT #XYZ123

KSA #1: Ability to do the work of a fabric worker without more than the normal supervision (screen out).

Because of (1) my demonstrated ability to work without more than normal supervision and, furthermore, because of (2) my proven ability to supervise the work of others involved in fabric work and parachute rigging, I was handpicked to manage the Supply and HALO Section from 2002-03 which placed me in charge of seven personnel. As a Senior Parachute Rigger (Chest and Back), Certificate # XYZ, Seal Symbol - BYT, I applied my extensive experience with MC-4, FF2, and AR2 which are used by the HALO School. While supervising the packing, maintenance, and repair of parachutes, applied my expertise in all aspects of parachute utilization including my extensive participation as a jumper in military static line and free fall parachute operations in order to expertly evaluate repairs and modification to life support systems.

In my more than five years of experience as a parachute rigger from 1998-02 and then as a supervisor of parachute riggers and fabric workers from 2002-03 , I demonstrated my strong personal initiative and ability to work with less than normal supervision as I achieved international stature in the parachuting field. On my own initiative and always requiring less than normal supervision, I obtained the following badges and decorations signifying my expertise with all aspects of parachuting as well as my highly motivated nature which requires no external motivational force to stimulate my strong desire for excellence in all endeavors:

- South African Defense Force (SADF) Parachutist Badge
- Royal Netherlands Marine Corps Parachute Badge B
- Royal Netherlands Aeronautical Association Parachute Badge A
- Saudi Arabian Parachutist Badge
- Italian Parachutes Badge
- Australian Army Parachutist Badge
- Singapore Basic Parachutist Badge
- Turkish Parachutist Badge
- Bronze German Armed Forces Parachutist Badge
- Senior Parachutist Badge
- Parachutist Badge
- Military Free Fall Parachutist Badge
- Parachute Rigger Badge

Numerous medals which I earned while excelling in the parachuting field attest to my strong personal initiative, my highly motivated nature, and my ability to work without more than normal supervision.

- The recipient of four Army Achievement Medals, I was awarded one of those medals for participating in a Military Freefall Operation with the ARAB's Resupply Parachute System.
- I earned an Army Commendation Medal based on my exceptional performance as a member of a Rigger Platoon with the 1st Special Warfare Training Group (Airborne).
- In the citation for that medal which I received for my work in 1999 as a HALO

Parachute Rigger, the recommendation for the award noted that I had **"discovered a manufacturer defect on the Automatic Ripcord Release (APR) on the Ram-Air parachute system."** I discovered this defect while working with less than normal supervision and while exercising my customary diligence and attention to detail in the performance of my job duties. As a parachute rigger and fabric worker, I became accustomed to performing all tasks with the attitude that there was "no room for error" because a miscalculation or negligent action on the part of a parachute rigger could one day cost the life of a parachutist.

Fabric Worker, WG-07 Announcement #XYZ123 Page Two of KSA #1

- One of the medals which I received during my period as a Parachute Rigger particularly praised my ability to take charge and work with less than normal supervision. In the citation for that Army Achievement Medal, for example, I was cited for excellence as a safety swimmer during the conduct of the deliberate parachute water operation. I was also assigned as Equipment NCO for the deployment to Key West, FL, and the same citation praised me saying that **"he was the first individual who successfully returned every piece of equipment."**

- While acting as supervisor of the HALO Section from 2002-03, I received a respected Army Achievement Medal for my exemplary performance. In particular I was singled out for my highly motivated nature, personal initiative, and ability to work with less than normal supervision while simultaneously supervising the work of seven other personnel. In the accompanying citation for the medal, was described in these words: *"Sgt. Waugh is a self-starter. He took it upon himself to take charge of an* inexperienced HALO crew and to identify numerous deficiencies; he then executed highly successful HALO Section meeting all mission requirements and exceeding all expectations." "Sgt Waugh is a consistent top performer, constantly seeking new and more *effective methods in performing his duties."*

"Screen out" means this is the most important of all KSAs you are asked to write.

My training and education related to this KSA includes:
College education:
I have completed more than three years of college courses including 1 ½ years of college courses at Clemson University, SC and 1 ½ years of college course work at the University of Virginia, VA. That course work provided me with a foundation of concepts and knowledge which promoted my ability to work independently and without more than normal supervision in all types of work situations.

Technical training:
Technical training which refined my knowledge:
USASOC Jump Master Course, 2001
Military Free Fall Parachutist Course, 2000
SERE High Risk Course, 2000
MC-5 Ram Air Parachute Systems Course, 2001
Air Drop Load Inspector Certification Course, 1999
Automatic Ripcord Release Assembly, 1999
Primary Leadership Development Course, 1998
Parachute Rigger Course, 1995
Airborne Course, 1995

Want to explore opportunities for employment in the federal system? Visit your closest Civilian Personnel Office or visit the World Wide Web site at http://www.fedjobs.com.

FABRIC WORKER

RICHARD S. WAUGH

SSN: 000-00-0000

FABRIC WORKER, WG-07 ANNOUNCEMENT #XYZ123

KSA #2: Knowledge of parachute construction.

Because of my expert knowledge of parachute construction which I gained in more than five years of experience as a parachute rigger and as a parachutist, I was hand-picked to manage the Supply and HALO Section from 2002-03 which placed me in charge of seven personnel. As a Senior Parachute Rigger (Chest and Back), Certificate #XYZ, Seal Symbol – BYT, I applied my extensive experience with MC-4, FF2, and AR2 which are used by the HALO School. While supervising the packing, maintenance, and repair of parachutes, applied my expertise in all aspects of parachute utilization including my extensive participation as a jumper in military static line and free fall parachute operations in order to expertly evaluate repairs and modification to life support systems.

I received a respected Army Achievement Medal for my exemplary performance as supervisor of the parachute rigging section from 2002-03. The accompanying citation for the medal praised my knowledge of parachute construction in these words:
"Sgt. Waugh took it upon himself to take charge of an inexperienced HALO crew and to identify numerous deficiencies; he then executed a highly successful HALO Section meeting all mission requirements and exceeding all expectations."

"Sgt. Waugh's superb working knowledge of parachute systems and equipment has increased the operational excellence and capability of the Rigger Section. The energetic and conscientious dedication he displayed in transforming his work group to a valuable operating element within three months of assuming charge set the example and pace for the entire Rigger Section."

"Sgt. Waugh has a sound working knowledge and understanding of the complicated Ram-Air Parachute System."

The recipient of four Army Achievement Medals, I was awarded one of those medals for participating in a Military Freefall Operation with the ARAB's Resupply Parachute System. An accomplished parachutist, I am an expert in testing and evaluating parachutes through military static line and free fall operations and, through my extensive parachutist experience, I have acquired expertise in evaluating repairs and modifications of life support systems because I bring first hand knowledge of the problems encountered in utilizing those systems.

My knowledge of parachute construction can be demonstrated by the fact that I have acquired numerous badges through my expertise in utilizing parachutes properly. Those badges include the Senior Parachutist Badge, the Parachutist Badge, the Military Free Fall Parachutist Badge, and Parachute Rigger Badge. Other badges I have earned include the following:
- South African Defense Force (SADF) Parachutist Badge
- Royal Netherlands Marine Corps Parachute Badge B
- Royal Netherlands Aeronautical Association Parachute Badge A
- Saudi Arabian Parachutist Badge

- Italian Parachutes Badge
- Australian Army Parachutist Badge
- Singapore Basic Parachutist Badge
- Turkish Parachutist Badge
- Bronze German Armed Forces Parachutist Badge

I earned one Army Commendation Medal based on my exceptional knowledge of parachute construction which I demonstrated as a member of a Rigger Platoon with the 1st Special Warfare Training Group (Airborne). In the citation for that medal which I received for my work in 1999 as a HALO Parachute Rigger, the recommendation for the award noted that I had "discovered a manufacturer defect on the Automatic Ripcord Release (APR) on the Ram-Air parachute system." I discovered this defect through my expert knowledge of parachute construction.

In my job as Parachute Rigger and Manager of the HALO Section in charge of seven parachute riggers (2002-03), I continuously demonstrated my knowledge of parachute construction. I also supervised parachute riggers in performing repairs, alterations, and modifications on various types of Troop and/or Emergency type personnel and small cargo parachutes and related items and components including the T-10, MC-1 series, and Ram Air Parachutes. As Section Supervisor of parachute rigging operations, I functioned in a quality assurance role at all times while performing supervisory oversight of parachute rigging operations. Performed an initial 100% Technical Rigger Type Inspection on air items and related equipment and recorded all repair on parachutes. Utilizing patterns, marked and cut replacement sections for various parachutes and trained other personnel to do so. Replaced, repairs, or fabricated items on different canopies. Darned, patched sections, replaced sections, and entire gores as needed. Made necessary repairs on examining for defects. Using required commercial electric sewing machines, sewed repairs in place as directed by the repair manuals. Reported all repairs and modifications correctly ensuring that completed work met all specifications and regulations upon final inspection.

*Emphasize your
achievements!*

My training and education related to this KSA includes:

USASOC Jump Master Course, 2001
MC-5 Ram Air Parachute Systems Course, 2001
Military Free Fall Parachutist Course, 2000
SERE High Risk Course, 2000
Automatic Ripcord Release Assembly, 1999
Air Drop Load Inspector Certification Course, 1999
Primary Leadership Development Course, 1998
Parachute Rigger Course, 1995
Airborne Course, 1995

GUIDANCE COUNSELOR

ROGER JAMES GEARY

SN: 000-00-0000

GUIDANCE COUNSELOR, GS-09 ANNOUNCEMENT #XYZ123

Here he gives an example of
how his ability averted loss of
human life.

KSA #1: Knowledge of varied education programs.

In completing my B.S. degree in Psychology at Wake Forest University, I completed numerous courses which provided me with insight into varied education programs. These and other courses were particularly helpful to me in gaining insight into varied education programs:

- Psychological Counseling
- Tests and Measurement
- Memory and Cognition
- Theories of Personality
- Principles of Learning

While serving in the U.S. Army and advancing to the rank of CW4, I was continuously involved in developing and implementing varied education programs for adult learners in numerous career fields. I gained expertise related to tests and measurement, educational program administration, curriculum development and design, guidance and counseling, career planning and career counseling, and became skilled at providing occupational information related to vocational and career choices. In subsequent positions as a civilian since departing from the U.S. Army, I have gained valuable insights into career opportunities in the private sector and public sector which would make me a valuable resource as a guidance counselor.

As Aviation Maintenance Technician from 2000-04, I was continuously involved in guidance counseling while in charge of the technical training and professional development of up to 42 personnel in the only Airborne Aviation Intermediate Maintenance (AVIM) Armament Platoon in the Army. Managed a Skill Qualifications Testing (SQT) program which prepared personnel for annual testing of their knowledge of their primary career field. Made significant contributions through my ability to train, counsel, motivate, and develop others. After platoon equipment returned from the Persian Gulf, I immediately identified shortcomings and deficiencies in personnel capability as well as in equipment. One problem was the very high number of newly assigned and relatively untrained armament mechanics. I immediately began a training program which developed the skills of those mechanics and which provided cross-training in the AH-64 Apache. As part of this training program, I counseled all individuals and provided career guidance and planning help. One formal performance evaluation said this: "Geary's comprehensive systems of training subordinates has contributed immensely to their professional development and unit readiness. The unit's flawless aviation safety record is also attributable to Geary's excellent training and insistence on the highest standards." As the Technical Advisor for the Hydraulic, Welding, Powertrain, Powerplant, and Airframe shops, I provided career counseling to individuals in those and other career fields. In a formal performance evaluation of my work as a Production Control Officer from 1997-00, was cited for "a remarkable ability to train subordinates on highly technical maintenance procedures and to incorporate a training program that makes an everyday task a learning process."

KSA #2: Knowledge of the techniques used in educational counseling of adults.

In completing my B.S. degree in Psychology at Wake Forest University, I completed numerous courses which provided me with insight into the techniques used in the educational counseling of adults. These and other courses were particularly helpful to me in gaining insight into varied education programs:

Psychological Counseling   Tests and Measurement
Memory and Cognition   Theories of Personality
Principles of Learning   Human Resources Management
Industrial and Organizational Psychology

Throughout my military career in which I rose to the rank of CW4, I was continuously in roles in which I functioned as Training Manager, Career Advisor, and Guidance Counselor. I gained hands-on experience in tests and administration and I conducted training and then evaluation of individuals and groups related to their aptitude and skill proficiency. I gained more than 20 years of experience in working with adult learners as I developed and implemented programs of varying complexity, and I was the author of numerous curricula for adult educational programs. My working with adult learners gave me insights into the teaching methods most effective with adult learners.

As Training Manager for 46 aviators, I was in charge of providing career and professional guidance while evaluating them in all activities related to their jobs. Responsible for planning, coordinating, and supervising training in all mission related areas. Evaluated crew members on the proficiency and the safety aspects of all aviation tasks, especially combat operations. Was extensively involved in tests and measurements as I conducted inflight and oral evaluations; administered the aviator annual written exam (AAPART); and planned, coordinated, and monitored all unit instrument training programs. Also served as unit standardization officer in charge of monitoring the unit's aircrew training manual (ATM) program to include coordinating the activities and standardization of instructor pilots. Advised the commander on individual aviator training and served on the squadron's standardization council which essentially made policy and procedures related to the standardized training of aviators. Developed, coordinated, and implemented aviator training programs which became the model for other organizations to follow. Was cited in a formal performance evaluation for my outstanding instrument training program and for my aircrew training manual implementation. Was praised formally for my expertise in administering instrument flight evaluations, flight training, and written exams to aviators.

In my previous job as Production Control Manager from 1997-00, I was cited in a formal performance evaluation for "a remarkable ability to train subordinates on highly technical maintenance procedures and to incorporate a training program that makes an everyday task a learning process."

Guidance Counselor, GS-09 Announcement #XYZ123 KSA #2

This individual wanted to get out of a marketing job and back into the kind of work he performed while in the military.

HEALTH TECHNICIAN

DEIDRE M. ATKINSON

SSN: 000-00-0000

HEALTH TECHNICIAN (OPHTHALMOLOGY), GS-07 ANNOUNCEMENT #XYZ123

**Health Technician,
GS-07
Announcement #XYZ123
KSA #1**

KSA (1): Knowledge of methods and practices used in the diagnosis and treatment of disorders and diseases of the eye.

During my tenure at the Eye, Ear, Nose, and Throat (EENT) clinic of U.S. Naval Hospital Pensacola, FL, (2003-present), frequently performed or assisted in the full range of diagnostic testing procedures. Performed opthalmalogical pre-screening, comprised of tests for visual acuity, depth perception, and color-blindness. Positioned and instructed the patient regarding each type of visual field test. Used the auto-refractor to measure nearsightedness and/or farsightedness and provide an estimate of the prescription needed for the patient's corrective lenses, and conducted NCT testing for glaucoma.

Conducted triage on clinic patients, prioritizing cases according to the nature and severity of the patient's condition and directing urgent or emergency cases to the physician's attention. Checked eyes for corneal abrasions and other types of eye trauma; disinfected the area of examination, changed dressings, and removed sutures. Prepared the patient for ophthalmological procedures and performed set up of instruments and equipment, using sterile technique as appropriate. Provided patient education related to proper aftercare, such as reapplication of topical medication and changing of the dressing in the case of minor corneal abrasions.

Education and Training Related to the KSA:
* Annual update courses in: Infection Control, Sexual Harassment, Sterilization, and Customer Service, 2004
* Advanced Cardiac Life Support (ACLS) course, American Heart Association, 2004
* Community CPR (adult, child, and infant), American Red Cross, 2003
* Emergency Medical Technician (EMT) certification course, 2002
* Intra-oral Radiography Course, 2002
* Patient Relations Course, 2001
* Dental Specialist Correspondence Course, 2001
* Professional Development for Nurses Assistants, 2000
* Naval Hospital Corps School, 1999 (Included approximately 80 hours of instruction in each area, including but not limited to: Medical Terminology, Pharmacology, Emergency Patient Care, and Anatomy & Physiology)

KSA (2): Ability to set up surgical materials, instruments, and medications.

As a GS-03 Dental Assistant at Lemoore Dental Clinic in California (2002-03), I worked in the Operating Room. I set up and ensured adequate supplies of all surgical materials and prepared instrument trays and medications as well as assisting in oral surgery and other surgical procedures. Maintained and disinfected all equipment and instruments necessary for surgical, orthodontic, endodontic, prosthodontic, and general dentistry procedures, using both cold and hot sterilization methods.

Served as first surgical assistant and scrub assistant to the surgeon in surgical procedures. Assisted in minor surgeries, holding and handling instruments, performing retraction, and holding and cutting sutures.

- In a letter of recommendation from my supervisor, was described as "without peer. Her sense of purpose and motivations ensure rapid room "turnover" between cases and full set up of all equipment, supplies, and instruments."
- Cited in an official evaluation for my "exceptional skills while performing in the operating room," as well as for "exceptional coordination of hospital Operating Room cases with medical staff."

Performed sterilization and setup of and utilized the full range of dental instruments and surgical equipment, including but not limited to the following:

- mouth mirrors   explorers   cotton pliers   periodontal   probe
- saliva ejectors   pulp testers   dental chisels   root elevators
- aspirating syringes   extracting forceps   spoon excavators
- rubber dam instruments (holder, punch, clamp, and forceps)
- dental burs, both excavating and surgical
- periodontal instruments (curettes, hose, files, probes, and knives)
- endodontic instruments (broaches, reamers, files, and pluggers)
- prosthodontic instruments (impression trays, dental casts, articulators, and the alcohol blow torch

Education and Training Related to the KSA:
- Annual update courses in: Infection Control, Sexual Harassment, Sterilization, and Customer Service, 2004
- Advanced Cardiac Life Support (ACLS) course, American Heart Association, 2004
- Community CPR (adult, child, and infant), American Red Cross, 2003
- Emergency Medical Technician (EMT) certification course, 2002
- Intra-oral Radiography Course, 2002
- Patient Relations Course, 2001
- Dental Specialist Correspondence Course, 2001
- Professional Development for Nurses Assistants, 2000
- Naval Hospital Corps School, 1999 (Included approximately 80 hours of instruction in each area, including but not limited to: Medical Terminology, Pharmacology, Emergency Patient Care, and Anatomy & Physiology)

HEALTH TECHNICIAN

DEIDRE M. ATKINSON
SSN: 000-00-0000
HEALTH TECHNICIAN (OPHTHALMOLOGY), GS-07 ANNOUNCEMENT #XYZ123

KSA (3): Knowledge of medical terminology.

Throughout my medical career, both in the Navy and the Civil Service, I have demonstrated the extensive knowledge of medical terminology that I was required to know as a medical professional.

While working as a Nursing Assistant at Kings Bay Memorial Hospital in Kings Bay, GA (1996-97), exhibited my knowledge of medical terminology on a daily basis while providing total patient care to preoperative and postoperative patients in the Cardiac Care Unit/Intensive Care Unit (CCU/ICU), as well as in the Medical/Surgical and Ambulatory Care Units. Utilized medical terminology in the process of updating patient charts, ordering laboratory tests.

As a GS-03 Medical Clerk at U.S. Naval Hospital Hawaii, (1994-96), utilized my knowledge of medical terminology while taking patient histories, making charts for new patients, and updating, maintaining, and ensuring the accuracy and completeness of patient charts.

As a Medical Technician (Corpsman) in the U.S. Navy at Naval Hospital Pensacola, FL (1999-2001), I demonstrated my knowledge of medical terminology while stationed at providing medical care to patients in a number of different areas, including the hospital's Emergency Room, Obstetrics/Gynecology Clinic, and Eye, Ear, Nose, and Throat (EENT) Clinic. Prepared medical charts for new patients and updated, maintained, and filed charts. Completed approximately 80 hours of instruction in Medical Terminology as part of my Hospital Corps training program.

Education and Training Related to the KSA:
- Annual update courses in: Infection Control, Sexual Harassment, Sterilization, and Customer Service, 2004
- Advanced Cardiac Life Support (ACLS) course, American Heart Association, 2004
- Community CPR (adult, child, and infant), American Red Cross, 2003
- Emergency Medical Technician (EMT) certification course, 2002
- Intra-oral Radiography Course, 2002
- Patient Relations Course, 2001
- Dental Specialist Correspondence Course, 2001
- Professional Development for Nurses Assistants, 2000
- Naval Hospital Corps School, 1999 (Included approximately 80 hours of instruction in each area, including but not limited to: Medical Terminology, Pharmacology, Emergency Patient Care, and Anatomy & Physiology)

KSA (4): Ability to perform audiological examinations and evaluations.

Health Technician, GS-03
Announcement #XYZ123
KSA #4

While serving in the U.S. Navy at the Eye, Ear, Nose, and Throat (EENT) clinic of Naval Hospital Pensacola, FL, (1999-2001), visually inspected the patient's ear to check for fluid discharge or excessive buildup of wax. Conducted hearing tests to determine if the patient was experiencing any loss of hearing. Instructed the patient listen to a series of high and low tones through headphones and raise their right or left hand when they heard the tone. Evaluated their responses to determine the nature and extent of any hearing loss, as well as which ear was effected, if the hearing loss was not bilateral.

Performed triage on clinic patients, prioritizing according to the severity of their medical condition and notifying the doctor immediately in the event that an urgent or emergency situation arose. Worked with children, using a variety of probes to remove items lodged in the ear canal. Assisted the doctor in various minor surgeries. Performed lavage, flushing the ear canal with saline solution to cleanse the ear. Placed medication in the ear canal.

Education and Training Related to the KSA:
- Annual update courses in: Infection Control, Sexual Harassment, Sterilization, and Customer Service, 2004
- Advanced Cardiac Life Support (ACLS) course, American Heart Association, 2004
- Community CPR (adult, child, and infant), American Red Cross, 2003
- Emergency Medical Technician (EMT) certification course, 2002
- Intra-oral Radiography Course, 2002
- Patient Relations Course, 2001
- Dental Specialist Correspondence Course, 2001
- Professional Development for Nurses Assistants, 2000
- Naval Hospital Corps School, 1999 (Included approximately 80 hours of instruction in each area, including but not limited to: Medical Terminology, Pharmacology, Emergency Patient Care, and Anatomy & Physiology)

INSURANCE MANAGEMENT SPECIALIST

LEONARD J. KOWALSKI

SSN: 000-00-0000

INSURANCE MANAGEMENT SPECIALIST, GS-12 ANNOUNCEMENT #XYZ123

KSA #1: Knowledge of Federal, Departmental and Risk Management Agency crop insurance program laws, policies, regulations, and procedures including delivery service contracts and procedures applicable to the acquisition and administration of reinsurance agreements, customer education, and claims mechanisms.

Overview of knowledge in this KSA:

For the past 16 years I have served the Department of Agriculture through applying my expert knowledge of Federal, Departmental and Risk Management Agency crop insurance program laws, policies, regulations, and procedures including delivery service contracts and procedures related to reinsurance agreements, customer agreements, and claims mechanisms. I have excelled in all aspects of my job. For example, in March 2004 I was awarded a Certificate of Appreciation from the U.S. Department of Agriculture because of my success as a Special Project Team Leader when I applied my loss adjusting knowledge while providing leadership in clearing up controversial claims in Wilmington which arose from crop damage due to floods. In that instance, and on numerous other occasions, I have applied my technical expertise in the claims and loss adjustment area while also performing liaison activities related to program delivery responsibilities with the Reinsurance Services Division. I offer vast experience in program management and delivery, customer education, and claims administration oversight related to insurance management and risk management in 13 states.

Experience related to this KSA:

Since 2002, I have worked as an Insurance Management Specialist with the Department of Agriculture Branch Office. While training state and county farm service personnel and loss adjusters, I work in underwriters in providing rate, yield, or coverage determinations through application and interpretation of operating procedures, standards, actuarial principles, and agronomic expertise. In addition to evaluating and validating data for yield calculation required to generate actuarial listings as well as assign Regional Service Office determined yields for insured growers not on a listing, I perform first-level review of reconsideration of actuarial determinations and underwriting decisions made by FCIC or reinsurance companies. I routinely work with the Program Services Branch on reviews and analytical studies of new crop programs, and I play a key role in recommending policy and procedural changes while also continuously reviewing marketing strategies. While conducting activities in a 13-state area, I am continuously in a problem-solving mode as I research and evaluate claims and service situations, unresolved or disputed claims, while also providing technical oversight of crop data resource materials and procedures related to sound crop insurance risk management strategies.

When in doubt, be specific and provide details!

- In my current job I have served as USDA representative between the West Virginia State USDA and county offices by providing classroom instruction to Department of Agriculture employees from 14 states on the state and county levels of the changes in policies and procedures concerning Federal Crop and Reinsurance programs. As part of the instruction I arranged for on-site training in the field setting. In order to prepare myself for instructing, I conducted state-of-the-art research into crop insurance programs and prepared lesson plans which incorporated information of crop insurance programs including reinsurance, claims, and customer education.

- In addition to providing training to USDA employees, I have trained USDA employees at the state and county level in NC, VA, WV, PA, and NJ on program changes. Specifically I instructed USDA personnel on how to implement the new ASCS/USDA catastrophic disaster program along with how to properly evaluate crop conditions and crop damage.
- I have supervised loss adjustment in claims processing by USDA employees in NC, VA, WV, PA, and NJ to insure that the policies of government farm programs are followed. I trained USDA recorders so that they could become certified as crop appraisers. I also worked in the field with USDA employees on new crop expansion in NC, NJ, and PA for blueberries, tomatoes, and potatoes.

In my previous job from 1996-02 as Crop Insurance Specialist, I supervised an average of 20 individuals in handling the responsibility for establishing and implementing Federal Crop Insurance programs.

Education and training related to this KSA:

In addition to holding an A.A. from the Devry Agriculture and Technical School, I believe the following education and training have enhanced my knowledge in the area of this KSA:

- 2004, Managing Work Force Diversity and Managing Change
- 2000, Creative Problem Solving
- 1998, Improving Communication with the Public
- 1997, Loss Adjuster Certification
- 1995, Federal Crop Insurance Certification (13 crops)
- 1994, Instructor Training
- 1990, Agents Certification Training

INSURANCE MANAGEMENT SPECIALIST

LEONARD J. KOWALSKI

SSN: 000-00-0000

INSURANCE MANAGEMENT SPECIALIST, GS-12 ANNOUNCEMENT #XYZ123

KSA #2: Ability to gather, analyze, and evaluate crop insurance programs and data, and develop appropriate recommendations.

Overview of knowledge in this KSA:

I am considered one of the USDA's foremost experts in the area of gathering, analyzing, and evaluating crop insurance programs and data and developing appropriate recommendations. Furthermore, over the past nearly 16 years I have conducted literally hundreds of investigations and evaluations of program and administrative operations related to crop insurance programs to ensure that government assets were protected against waste, loss, or misuse.

Experience related to this KSA:

In my current job, 2002 to present, I work with underwriters in providing rate, yield, or coverage determinations through application and interpretation of operating procedures, standards, actuarial principles, and agronomic expertise. In addition to evaluating and validating data for yield calculation required to generate actuarial listings as well as assign Regional Service Office determined yields for insured growers not on a listing, I perform first-level review of reconsiderations of actuarial determinations and underwriting decisions made by FCIC or reinsurance companies. I routinely work with the Program Services Branch on reviews and analytical studies of new crop programs, and I play a key role in recommending policy and procedural changes while also continuously reviewing marketing strategies. While conducting activities in a 13-state area, I am continuously in a problem-solving mode as I research and evaluate claims and service situations, unresolved or disputed claims, while also providing technical oversight of crop data resource materials and procedures related to sound crop insurance risk management strategies.

This KSA goes back job-by-job.

I have played a key role in new crop expansions in NC, NJ, and PA. These crops have been cabbage, blueberries, and sweet potatoes. I have performed the field work by gathering the production information pertaining to the insurability of these crops in these geographical areas. While performing this field work, I have conducted farm surveys which required me to coordinate with producers and growers and with grower groups in order to write policies for those crops. Since I have played a key role in writing the guidelines for crop insurance, I would be an expert loss adjuster in the future for those crop programs as well as for numerous other crops for which I have had extensive loss adjustment experience.

In my previous job from 1996-02 as Crop Insurance Specialist, I supervised an average of 20 individuals in handling the responsibility for establishing and implementing Federal Crop Insurance programs. This involved me constantly in expertly interpreting policies and procedures and in applying guidance to subordinates, peers, and farmers relating to all phases of crop insurance programs. It was my responsibility to assign, control, and review all loss adjustment work in the area. As the most knowledgeable and most experienced loss adjuster, it was also my responsibility to handle the most controversial claims as I also routinely conducted inspections of crops, evaluated farming management and practices, reviewed all contract folders for accuracy, and reviewed contract service programs in order to make recommendations for improving overall effectiveness. With a reputation as a highly articulate technical expert, I became highly respected for my ability to communicate highly technical concepts in an understandable manner while providing program information to reinsurance specialists, private companies, Federal and state agencies, agri-business concerns, and underwriters.

In my job from 1994-96 as a Crop Insurance Specialist/Distribution Director, I supervised a total of 30 employees who were supervisors and loss adjusters in District 11. I personally reviewed and handled all controversial and difficult claims while working closely with USDA agencies, handling public relations with farmers and farm organizations, and making recommendations on a wide range of matters ranging from personnel administration to controversial claims management.

In my job from 1991-94 as a Crop Insurance Field Representative, I supervised up to 35 loss adjusters while earning rapid promotion from a Supervisor position to Assistant to the District Director. I became certified on 13 crops and during this period of time I worked claims on nine insurance crops while continuously reviewing and auditing controversial claims. While training and supervising other loss adjusters, it was my responsibility to handle the most controversial and difficult claims, and I received praise on numerous occasions for the skillful manner in which I combined my claims and loss adjustment expertise with my communication skills in resolving stubborn problems and difficult situations.

Education and training related to this KSA:

In addition to holding an A.A. from the Devry Agriculture and Technical School, I believe the following education and training have enhanced my knowledge in the area of this KSA:

- 2004, Managing Work Force Diversity and Managing Change
- 2000, Creative Problem Solving
- 1998, Improving Communication with the Public
- 1997, Loss Adjuster Certification Training
- 1995, Federal Crop Insurance Certification (13 crops)
- 1994, Instructor Training
- 1990, Agents Certification Training

INSURANCE MANAGEMENT SPECIALIST

LEONARD J. KOWALSKI

SSN: 000-00-0000

INSURANCE MANAGEMENT SPECIALIST, GS-12 ANNOUNCEMENT #XYZ123

KSA #3: Ability to coordinate and work with individuals and groups to accomplish work objectives and assignments.

Overview of knowledge in this KSA:

I believe my excellent track record of promotion as well as my numerous accomplishments with the USDA are due not only to my technical expertise but also to my ability to work well with others, both as a team leader and team member.

Experience related to this KSA:

Since 2002 to the present, I have worked as an Insurance Management Specialist with the Department of Agriculture. I continuously coordinate with individuals and groups in 13 states while training state and county farm service personnel and loss adjusters. I also work with underwriters in providing rate, yield, or coverage determinations through application and interpretation of operating procedures, standards, actuarial principles, and agronomic expertise. In addition to evaluating and validating data for yield calculation required to generate actuarial listings as well as assign Regional Service Office determined yields for insured growers not on a listing, I perform first-level review of reconsiderations of actuarial determinations and underwriting decisions made by FCIC or reinsurance companies. I routinely work with the Program Services Branch on reviews and analytical studies of new crop programs, and I play a key role in recommending policy and procedural changes while also continuously reviewing marketing strategies. While overseeing activities in a 13-state area, I am continuously in a problem-solving mode as I research and evaluate claims and service situations, unresolved or disputed claims, while also providing technical oversight of crop data resource materials and procedures related to sound crop insurance risk management strategies.

This is somewhat different from the standard "management" or "supervisory" KSA.

In my current job I also have served as USDA representative between the West Virginia State Department of Agriculture and county offices by providing classroom instruction to employees from 14 states on the state and county levels of the changes in policies and procedures concerning Federal Crop and Reinsurance programs. As part of the instruction I arranged for on-site training in the field setting. In order to prepare myself for instructing, I conducted state-of-the-art research into crop insurance programs and prepared lesson plans which incorporated information of crop insurance programs including reinsurance, claims, and customer education. In addition to training USDA employees, I have trained USDA employees at the state and county level in NC, VA, WV, PA, and NJ on program changes. Specifically I instructed personnel on how to implement the new ASCS/USDA catastrophic disaster program along with how to evaluate crop conditions and crop damage.

I offer a proven ability to coordinate and work with individuals including state and county farm service personnel as well as loss adjusters. I have supervised loss adjustment in claims processing by USDA employees in NC, VA, WV, PA, and NJ to insure that the policies of government farm programs are followed. I trained USDA recorders so that they could become certified as crop appraisers. I also worked in the field with USDA employees on new crop expansion in NC, NJ, and PA for blueberries, tomatoes, and potatoes.

In my previous job from 1996-02 as Crop Insurance Specialist, I supervised an average of 20 individuals in handling the responsibility for establishing and implementing Federal Crop Insurance programs. This involved me constantly in expertly interpreting policies and procedures and in applying guidance to subordinates, peers, and farmers relating to all phases of crop insurance programs. It was my responsibility to assign, control, and review all loss adjustment work in the area. As the most knowledgeable and most experienced loss adjuster, it was also my responsibility to handle the most controversial claims as I also routinely conducted inspections of crops, evaluated farming management and practices, reviewed all contract folders for accuracy, and reviewed contract service programs in order to make recommendations for improving overall effectiveness. With a reputation as a highly articulate technical expert, I became highly respected for my ability to communicate highly technical concepts in an understandable manner while providing program information to reinsurance specialists, private companies, Federal and state agencies, agri-business concerns, and underwriters.

In my job from 1994-96 as a Crop Insurance Specialist/Distribution Director, I supervised a total of 30 employees who were supervisors and loss adjusters in District 08. I personally reviewed and handled all controversial and difficult claims while working closely with USDA agencies, handling public relations with farmers and farm organizations, and making recommendations on a wide range of matters ranging from personnel administration to controversial claims management.

In my job from 1991-94 as a Crop Insurance Field Representative, I supervised up to 35 loss adjusters while earning rapidly promotion from a Supervisor position to Assistant to the District Director. I became certified on 13 crops and during this period of time I worked claims on nine insurance crops while continuously reviewing and auditing controversial claims. While training and supervising other loss adjusters, it was my responsibility to handle the most controversial and difficult claims.

Education and training related to this KSA:
In addition to an A.A. from the Devry Agriculture and Technical School, I believe the following education and training have enhanced my knowledge in this area:
- 2004, Managing Work Force Diversity and Managing Change
- 2000, Creative Problem Solving
- 1998, Improving Communication with the Public
- 1997, Loss Adjuster Certification Training
- 1995, Federal Crop Insurance Certification (13 crops)
- 1994, Instructor Training
- 1990, Agents Certification Training

INTELLIGENCE OPERATIONS SUPERVISOR

ARMANDO C. RODRIGUEZ

SSN: 000-00-0000

INTELLIGENCE OPERATIONS SUPERVISOR, GS-12 ANNOUNCEMENT #XYZ123

KSA (1): Ability to analyze specific geographic and/or functional area(s) to identify significant factors, gather pertinent data, and develop solutions.

As an Intelligence Operations Supervisor at Fort Hood, I supervise 15 Intelligence Specialists while managing the collection, editing and dissemination of intelligence reports, overseeing the analysis of specific geographic and/or functional areas to identify significant factors and gathering pertinent data in order to develop solutions. Received a citation for my attention to detail and ability to effectively handle time-sensitive projects while analyzing and editing more than 150 intelligence reports during a large-scale field exercise to identify significant factors. During the same exercise, demonstrated expertise and knowledge, supervising the gathering of pertinent data through the successful interrogation of over 100 prisoners of war, and developed situations based on the information obtained. Praised in official performance evaluations for "professionalism and composure during stressful and demanding situations".

During my tenure as an Instructor at The Presidio, I received several medals and commendations for my work as an interpreter and instructor at the Defense Language Institute, as well as for my participation in several highly-visible special projects. Acted as interpreter for a visiting Arabic airborne commander, and wrote and published a Arabic-language "survival packet" which was distributed for use throughout the Army's quick-response community. Was awarded the Joint Service Commendation Medal for my expertise during a NATO exercise.

In my prior position as Interrogation and Section Supervisor in Afghanistan, I trained and supervised 45 people in an organization which conducted extensive peacetime operations, collecting intelligence information vital to national security. Was promoted on the basis of my accomplishments as Senior Interrogator and Assistant Supervisor, responsible for an 15-person debriefing section. Debriefed human intelligence sources, using my command of the Arabic language to analyze the information provided and identify significant factors. I then developed situations and prepared reports based on this and other information collected by my office.

As an Interpreter for the Counterintelligence professionals in Afghanistan, I interpreted from Arabic to English and English to Arabic while conveying ideas orally in an effective manner. I also conveyed ideas orally in an effective manner while interpreting polygraph questions.

To summarize, the ability to analyze specific geographic and/or functional areas to identify significant factors, gather pertinent data, and develop solutions has been a constant requirement in every position I have held during my military career, from my early days as a Reconnaissance Sergeant and Debriefer, through advancement to Senior Interrogator and Interrogation and Exploitation Section Supervisor, Instructor at the Defense Language Institute, and finally as Intelligence Operations Supervisor at Fort Hood. I have attended numerous military training programs and received many awards and commendations for my knowledge, skills, and abilities in these areas.

Education and Training related to this KSA:

In addition to my military training, I possess the following degrees, many of which are directly related to this KSA.

- Bachelor of Arts degree, History – Texas Southern University of Houston (September, 2002).
- Bachelor of Arts degree, Communication – Norfolk State University (1999).
- Associate of Arts degree, Liberal Arts — Texas Southern University (1996).
- Associate of Applied Science degree, Criminal Justice – Virginia Highlands Community College (1994).
- Associate of Arts degree, Liberal Arts – Virginia Highlands Community College (1992).
- Associate of Applied Science, Law Enforcement – Kilgore College (1990).
- Associate of Applied Science, Automotive Service and Repair – Kilgore College (1989).

Have excelled in numerous military training programs related to this KSA, to include the following Interrogation, Intelligence, Leadership and Engineering courses: Reid Interrogation Course (2003), Kinesics Intelligence Course (2003), Laboratory for Scientific Interrogation (2002), British Specialist Prisoner Handling (2001), Military Language Instructor Training (2001), Strategic Debriefing (2000), British Joint Services Tactical Quest (2000), Senior Leadership Course (1999), Interrogator Course (1998), Ranger Platoon Confidence Training (1997), Primary Leadership Development Course (1994), Combat Engineer Training (1993).

Language Courses and Languages spoken which strengthen my ability to analyze specific geographic and/or functional areas to identify significant factors, gather pertinent data, and develop solutions:

In February/March 2000, I will be enrolled in an intensive Arabic Language Course and the American Language Course (1999). In addition to these courses, I have strong linguistic abilities through experience in the German, Hungarian, Italian as well as my native language—Spanish.

INTELLIGENCE OPERATIONS SUPERVISOR

ARMANDO C. RODRIGUEZ

SSN: 000-00-0000

INTELLIGENCE OPERATIONS SUPERVISOR, GS-12 ANNOUNCEMENT #XYZ123

KSA (2): Skill in the use of various research tools such as bibliographies, regulations, statistics, automated databases, etc.

In the course of my job as Intelligence Operations Supervisor at Fort Hood, it is necessary for me to constantly utilize various different research tools while also training and supervising 15 Intelligence Specialists in using various tools. In order to perform my job effectively, I must be able to refer to bibliographies, regulations, statistics, and automated databases in order to assess and prioritize collected intelligence data and identify significant factors.

In my current position as Intelligence Operations Supervisor for the 2-29th Intelligence Division, I am responsible for training and supervising 25 Intelligence Specialists in utilizing ADP systems and databases while supporting the work of the Army's only airborne interrogation company. As Supervisor of 15, I oversee the utilization of the most sophisticated ADP systems and databases used in the Intelligence Community while managing the collecting, editing, and dissemination of intelligence reports and controlling the utilization and maintenance of more than $225,000 worth of equipment. Demonstrated knowledge and expertise of ADP systems and databases while supervising the interrogation of more than 100 prisoners of war during a large-scale field exercise, and was awarded a citation for my attention to detail and ability to handle time-sensitive projects while editing over 150 intelligence reports as part of the same exercise. My knowledge of ADP systems and databases contributed to the effectiveness of individual and group training, while emphasizing the importance of setting and achieving high standards.

While an Instructor for the Defense Language Institute at The Presidio from 1998-01, I acquainted students with the software and hardware used in the Intelligence Community while planning and organizing the work of students involved in sophisticated executive-level language training programs. On numerous occasions, I was handpicked to take on special projects which required my ability to utilize sophisticated ADP systems and databases for planning and organizational purposes. I received a Certificate of Achievement for planning and coordinating an event providing more than 3,250 civilian students and teachers with the opportunity to visit the facility and resulting in numerous recruiting contacts. In addition, I planned, wrote, and published a Arabic-language "crisis survival package" which was distributed for use throughout the Army's quick response community, and planned and developed a Arabic Headstart Course which was praised by students and other instructors. While achieving recognition for these special projects, I was also responsible for conducting Arabic language instruction for as many as 45 students and providing my students with counseling for academic, personal and career issues. Was awarded the Joint Service Commendation Medal for my expertise during a NATO exercise.

As Interrogation and Exploitation Section Supervisor in Afghanistan, from 1995-98, I interfaced with ADP systems and databases as I planned and executed the training of 45 people and supervised them in an organization which conducted extensive peacetime operations, collecting intelligence information vital to national security. Using ADP systems and databases for planning and control purposes, I oversaw a project to relocate the unit following a base closure, and orchestrated resettlement and immigration affairs for human intelligence sources. While Senior Interrogator at the same post, I supervised, planned, and organized the work of an 15-person debriefing unit, with major duties which included the debriefing of human intelligence sources in Arabic as well as drafting reports, assessing and prioritizing potential information sources, and acting as an interpreter.

Furthermore, pursuing a total of six degrees while simultaneously serving my country at various posts and positions around the world also required me to possess skill in the use of various research tools. Many of these courses were completed by correspondence, and I had to depend heavily on my own research skills, as I was unable to rely on the resources of a major university.

Education and Training related to this KSA:
In addition to my military training, I possess the following degrees, many of which are directly related to this KSA.
- Bachelor of Arts degree, History – Texas Southern University of Houston (September, 2002).
- Bachelor of Arts degree, Communication – Norfolk State University (1999).
- Associate of Arts degree, Liberal Arts — Texas Southern University (1996).
- Associate of Applied Science degree, Criminal Justice – Virginia Highlands Community College (1994).
- Associate of Arts degree, Liberal Arts – Virginia Highlands Community College (1992).
- Associate of Applied Science, Law Enforcement – Kilgore College (1990).
- Associate of Applied Science, Automotive Service and Repair – Kilgore College (1989).

Have excelled in numerous military training programs related to this KSA, to include the following Interrogation, Intelligence, Leadership and Engineering courses: Reid Interrogation Course (2003), Kinesics Intelligence Course (2003), Laboratory for Scientific Interrogation (2002), British Specialist Prisoner Handling (2001), Military Language Instructor Training (2001), Strategic Debriefing (2000), British Joint Services Tactical Quest (2000), Senior Leadership Course (1999), Interrogator Course (1998), Ranger Platoon Confidence Training (1997), Primary Leadership Development Course (1994), Combat Engineer Training (1993).

Language Courses and Languages spoken which strengthen my ability to analyze specific geographic and/or functional areas to identify significant factors, gather pertinent data, and develop solutions:

In February/March 2000, I will be enrolled in an intensive Arabic Language Course and the American Language Course (1999). In addition to these courses, I have strong linguistic abilities through experience in the German, Hungarian, Italian as well as my native language—Spanish.

INTELLIGENCE OPERATIONS SUPERVISOR

ARMANDO C. RODRIGUEZ

SSN: 000-00-0000

INTELLIGENCE OPERATIONS SUPERVISOR, GS-09 ANNOUNCEMENT #XYZ123

KSA (3): Ability to plan and organize work.

In my current position as Intelligence Operations Supervisor for the 2-29th Intelligence Division, I am responsible for planning and organizing the work of the U.S. Army's only airborne interrogation company. As Supervisor of 15 Intelligence Specialists, I plan and organize their work while managing the collecting, editing, and dissemination of intelligence reports and controlling the utilization and maintenance of more than $225,000 worth of equipment. Demonstrated knowledge and expertise while supervising the interrogation of more than 100 prisoners of war during a large-scale field exercise, and was awarded a citation for my attention to detail and ability to handle time-sensitive projects while editing over 150 intelligence reports as part of the same exercise. My planning and organizational skills contributed to the effectiveness of individual and group training, while emphasizing the importance of setting and achieving high standards.

While an Instructor for the Defense Language Institute at The Presidio from 1998-01, I continuously planned and organized the work of students involved in sophisticated executive-level language training programs. On numerous occasions I was handpicked to take on special projects which required excellent planning, organizational, and management skills; I received a Certificate of Achievement for planning and coordinating an event providing more than 3,250 civilian students and teachers with the opportunity to visit the facility and resulting in numerous recruiting contacts. In addition, I planned, wrote, and published a Arabic-language "crisis survival package" which was distributed for use throughout the Army's quick response community, and planned and developed a Arabic Headstart Course which was praised by students and other instructors. While achieving recognition for these special projects, I was also responsible for conducting Arabic language instruction for as many as 45 students and providing my students with counseling for academic, personal and career issues. Was awarded the Joint Service Commendation Medal for my expertise during a NATO exercise.

As Interrogation and Exploitation Section Supervisor in Afghanistan, from 1995-98, I planned and executed the training of 45 people and supervised them in an organization which conducted extensive peacetime operations, collecting intelligence information vital to national security. I oversaw a project to relocate the unit following a base closure, and orchestrated resettlement and immigration affairs for human intelligence sources.

While Senior Interrogator at the same post, I supervised, planned, and organized the work of an 15-person debriefing unit, with major duties which included the debriefing of human intelligence sources in Arabic as well as drafting reports, assessing and prioritizing potential information sources, and acting as an interpreter.

As an Interpreter for the Counterintelligence professionals in Afghanistan, I interpreted from Arabic to English and English to Arabic while conveying ideas orally in an effective manner. I also conveyed ideas orally in an effective manner while interpreting polygraph questions.

Education and Training related to this KSA:

In addition to my military training, I possess the following degrees, many of which are directly related to this KSA.

- Bachelor of Arts degree, History – Texas Southern University of Houston (September, 2002).
- Bachelor of Arts degree, Communication – Norfolk State University (1999).
- Associate of Arts degree, Liberal Arts — Texas Southern University (1996).
- Associate of Applied Science degree, Criminal Justice – Virginia Highlands Community College (1994).
- Associate of Arts degree, Liberal Arts – Virginia Highlands Community College (1992).
- Associate of Applied Science, Law Enforcement – Kilgore College (1990).
- Associate of Applied Science, Automotive Service and Repair – Kilgore College (1989).

Have excelled in numerous military training programs related to this KSA, to include the following Interrogation, Intelligence, Leadership and Engineering courses: Reid Interrogation Course (2003), Kinesics Intelligence Course (2003), Laboratory for Scientific Interrogation (2002), British Specialist Prisoner Handling (2001), Military Language Instructor Training (2001), Strategic Debriefing (2000), British Joint Services Tactical Quest (2000), Senior Leadership Course (1999), Interrogator Course (1998), Ranger Platoon Confidence Training (1997), Primary Leadership Development Course (1994), Combat Engineer Training (1993).

Language Courses and Languages spoken which strengthen my ability to analyze specific geographic and/or functional areas to identify significant factors, gather pertinent data, and develop solutions:

In February/March 2000, I will be enrolled in an intensive Arabic Language Course and the American Language Course (1999). In addition to these courses, I have strong linguistic abilities through experience in the German, Hungarian, Italian as well as my native language—Spanish.

LIBRARY TECHNICIAN

REBECCA MARIE SCHOFIELD

SSN: 000-00-0000

LIBRARY TECHNICIAN, GS-05/07 ANNOUNCEMENT #XYZ123

**Library Technician,
GS-05/07
Announcement #XYZ123
KSA #1**

KSA #1: Knowledge of basic cataloging and filing principles.

In my present position as a Library Technician (2003-present), I must show the knowledge of basic cataloging and filing principles on a daily basis. At the Johnson Memorial Library, the main post library, at Ft. Drum, NY, approximately 1,000 patrons use the facility on a daily basis. Approximately half of my time is spent processing new materials (to include books, videocassettes, compact disks) into the library system. Therefore, I am spending a great deal of my time seeing that these items are properly cataloged and thus can be shelved properly. One of the first steps in the cataloging process is to search the Online Computer Library Center (OCLC) database for cataloging information on newly acquired materials. I review machine-readable records (MARC) for errors and omissions in the data and then make the appropriate corrections and additions by applying my knowledge of the Dewey Decimal Classification and Anglo-American Cataloging Rules 2 (AACR2) and then using the MARC format and bibliographic data elements.

Helped input, update, and correct records on the new Automated Information System daily. Downloaded records from OCLC not found in SIRSI database and converted data for downloading to SIRSI.

A librarian will probably have
to prepare this KSA.

As a Supply Clerk at the 44th General Hospital in Munich, Germany (2000-03), maintained a complete inventory of forms, this included seeing that every blank form used throughout the hospital was properly cataloged and an up-to-date count maintained at all times. I was solely responsible for providing this support to the hospital itself as well as three outlying clinics. I cataloged and filed each type of form and ensured adequate levels were available as needed. When supplies reached certain prescribed levels, I ordered new inventories from a government printing office.

Education, training, and awards:

Completed U.S. Army-sponsored training programs where emphasis was placed on increasing knowledge related to basic cataloging and filing principles:

Fifth Annual Conference for Library Support staff, University of Michigan, 2003

OCLC Prism Training, Ft. Drum, NY, 2002

- Received "on the spot" cash awards in 1998 and again in 2002 for professionalism and job knowledge.
- Was given "time-off awards" in 2000 and 2001 in recognition of my contributions.
- Was promoted in December 1999 on the basis of the results of a "desk audit."

KSA #2: Ability to meet and deal with a variety of individuals in a variety of situations.

At Johnson Memorial Library, Ft. Drum, NY (2002-03), I was assigned regular "front desk" shifts which involved constant contact with the public. Although I was assigned to conduct the processing of new materials, because of staff shortages and the volume of use of the library facility, I was assigned to two regular four-hour shifts each week to supplement circulation staff. In this capacity my ability to meet and deal with the public was demonstrated while in contact with military and civilian personnel as well as family members to whom I provided basic library services.

Another aspect of dealing with a variety of individuals is the part of my job (2002) that involves providing the three other branches with answers to technical service questions and to solicit information from them to be used in reports or to answer patron's inquiries.

As the Supply Clerk at 44th General Hospital (2000-02), I was in daily contact with a variety of individuals from all the various departments within the hospital. Each department had its own set of forms which were unique to its internal operations. So I had to be aware that each department had its own needs and requirements and I had to be able to meet the individual department needs and keep each supplied.

In an earlier position as a Supply Clerk (1997-00), for the 2nd Armor Division in Mannheim, Germany, I was involved in an almost entirely military work setting where I handled the division's DA Form 12 Series Table of Organization and Equipment (TOE).

From April to September 1996 I was a Customer Service Clerk for AAFES (Army and Air Force Exchange Service) Okinawa. At the main post exchange in a major military community I dealt with a large number of individual customers daily either in person, by phone, or through correspondence. My range of duties required constant contact while doing everything from making refunds, exchanges or adjustments, to assisting customers, to preparing deferred payment and layaway payments.

Education, training, and awards:
- Training directly related to the development of the ability to deal with individuals included government training on:
  > Managing Difficult Customers, Ft. Drum, NY, 2002
  > Stress Management for Women, 2001
  > Customer Care I, 2001
- AAFES **"Employee of the Month"** for ability to deal with customers politely and tactfully, August 2000.
- Received **"on the spot"** cash awards in 1998 and again in 2002 for professionalism and job knowledge.
- Was given **"time-off awards"** in 2000 and 2001 in recognition of my contributions.
- Was promoted in December 1997 on the basis of the results of a "desk audit."

Library Technician, GS-05/07 Announcement #XYZ123 KSA #2

Be very detailed about any education or training which is relevant.

LINGUIST

ELIZABETH SMITH MARKHAM

SSN: 000-00-0000

LINGUIST, GS-09 ANNOUNCEMENT #XYZ123

KSA: Ability to plan, organize and coordinate foreign language training.

Overview of knowledge in this area:

Through my extensive study of foreign languages, combined with 23 years experience as an Army linguist, and leadership assignments at DLI and the Foreign Language Training Center Europe, I have developed an in-depth and unique ability to plan, organize, and coordinate foreign language training. I believe my promotion to Command Sergeant Major is an indication of my exceptional problem-solving skills and operations management abilities in the area of language training activities.

Experience related to this KSA:

In my previous job at the Defense Language Institute of Monterey, I demonstrated my ability to plan, organize, and coordinate language training activities for initial acquisition. Indeed, this job is probably my "showcase" job in terms of displaying my expertise in planning, organizing, and coordinating language training. This was one of the most difficult jobs I ever held because the battalion had a unique mission which required above-average flexibility and innovation, and also because this was a very large (1600 soldiers) organization which placed enormous pressure on soldiers to learn a foreign language for the first time. In this job I drew on my personal experience in learning Czech, Polish, German, and Latin as I attempted to understand the needs and feelings of the student body and determine necessary changes in training activities. I provided feedback to the U.S. Army Training and Doctrine Command (TRADOC) about the initial entry training program. I was able to draw on my previous experiences as a Technical Language Assistant at the Defense Language Institute (DLI) and as First Sergeant of the Foreign Language Training Center Europe in planning, organizing, and coordinating language training activities for initial acquisition. As a result of my outstanding performance in this job, I earned a reputation as a leading authority in the area of planning, organizing, and coordinating language training activities for initial acquisition. I believe constant interaction with the student body is a key to solving instructional and training program issues, especially in initial acquisition training.

Also in my most recent job as Command Sergeant Major, I improved the foreign language proficiency scores of linguists assigned to the organization by establishing a refresher and enhancement language training program. I established this program after identifying shortfalls in student capabilities and scores, and then I instituted the program. I also authored and communicated a policy which focused the organization's attention on foreign language training, and I improved the utilization of linguists by implementing a program which more rapidly assigned personnel to positions at the National Security Agency. I designed and directed implementation of a program which selected the most qualified and motivated NCOs to represent our organization at the U.S. Army Foreign Language Olympics. I was continuously in a problem-solving and opportunity-finding mode at this job. For example, when I arrived at this job in July 2002, I studied existing policies and procedures and developed numerous programs which improved morale, increased training effectiveness, and boosted training results in formal evaluations.

Emphasize your results!

In my job as First Sergeant of the Foreign Language Training Center, I played a key role in planning, organizing, and coordinating language training activities. Part of my job was to organize and supervise a 70-person staff consisting of military and foreign civilian language instructors with disparate backgrounds. One of the main problems I had to solve was not a classroom problem but a billeting and barracks maintenance problem which was affecting student morale and performance. While managing a contract for $500,000 I worked with a German contractor who at first refused to do many tasks which I felt were essential to student health and welfare. After extensive negotiation, I convinced the German contractor to proceed with numerous activities which I felt were essential, and I was credited by my peers as solving some stubborn operational problems which faculty and students thought were related to training effectiveness. With a reputation as an innovative administrator who is always seeking new ways of planning and organizing language training activities, I conceived of a language utilization and cultural immersion program after the breakup of the Soviet Union which permitted students to go on tours throughout the former Warsaw Pact.

Give dates and details.

Education and training related to this KSA:

My civilian education includes a Master's degree from Dubois University where I concentrated in Business Management Courses, and I also hold a BA from the University of Rhode Island where my chief undergraduate subjects were foreign language courses.

My military training and education related to foreign language training and development is vast and multifaceted. I excelled in studies of Polish and Czech at the Defense Language Institute and I studied Basic Traffic Analysis and completed the Advanced Noncommissioned Officer course for EW Cryptologic Supervisors at the U.S. Army Security Agency Training Center. I am certified as a Professional Language Analyst in Polish and Czech by NSA. I am a graduate of the Senior Cryptologic Supervisor Course and I am a Distinguished Graduate of the Advanced EW/Crypto Course for NCOs (ANCOC).

Courses I completed in the military which helped me gain the ability to plan, organize, and coordinate language training activities for initial acquisition included the following:
- the First Sergeant's Course, 2001; I maintained 100% academic average.
- the Sergeant's Major Course, 2000; I completed two-year nonresident program in one year.
- Cryptologic Supervisor Course, 1996; was Distinguished Graduate.
- the Advanced Noncommissioned Officer Course, 1993; was Distinguished Graduate.
- the Czech Basic Course, Defense Language Institute, 1990-91; was Distinguished Graduate.
- the Polish Basic Course, Defense Language Institute, 1988-89; won the Polish Department Book Award.

MAINTENANCE TECHNICIAN

GEORGE S. ZANE

SSN: 000-00-0000

MAINTENANCE TECHNICIAN, WG-07/09 ANNOUNCEMENT #XYZ123

KSA #1: Ability to use and maintain tools and equipment.

In my capacity of Ordnance Equipment Mechanic with the U.S. Air Force Reserves since 2000, I have become qualified and certified to use the following test sets:

- DSM-151B for AIM-7E and F electronic, hydraulic function, performance, and operational use
- AN/DSM-162 for determining if AIM-7E, F, and M missile guidance units are functioning properly
- TS4044/D for determining if AIM-BE, J, M, and P missile guidance units are functioning properly
- GCU-26E for checking AIM missile coolant pressure tank recharging unit

My responsibilities extend to cover all associated munitions handling and support equipment for which I evaluate solid state circuits, electromechanical, pneumatic, hydraulic, and explosive components and systems using precision measuring tools and equipment. I interpret and apply information gained from blueprints, schematics, and technical drawings.

Give specifics.

I regularly and routinely use tools and equipment which include, but are not limited to, the following:

lineman's and common pliers	3/8" ratchet drive	7/16" socket
6" and 8" adjustable wrench	7" vise grips	flashlight
3/8" and 5/16" box-end wrench	1/4" t-handle wrench	1/4" air fastener bit
1/8" and 5/64" Allen wrench	1/8", 7/32", 1/4" and 5/16" apex	
torque wrench	lanyard kits	sledge hammer
bomb lift adapter with hook	MK-82 slings	levels
bomb rotating tool	slings	nail can
claw hammer	banding cutter	crosscut saw
spanner wrenches	hydraulic jack	light cables
ATU-35 tool	swaging tool	air ratchet
alignment tool	adapter ratchet	adapter socket
safety wire		

4" common, 6" common, and 3" Phillips screwdrivers
ear plugs, safety glasses, hard hat, face shield, foam ear plugs, and safety glasses
mobility equipment: tie-down straps, rail assemblies, chock assemblies, trolley assemblies, ramps, boom adapters, load binders, load chains, and pallets
communications equipment: notebook computer, laser jet printer, hand-held radios, and control radio mobility box

Education and Training Related to this KSA:

Attended courses including the Air Force Combat Ammunition Planning and Production Course, 80 hours, July 2003; a Total Quality Management (TQM) course; and the Munitions Supply Technical School, Schriever AFB, CO, 2000 (285 hours).

GEORGE S. ZANE

SSN: 000-00-0000

MAINTENANCE TECHNICIAN, WG-07/09 ANNOUNCEMENT #XYZ123

KSA #2: Knowledge of equipment assembly, installation, and repair.

My knowledge of equipment assembly, installation and repair is a vital element in my present job with the U.S. Air Force Reserves (2000 to present) where I am a Materials Expediter and Ordnance Equipment Mechanic. I manage, monitor, account for, identify, store, issue, distribute, deliver, procure, and dispose of Air Force munitions. These munitions include unguided bombs, dispensers, mines, rockets, aircraft systems, small arms ammunition, guided munitions, and chemical munitions. My unit's primary mission is to provide safe and timely delivery of nonnuclear munitions, training munitions, and components which support the F-16C and D Fighting Falcon combat training aircraft.

My responsibilities extend to include all associated munitions handling and support equipment. While troubleshooting I evaluate solid state circuits, electromechanical, pneumatic, hydraulic, and explosive components and systems using precision measuring tools and equipment. I interpret and apply information gained from blueprints, schematics, and technical drawings. Inspect munitions for serviceability and apply all relative quality assurance procedures. I also oversee the Munitions Critical Item Program, non-nuclear combat operations, annual munitions forecasts, automation policy, distribution of munitions allocations, support planning and pre-directs, financial accounting, manual conventional munitions operations, and management of nuclear accounts. I accomplish the details of item accounting, inventory stock control, requirements computations, and determination of allowances.

While managing non-nuclear munitions, I recondition, deliver, maintain, test, and assemble guided and unguided munitions. When controlling nuclear munitions, I handle, store, and transport them according to existing safety directives and operating procedures. Inventory control and documentation actions include conducting/documenting inventories and any discrepancies which may occur. Operate the Combat Ammunition System and Maintenance Classification programs.

Education and Training Related to this KSA:
Attended courses including the Air Force Combat Ammunition Planning and Production Course, 80 hours, July 2003; a Total Quality Management (TQM) course; and the Munitions Supply Technical School, Schriever AFB, CO, 2000 (285 hours).

MAINTENANCE TECHNICIAN

GEORGE S. ZANE
SSN: 000-00-0000

MAINTENANCE TECHNICIAN, WG-07/09 ANNOUNCEMENT #XYZ123

**Maintenance Technician,
WG-07/09
Announcement #XYZ123
KSA #3**

KSA #3: Work practices.

In my current position as U.S. Air Force Reserve Materials Expediter/Ordnance Equipment Mechanic (2000 to present) and earlier as a Service Clerk with Service Merchandise (1993-2000), keeping supplies, equipment and the physical facility clean and neat are vital to the safety and productivity of the respective daily activities.

Presently serving as a Materials Expediter/Ordnance Equipment Mechanic with the U.S. Air Force Reserves (from 2000 to present), I have accumulated approximately 3,200 hours as a Munitions Supply Specialist (two years) and 1,496 hours as a Munitions System Specialist (1-1/2 years). In these capacities I manage, monitor, account for, identify, store, issue, distribute, deliver, procure, and dispose of Air Force munitions. These munitions include unguided bombs, dispensers, mines, rockets, aircraft systems, small arms ammunition, guided munitions, and chemical munitions. My unit's primary mission is to provide safe and timely delivery of non-nuclear munitions, training munitions, and components which support the F-16C and D Fighting Falcon combat training aircraft.

My responsibilities extend to include all associated munitions handling and support equipment. I am skilled in following prescribed work practices and instructions in order to maintain specific components in the munitions field. In my job I must be trained, certified and familiar with the operation of various components and the manner in which each of them interacts with various other related parts. Additionally, during the testing phase reconfiguration of munitions and preloaded launch racks may be required and can not be completed safely and competently unless the proper Technical Orders, checklists, manuals and other available guidelines are used and followed.

Sometimes writing a KSA worded so vaguely can be challenging!

I fully understand that the importance of safety practices in the workplace can not be overstated especially when dealing with explosives and with electricity. I am fully aware of the technical practices which call for functional testing and troubleshooting of weapons systems with applied voltage. I have been instrumental in making suggestions and recommendations as to more efficient and/or safer methods based on my experiences and knowledge of munitions maintenance and which have led to the success of the team during two important OREs (Ordnance Readiness Exercises) and two ORIs (Ordnance Readiness Inspections).

Education and Training Related to this KSA:
- Received a bachelor's degree in Business Administration, Cambridge College, Miami, FL, fall 2002. Earned an Associate in Applied Science degree in Logistics Operations Management, Community College of the Air Force, Eglin AFB, FL, 2000.
- Attended courses including the Air Force Combat Ammunition Planning and Production Course, 80 hours, July 2000; a Total Quality Management (TQM) course; and the Munitions Supply Technical School, Schriever AFB, CO, 2000 (285 hours).

KSA #4: Technical Practices.

Presently serving as a Materials Expediter/Ordnance Equipment Mechanic with the U.S. Air Force Reserves (from 2000 to present), I have accumulated approximately 3,200 hours as a Munitions Supply Specialist (two years) and 1,496 hours as a Munitions System Specialist (1-1/2 years). In these capacities I manage, monitor, account for, identify, store, issue, distribute, deliver, procure, and dispose of Air Force munitions. These munitions include unguided bombs, dispensers, mines, rockets, aircraft systems, small arms ammunition, guided munitions, and chemical munitions. My unit's primary mission is to provide safe and timely delivery of non-nuclear munitions, training munitions, and components which support the F-16C and D Fighting Falcon combat training aircraft.

My responsibilities extend to include all associated munitions handling and support equipment. I am skilled in following prescribed work practices and instructions in order to maintain specific components in the munitions field. In my job I must be trained, certified and familiar with the operation of various components and the manner in which each of them interacts with various other related parts. Additionally, during the testing phase reconfiguration of munitions and preloaded launch racks may be required and can not be completed safely and competently unless the proper Technical Orders, checklists, manuals and other available guidelines are used and followed.

In KSAs, he borrows some language from KSA 3.

I fully understand that the importance of safety practices in the workplace can not be overstated, especially when dealing with explosives and with electricity. I am fully aware of the technical practices which call for functional testing and troubleshooting of weapons systems with applied voltage can lead to possible electrocution, fire or even detonation of munitions if safety practices are ignored. Human error must be minimized because one step missed in checking or assembly procedures or an incorrect test adjustment setting could be fatal. The time element is also essential in some procedures when dealing with explosives.

I have been instrumental in making suggestions and recommendations as to more efficient and/or safer methods based on my experiences and knowledge of munitions maintenance. Some of my suggestions have led to the success of the team during two important OREs (Ordnance Readiness Exercises) and two ORIs (Ordnance Readiness Inspections).

Education and Training Related to this KSA:
Attended courses including the Air Force Combat Ammunition Planning and Production Course, 80 hours, July 2003; a Total Quality Management (TQM) course; and the Munitions Supply Technical School, Schriever AFB, CO, 2000 (285 hours).

MEDICAL SUPPLY TECHNICIAN

ALLISON CARTER JENSON

SSN: 000-00-0000

MEDICAL SUPPLY TECHNICIAN, GS-07 ANNOUNCEMENT #XYZ123

**Medical Supply
Technician, GS-07
Announcement #XYZ123
KSA #1**

KSA #1: Knowledge of aseptic principles and techniques.

In my jobs as Chairside Dental Assistant with Dr. Francis from 2001-03 and with Dr. Sweeney from 2000-01, assisted doctors in chairside duties.

Demonstrated knowledge of proper infection control procedures as needed by OSHA regulations, knowledge of disease transmission, droplet infection and indirect transmission, in order to prevent cross contamination to prevent the spread of disease through indirect contact and through personal contact. Demonstrated knowledge about preventing the spread of STDs such as AIDS, herpes, syphilis and gonorrhea which can be spread through contaminated blood, saliva, or mucous membranes. Demonstrated knowledge of carrier contact such as people with typhoid fever, tuberculosis, hepatitis B, herpes, and AIDS. Utilized proper protective and safety habits by wearing gloves, protective eye wear, and NOISN approved mask when handling contaminated materials.

Knowledge is not the same as experience. You can have knowledge about an area in which you have no experience.

Conducted training for new personnel on office equipment and material including Bio Hazardous Materials Shipment. Assisted in all phases of general dentistry including prosthodontics, surgical removal of impacted third molars, pediatrics, and amalgam and composite fillings. Charted and maintained patient records. Exposed and developed dental radiographs. Also assisted in endodontics, prosthodontics, and utilization of nitrous oxide, and application of sealants. Prepared new patient documentation and evaluations of diet, dental habits, and vital signs. Assisted in crown and bridge work, prosthetics, non-surgical periodontal therapy, and restorative and cosmetic dentistry.

KSA #2: Knowledge of the full range of medical supplies, instruments, equipment and the specific cleaning, sterilizing, and store requirements of each.

In my jobs as Chairside Dental Assistant with Dr. Francis from 2001-03 and with Dr. Sweeney from 2000-01, assisted doctors in chairside duties and was also involved in tasks related to prosthodontics, surgical removal of impacted third molars, pediatrics, and amalgam and composite fillings. Charted and maintained patient records. Exposed and developed dental radiographs. Also assisted in endodontics, prosthodontics, and utilization of nitrous oxygen, and application of sealants. Prepared new patient documentation and evaluations of diet, dental habits, and vital signs. Assisted in crown and bridge work, prosthetics, non-surgical periodontal therapy, and restorative and cosmetic dentistry.

Demonstrated my knowledge of hydrocolloid impression materials, mixing, measuring cleaning and safety precautions as well as well as knowledge of reversible hydrocelloids such as agar impression materials. Also demonstrated knowledge of irreversible hydrocolloids such as alginates. Became knowledge of the different temperatures at which agar impression materials become a solid and a liquid. Was skilled in setting times for normal set and fast set alginate. Demonstrated my knowledge of thermoplastic, impression compound, stick compound, and tray compound. Demonstrated familiarity with zinc oxide impression pastes, bit registration pastes, surgical pastes. Also demonstrated knowledge in elastomenic impression materials (rubber based impression materials) such as polysulfide, silicone, polysiloxane, polyethers, gypsum products and visible light-care impression materials. Worked with different classification of gypsum products, mixing ratio of gypsum products (water/powder ratio), setting time of gypsum products. Demonstrated familiarity with different alloys: base-metal, porcelain bonding, noble metal alloy as well as with soldering and welding.

Medical Supply Technician, GS-07 Announcement #XYZ123 KSA #2

NURSE: PATIENT ADVOCATE

HEATHER PHILLIPS

SSN: 000-00-0000

NURSE: PATIENT ADVOCATE, GS-09 ANNOUNCEMENT #XYZ123

KSA #1: Knowledge of Professional Nursing Care principles, practice, and procedures.

In my current position as a Psychiatric Charge Nurse, I am expected to be a patient advocate and to provide care for the patient with mental and emotional disorders, sometimes in conjunction with physical disorders. I contribute to the effectiveness of patient care for emotionally and mentally disturbed patients by handling patient assessment interviews, collecting and evaluating psychological and health histories, monitoring behaviors, and documenting instances of ill health and inappropriate behaviors while supervising other RNs, LPNs, and MHT. As a Staff Nurse in medical/surgical and oncology, I provided the same type of assessment and care; only the disorders and ailments were mostly of a physical nature and required more technical skill with IV pumps, chest tubes, wound care, etc.

My positions which have helped me acquire expert knowledge of professional nursing care principles, practice, and procedures are these:
- **Psychiatric Charge Nurse**, Grandview Hospital, Tampa, FL (2003-present)
- **Staff Registered Nurse**, Mercy Regional Medical Center, Tempe, AZ (2002) and Wisteria General Hospital, Austin, TX (1999-2000)
- **Psychiatric Staff Nurse/Mental Health Technician.** Memorial Medical Center, Austin, TX (1998-99)

In all of the above positions, I used my initiative and independent judgment to plan and implement professional nursing care for patients in accordance with hospital policies and NANDA. I established cooperative interpersonal relationships with other hospital staff and medical staff members. Among my responsibilities, I used the nursing process and performed the initial nursing history and assessment, developed a nursing care plan, and also developed and implemented nursing orders. I evaluated patient care depending on the patient's response to that care and revised the nursing care plan accordingly. I recognized and informed appropriate personnel of changes in a patient's condition. For psychiatric patients, I followed established protocols, and I worked closely with other members of the total treatment team in the formulation of the total care plan for patients. I focused on motivating and redirecting the behavior of psychiatric patients, and I participated in group therapy sessions while also providing one-to-one counseling sessions with patients. I administered prescribed medications by oral, intramuscular, subcutaneous and topical routes, and I also prepared patients for diagnostic examinations. I identified and performed patient teaching specific to each patient's needs and initiated and completed patient discharge plan. I followed infection control procedures and practiced proper aseptic techniques at all times while also maintaining appropriate records and documents.

In my most recent position as a Psychiatric Registered Nurse, I have functioned as a Charge Nurse and am responsible for coordinating and supervising day-to-day nursing activities in the psychiatric nursing unit while ensuring the quality of patient care through close observation of all unit activities. I routinely assist emergency room staff in evaluating patients to determine whether they meet Psychiatric admission criteria and provide a complete nurse assessment upon admission.

Overview of skills and knowledge:
Through education, training, and experience, have acquired expert skills related to the following areas:

physical assessment	mental-spiritual assessment
observing signs/symptoms of illness	intravenous therapy
blood transfusion	water-seal drainage system
tracheostomy care	suctioning
bladder irrigation	colostomy care
wound care	crisis intervention
patient instruction	documentation of nursing care
supervising and coordinating health teams	blood glucose testing
Hemocults	reviewing lab tests
catheter insertion	Medications
catheter care	suprapubic catheter
oxygen therapies	volume spirometer
CPR	Hickman and Groshong catheters
subcutaneous infusion port	cast care

obtaining cultures: throat, wound, IV cannula
medication administration observing reaction/response
preparing patients for surgery, X-ray, and various tests

A Psychiatric Nurse was applying for this job.

Education and Training related to this KSA:
- Hold an Associate of Science in Nursing degree from Davidson State College, Austin, TX 1998.
- Graduated **magna cum laude** and was recognized as one of the class's top four students.
- Have completed professional development training related to providing nursing care in medical/surgical, oncology, and the mental health field.
- Am **Certified in Psychiatric Nursing** by American Nurse Association.
- Am a licensed Registered Nurse in FL and TX.

NURSE: NURSE/PATIENT ADVOCATE

HEATHER PHILLIPS

SSN: 000-00-0000

NURSE: PATIENT ADVOCATE, GS-09 ANNOUNCEMENT #XYZ123

KSA #2: Ability to communicate orally.

As a **Psychiatric Nurse** and **Charge Nurse**, I provide direct patient and family care using the nursing process and work in close cooperation with other members of the total treatment team in the formulation, implementation, and evaluation of the total care plans for patients. I establish cooperative interpersonal relationships with hospital and medical staff members in order to coordinate patient care, and I have responsibility for the milieu and contact with patients at all stages of daily life. I teach self care — medications, health care, and hygiene, and I also teach residents how to relate to others, solve problems, communicate clearly, and try out new ways of coping while helping clients progress toward less restricted living situations and less restrictive environments. I am responsible for informing patients and families about available mental health facilities, the nature of psychiatric illness and substance abuse, treatment approaches, and the prevention and reduction of stress as well as teaching anger management techniques and discharge planning procedures.

As a **Charge Nurse**, it is my responsibility to communicate to the staff what their duties, assignments, and responsibilities are. Assignments are made each day, and they must be orally communicated as well. I must inform not only my immediate staff of patient needs, but also I must contact various hospital staffs to arrange for tests, consults, and other needs that the patient might have. Throughout the day I am constantly communicating with the patient while simultaneously collecting data on their mental status. This is sometimes a difficult task due to the fact that some of my patients may be psychotic and sometimes quite paranoid. I must inform the doctor by telephone or in person of any changes in the patient's status that might suggest the need for immediate attention or intervention. It is my responsibility as a nurse to make sure the doctor has not overlooked or disregarded a problem, and this area of my oral communications responsibilities requires that I utilize the utmost tact, diplomacy, and delicacy so that the information I relay orally will be received in a positive and professional manner and so that all medical professionals remain firmly focused on quality patient care above all else.

As a **Charge Nurse** in my current position as a Psychiatric Nurse, my duties include ER admission assessments/screening. This requires me to collect data from and about the patient. I speak with not only the patient but quite often also with the family, staff, and other facilities such as nursing homes. After gathering the information, I must call the doctor and communicate a clear synopsis of the patient's problem so that the doctor can decide whether to admit the patient or not.

Another of my duties as a **Charge Nurse** which involves oral communications involves teaching nursing education classes. I utilize a lecture and discussion format and vary my style according to what is being taught and also according to the skills level of my students. Indeed, in an informal manner, I am constantly involved in teaching other nurses many concepts and skills. I am responsible for following up with patients, with the patient's family, and with the facility the patient will be assigned to.

I serve as a patient advocate, liaison, and communicator for the delivery of individualized, safe, quality care. I communicate on a regular basis with the unit manager to keep informed and up to date on information concerning the condition of patients, their problems, and any other issues which come up that directly affect a patient's care. I perform one-on-one counseling and group sessions with patients to facilitate a useful change in their life, and I focus on motivating and redirecting the behavior of psychiatric patients. I initiate trust building and establish rapport with the patient. Using the nursing process, I perform initial nursing history and assessment and I address the client's resistance if it becomes apparent due to care initiated at someone else's request or insistence, fears and misconceptions about therapy, or an unsatisfactory past therapeutic experience. I involve the patient as a full partner in the therapeutic process, identify and perform patient teaching specific to each patient's needs, teach patients about and prepare them for diagnostic procedures, and I participate in group therapy sessions and teach patient groups on anger management, discharge planning, medications, the nature of psychiatric illness and substance abuse, and social skills.

Communication skills are sought in many jobs.

In jobs prior to nursing, I greatly refined my communication skills. As a **Drug and Alcohol Abuse Counselor** from 1999-2000, I was continuously using my oral communication skills while working with patients as well as with their families and with medical professionals and referral sources. In my job prior to my current position as a Staff Registered Nurse, I also utilized my communication skills in order to communicate about highly technical matters in a nursing environment. I also used my oral communication skills as a Mental Health Nurse from 1998-99 while working with emotionally and mentally disturbed patients, and that job required extensive interviewing of patients as well as subsequent extensive consulting with medical professionals and others.

Education and Training related to this KSA:
- Hold an Associate of Science in Nursing degree from Davidson State College, Austin, TX, 1998.
- Graduated **magna cum laude** and was recognized as one of the class's top four students.
- Have completed professional development training related to providing nursing care in medical/surgical, oncology, and the mental health field.
- Am **Certified in Psychiatric Nursing**.
- Am a licensed Registered Nurse in FL, TX, and AZ.

NURSE: NURSE/PATIENT ADVOCATE

HEATHER PHILLIPS

SSN: 000-00-0000

NURSE: PATIENT ADVOCATE, GS-09 ANNOUNCEMENT #XYZ123

KSA #3: Ability to assign the work of other nursing personnel.

In my current position as the day **Charge Nurse** for the Adult Geriatric Unit, it my job to address the needs of the unit and make daily assignments to RNs, LPNs, and MHTs. The assignments are determined by acuity of unit, the needs of each patient, and the staff scope of practice. The duties are assigned orally first thing in the morning; they are also written on an assignment board to avoid any confusion. Throughout the day, it is not only my job to take care of patients and their records but also to oversee all staff to make sure all assigned tasks are completed in a timely manner.

As a **Psychiatric Nurse** and **Charge Nurse**, I direct other nursing professionals in providing patient and family care using the nursing process and work in close cooperation with other members of the total treatment team in the formulation, implementation, and evaluation of the total care plans for patients. I direct other nursing professions in establishing cooperative interpersonal relationships with hospital and medical staff members in order to coordinate patient care, and I have responsibility for the milieu and contact with patients at all stages of daily life. I train, supervise, and monitor other nursing professionals in teaching self care — medications, health care, and hygiene, and I also teach residents how to relate to others, solve problems, communicate clearly, and try out new ways of coping while helping clients progress toward less restricted living situations and less restrictive environments. I oversee other nursing professionals as they inform patients and families about available mental health facilities, the nature of psychiatric illness and substance abuse, treatment approaches, and the prevention and reduction of stress as well as teaching anger management techniques and discharge planning procedures.

As a **Charge Nurse** I am responsible for coordinating and supervising day-to-day nursing activities in the psychiatric nursing unit while ensuring the quality of patient care through close observation of all unit activities. I routinely assist emergency room staff in evaluating patients to determine whether they meet psychiatric admission criteria and provide a complete nurse assessment upon admission. I provide outstanding case management for adult and geriatric patients while ensuring that all standards of care were met and proper procedures followed. I continuously remain alert to potential emergency or high-risk situations so that appropriate actions can be taken. I keep up-to-date in areas including equipment familiarity as well as safety and procedural issues. I have earned the respect of physicians and other nursing staff for my skills, attitude, concern for patients, willingness to work long hours, and respect for confidentiality. In jobs prior to nursing, I greatly refined my communication skills.

As a **Drug and Alcohol Abuse Counselor** from 1999-2000, I was continuously using my oral communication skills while working with patients as well as with their families and with medical professionals and referral sources. In my job prior to my current position as a Staff Registered Nurse, I also utilized my communication skills in order to communicate about highly technical matters in a nursing environment. I also used my oral communication skills as a Mental Health Nurse from 1998-99 while working with emotionally and mentally disturbed patients, and that job required extensive interviewing of patients as well as subsequent extensive consulting with medical professionals and others.

Education and Training related to this KSA:

- Hold an Associate of Science in Nursing degree from Davidson State College, Austin, TX, 1998.
- Graduated **magna cum laude** and was one of the class's top four students.
- Have completed professional development training related to providing nursing care in medical/surgical, oncology, and the mental health field.
- Am **Certified in Psychiatric Nursing** by American Nurse Association.
- Am a licensed Registered Nurse in FL and TX.

NURSE: CHARGE NURSE

YOLANDA M. MARIN

SSN: 000-00-0000

CHARGE NURSE, GS-09 ANNOUNCEMENT #XYZ123

KSA #1: Ability to communicate orally.

As a Charge Nurse, provide direct patient and family care using the nursing process. Work in close cooperation with other members of the total treatment team in the formulation, implementation, and evaluation of the total care plans for patients. Establish cooperative interpersonal relationships with hospital and medical staff members in order to coordinate patient care. As a Psychiatric Nurse, have responsibility for the milieu and contact with patients at all stages of daily life. Teach self care: medications, health care, and hygiene. Also teach residents how to relate to others, solve problems, communicate clearly, and try out new ways of being. Help clients progress toward less restricted living situations and less restrictive environments. Am also responsible for informing patients and families about available mental health facilities, the nature of psychiatric illness and substance abuse, treatment approaches, and the prevention and reduction of stress as well as teaching anger management techniques and discharge planning procedures.

Perform one-on-one counseling sessions with patients to facilitate a useful change in their life. Focus on motivating and redirecting the behavior of psychiatric patients. Initiate trust building and establish rapport with the patient. Using the nursing process, perform initial nursing history and assessment. Address the client's resistance if it becomes apparent due to care initiated at someone else's request or insistence, fears and misconceptions about therapy, or an unsatisfactory past therapeutic experience. Involve the patient as a full partner in the therapeutic process. Identify and perform patient teaching specific to each patient's needs. Teach patients about and prepare them for diagnostic procedures. Participate in group therapy sessions and teach patient groups on anger management, discharge planning, medications, the nature of psychiatric illness and substance abuse, and social skills.

Also serve as a patient advocate, liaison, and communicator for the delivery of individualized, safe, quality care.

Communicate on a regular basis with the unit manager to keep informed and up to date on information concerning the condition of patients, their problems, and any other issues which come up that directly affect a patient's care.

Education and Training related to this KSA:
- Hold an Associate of Science in Nursing degree from Crawford Technical School, Chicago, IL, 1997.

KSA #2: Ability to plan, assign, and direct the work of other nursing personnel.

Perform Charge Nurse duties on a regular basis while supervising two or three Residential Care Specialists on the evening shift at the Residential Treatment Center. Use my initiative and independent judgment to plan and implement professional nursing care for patients in accordance with hospital policies. Am familiar with hospital policies regarding patient care. Also am responsible for knowing and following the chain of command. Am familiar with the resources available to me so that I can fill the role of Charge Nurse. Have established cooperative interpersonal relationships with other hospital staff and medical staff members. Among my responsibilities is knowing the position descriptions of nursing personnel supervised. In order to effectively delegate tasks I determine what needs to be done and what can be delegated to others. Evaluate the job performance of team members in order to determine who can best take care of each delegated task. Describe the tasks and assignments to the team members and make sure each member understands the tasks and assignments given to them and to test their listening skills. Provide the guidelines for them to report back and on how and when the assignments will be evaluated. Ensure that follow up and evaluation is as previously stated to each team member. Provide the authority, responsibility, and support needed to complete the assignment. I recognize and appreciate a job well done by giving praise that is specific, honest, sincere, and succinct. Acknowledge improvement in performance of a task and promote team synergy and cooperation. Am familiar with disruptive behaviors that may prevent coworkers from functioning well and effective in redirecting those behaviors. Endeavor to build and maintain morale to help coworkers work together smoothly. Attended and participated in the Taking Charge Workshop presented by the Education Department of Northwestern Medical Center.

Performed as a Charge Nurse as assigned at Rockefeller Regional Medical Center, supervising three or four Registered Nurses, one LPN or occasion, two Nursing Assistants, and a Unit Secretary. Became familiar with hospital policies governing patient care, the chain of command, available hospital resources, and position descriptions of nursing staff members supervised. Planned, assigned, and implemented nursing care for patients on the acute psychiatric unit, which treated adult patients and with substance and mental illness. Accompanied physicians on rounds, assisting them with planning, evaluating, and implementing patient care, based on the physician's medical care plans.

Education and Training related to this KSA:
- Hold an Associate of Science in Nursing degree from Crawford Technical School, Chicago, IL, 1997.

OFFICE CLERK

PAIGE L. FORBES

SSN: 000-00-0000

OFFICE CLERK, GS-05 ANNOUNCEMENT #XYZ123

Office Clerk, GS-05
Announcement #XYZ123
KSA #1

KSA #1: Ability to use computer systems and related software.

Overview of my work experience: In the jobs described below, I have received a **Certificate of Outstanding Performance** each and every year from 2003-present and have been cited each year for **performing all duties in an outstanding manner.** I have been commended on numerous occasions for my expertise in utilizing computer systems and related software as well as for my ability to rapidly master new tasks, new knowledge, and new projects. I have earned a reputation as a self-starter known for attention to detail and follow-through in every aspect of my job.

In my current position as **Supply Clerk**, NF-2, I review, analyze, and prepare a wide variety of documentation and paperwork while assuring that paperwork is always within guidelines established by regulatory authorities and other authorities. While maintaining, updating, and utilizing a variety of data systems and using personal computers, I operate a GTA computer with WordPerfect Software, Time Management Labor System software, Microsoft Office software to include Word, Excel, PowerPoint, and Access. I type all correspondence for the Supply and Warehouse Section using the WordPerfect and Word software. One of my responsibilities is to maintain the internal supply budget on Excel software and prepare flyers for the MWR Auction on PowerPoint. Furthermore, I maintain and prepare all NAF time cards using the Time Management Labor System software. In addition, I maintain the annual budget for the Supply & Warehouse and the Recycling Section, I use the internal software (NAF Financial Management Budget System). My knowledge of the computer and programs enables me to type all performance appraisals for all employees within the section, to type memoranda for the Chief, Technical Services Branch, to maintain and print all NAF time cards, to maintain annual budget for the Supply and Warehouse and Recycling Section and Forward to Budget Office. I have operated a Zenith Data System computer with ADEPT and WordPerfect software to maintain the NAF property book, adding property when received, deleting property whenever it is turned in or missing.

In my previous position, as **Personnel Clerk** for the Civilian Personnel Office at Ft. Hood, I prepared all NAF job announcements, contacted all eligible applications for interviews, and coordinated with activity managers for interviews while also preparing referrals. I informed selected applicants of their selection, I typed non-selection letters, and I also maintained files for applications and referrals.

Knowledge and Training related to this KSA:
- In 2003 I took a Microsoft Office course at Galveston Technical Community College. This course enabled me to use Word, Excel, PowerPoint, and Access to type a variety of material and documents for the Supply and Warehouse Section.
- In 2001 I took 116 hours of IBM Operations at Western Texas Technical College.
- In 2000 I took a NAF Financial Management Budget System Course at Ft. Hood, TX. This course gave me the knowledge, skills and ability to maintain the NAF budget for Supply and Warehouse, and the Recycling Section.

This secretary seeks a job in a medical and legal environment.

KSA #2: Ability to process a variety of medical and legal cases/records and documents.

Overview of my work experience: In the jobs described below, I have received a **Certificate of Outstanding Performance** each and every year from 2003-present and have been cited each year for **performing all duties in an outstanding manner.** I have been commended on numerous occasions for my expertise in preparing records and documents. Through my problem-solving and negotiating skills, I have in many instances resolved stubborn problems and difficult issues which could have resulted in serious liability problems involving theft, loss, etc.

In my current position as Supply Clerk, NF-2, I review, analyze, and prepare a wide variety of documentation and paperwork while assuring that paperwork is always within guidelines established by regulatory authorities and other authorities. While maintaining, updating, and utilizing a variety of data systems and using personal computers, I operate a GTA computer with WordPerfect Software, Time Management Labor System software, Microsoft Office software to include Word, Excel, PowerPoint, and Access. I type all correspondence for Supply and Warehouse Section using the WordPerfect and Word software. One of my responsibilities is to maintain the internal supply budget on Excel software and prepare flyers for the MWR Auction on PowerPoint. Furthermore, I maintain and prepare all NAF time cards using the Time Management Labor System software. In addition, to maintain the annual budget for Supply & Warehouse and the Recycling Section, I use the internal software (NAF Financial Management Budget System). My knowledge of the computer and programs enables me to type all performance appraisals for all employees within the section, to type memoranda for the Chief, Technical Services Branch, to maintain and print all NAF time cards, to maintain annual budget for Supply and Warehouse and Recycling Section and Forward to Budget Office. I have operated a Zenith Data System computer with ADEPT and WordPerfect software to maintain the NAF property book, adding property when received, deleting property whoever it is turned in or missing.

Be specific.

Knowledge and Training related to this KSA:
- In 2003 I took a Microsoft Office course at Galveston Technical Community College. This course enabled me to use Word, Excel, PowerPoint, and Access to type a variety of material and documents for the Supply and Warehouse Section.
- In 2001 I took 116 hours of IBM Operations at Western Texas Technical College. This gave me the knowledge, skills and ability to operate a computer.
- In 2000 I took a NAF Financial Management Budget System Course at Ft. Hood, TX. This course gave me the knowledge, skills and ability to maintain the NAF budget for Supply and Warehouse, and the Recycling Section.
- In 1999 I took 33 hours of word processing with Word at Galveston Technical Community College. This enabled me to type documents and material using Word.

OFFICE CLERK

PAIGE L. FORBES

SSN: 000-00-0000

OFFICE CLERK, GS-05 ANNOUNCEMENT #XYZ123

KSA #3: Ability to communicate orally.

Overview of my work experience: In the jobs described below, I have received a **Certificate of Outstanding Performance** each and every year from 2003-present and have been cited each year for **performing all duties in an outstanding manner.** I have been commended on numerous occasions for my outstanding oral communication skills as well as for excellent problem-solving, negotiating, and decision-making skills. Through my ability to communicate tactfully and graciously, to explain complex technical issues, and to train and motivate other employees, I have earned a reputation as an outstanding communicator in every aspect of my job.

In my current position as Supply Clerk, NF-2, I communicate with customers, vendors, and others in the process of performing my job. After I review, analyze, and prepare a wide variety of documentation and paperwork, I communicate orally with vendors, customers, and employees. I communicate orally with new or junior employees while training them to utilize a variety of data systems and using personal computers, I operate a GTA computer with WordPerfect Software, Time Management Labor System software, Microsoft Office software to include Word, Excel, PowerPoint, and Access. One of my responsibilities is to maintain the internal supply budget on Excel software and prepare flyers for the MWR Auction on PowerPoint. Furthermore, I maintain and prepare all NAF time cards using the Time Management Labor System software. In addition, to maintain the annual budget for Supply & Warehouse and the Recycling Section, I use the internal software (NAF Financial Management Budget System). My knowledge of the computer and programs enables me to type all performance appraisals for all employees within the section, to type memoranda for the Chief, Technical Services Branch, to maintain and print all NAF time cards, to maintain annual budget for Supply and Warehouse and Recycling Section and Forward to Budget Office. I have operated a Zenith Data System computer with ADEPT and WordPerfect software to maintain the NAF property book, adding property when received, deleting property whoever it is turned in or missing.

> Notice how often the communication KSA comes up.

In my position as Personnel Clerk, I communicated orally with potential employees after receiving applications and briefed them about positions available. I communicated extensively through telephone conversations with Activity Managers to coordinate pickup of referrals and selection of new employees. I also telephoned applicants when they were accepted for the position.

Knowledge and Training related to this KSA:
- In 2003 I took a Microsoft Office course at Galveston Technical Community College. This course enabled me to use Word, Excel, PowerPoint, and Access to type a variety of material and documents for the Supply and Warehouse Section.
- In 2001 I took 116 hours of IBM Operations at Western Texas Technical College.
- In 2000 I took a NAF Financial Management Budget System Course at Ft. Hood, TX. This course gave me the knowledge, skills and ability to maintain the NAF budget for Supply and Warehouse, and the Recycling Section.

KSA #4: Ability to communicate in writing.

Overview of my work experience: In the jobs described below, I have received a **Certificate of Outstanding Performance** each and every year from 2003-present and have been cited each year for **performing all duties in an outstanding manner.** I have been commended on numerous occasions for my ability to communicate in writing in a concise, articulate, and effective manner. I have earned a reputation as an excellent writer.

In my current position as Supply Clerk, NF-2, I communicate extensively in writing in the process of reviewing, analyzing, and preparing a wide variety of documentation and paperwork while assuring that paperwork is always within guidelines established by regulatory authorities and other authorities. In creating documents for written communication and transmission, I maintain, update, and utilize a variety of data systems and using personal computers. I operate a GTA computer with WordPerfect Software, Time Management Labor System software, Microsoft Office software to include Word, Excel, PowerPoint, and Access. I communicate in writing by typing all correspondence for Supply and Warehouse Section using the WordPerfect and Word software. One of my responsibilities is to maintain the internal supply budget on Excel software and prepare flyers for the MWR Auction on PowerPoint. Furthermore, I maintain and prepare all NAF time cards using the Time Management Labor System software. In addition, to maintain the annual budget for Supply & Warehouse and the Recycling Section, I use the internal software (NAF Financial Management Budget System). My knowledge of the computer and programs enables me to type all performance appraisals for all employees within the section, to type memoranda for the Chief, Technical Services Branch, to maintain and print all NAF time cards, to maintain annual budget for Supply and Warehouse and Recycling Section and Forward to Budget Office. I have operated a Zenith Data System computer with ADEPT and WordPerfect software to maintain the NAF property book, adding property when received, deleting property whoever it is turned in or missing.

> Sometimes the "oral" and "in writing" skills are joined in one KSA; sometimes they are separate as they are here.

Knowledge and Training related to this KSA:
- In 2003 I took a Microsoft Office course at Galveston Technical Community College. This course enabled me to use Word, Excel, PowerPoint, and Access to type a variety of material and documents for the Supply and Warehouse Section.
- In 2001 I took 116 hours of IBM Operations at Western Texas Technical College. This gave me the knowledge, skills and ability to operate a computer.
- In 2000 I took a NAF Financial Management Budget System Course at Ft. Hood, TX. This course gave me the knowledge, skills and ability to maintain the NAF budget for Supply and Warehouse, and the Recycling Section.
- In 1999 I took 33 hours of word processing with WordPerfect at Galveston Technical Community College. This enabled me to type documents and material using WordPerfect.

POLICE OFFICER

MAXWELL R. CAMERON

SSN: 000-00-0000

POLICE OFFICER, GS-07/11 ANNOUNCEMENT #XYZ123

KSA #1: Ability to do the work without more than normal supervision.

In my present position as a Police Officer GS-07-11 (2004-present), I demonstrate my ability to perform the work of the position without more than normal supervision on a daily basis. As Lead Officer for the Department of Veteran's Affairs (DoVA) in Lawton, OK, I act on my own judgment, providing supervision to as many as four employees in the absence of the Police Sergeant. Without direction from my superiors, I preserve the peace and prevent crime by providing a visible law enforcement presence while conducting vehicular and foot patrols of the DoVA premises, parking lot, access roads, and grounds. Conduct initial and follow-up investigations of all reported thefts, burglaries, assaults, threats, incidences of vandalism, narcotics violations, and other offenses on an independent basis, preparing written reports of my findings.

Earlier as a Platoon Sergeant for the 35th C Company, 56th MP Division, Fort Sills, OK (2003-04), I provided supervisory oversight and training to as many as 35 personnel. Independently performed foot and motorized patrols, providing a visible law enforcement presence to prevent and deter criminal activity. Without direct supervision, conducted interviews, obtained statements, and received complaints using my own judgment to determine appropriate response to information received. On my own initiative, apprehended, cited, used appropriate restraint measures, and detained law and traffic violators, as well as determining if probable cause was present to justify searches and seizures. Searched buildings and vehicles as well as conducting body searches, as required.

In a previous position as a Platoon Sergeant with a Military Police Company at Camp Humphreys, Korea, I supervised and trained up to 18 law enforcement personnel in all aspects of the duties and responsibilities of the position. On my own initiative, I processed and supervised the processing of crime scenes for the purpose of obtaining evidence, performed motorized and foot patrols, and responded to reports citing possible domestic/ family disturbances or incidents involving juveniles. Working with little or no direct supervision, I apprehended, cited, used appropriate force and restraints on, and processed law and traffic violators.

Education and Training related to this KSA:

Completed one year of an Associate's degree program in Criminal Justice, Oklahoma City Community College, Lawton, OK, 2001-2002; pursuing the completion of this degree as time and my work schedule allow.

Received advanced military training from the U.S. Army which included completion of: U.S. Army Military Police School, Military Police Non-Commissioned Officers Basic Course, Military Police Non-Commissioned Officer Advanced Course.

Finished the Basic Police Officer Training and Baton Instructor Course given at the Department of Veteran's Affairs Law Enforcement Training Center.

Graduated from the State Bureau of Investigation Division of Criminal Investigation Terminal Certification Course.

KSA #2: Ability to deal with a wide variety of people.

As a Police Officer GS-07/13 (2004-present), I demonstrate my ability to deal with a wide variety of people on a daily basis. As Lead Officer for the Department of Veteran's Affairs (DoVA) in Lawton, OK, I have regular and continuous contact with a wide variety of people from diverse cultural, ethnic, religious, and socioeconomic backgrounds. These individuals include, but are not limited to, Medical Center patients and their family members; doctors, nurses, medical technicians, and other hospital personnel; federal, state, and local law enforcement and emergency services personnel (including my subordinate officers); and visitors to the hospital, as well as witnesses and suspects involved in cases that are under investigation. In order to discharge the duties and responsibilities of my position, it is necessary that I deal with individuals from all of these populations in a fair and equitable manner, treating them courteously and respectfully. Use tact and diplomacy to defuse tense and potentially explosive situations; build a quick rapport with people from varied backgrounds, using my exceptional communication skills and law enforcement experience to handle complex interactions with a wide variety of people.

While serving as a Platoon Sergeant for Charlie Company, 56th MP Division, Fort Sills, OK (2003-04), I had regular and continuous contact on a daily basis with a wide range of military and civilian personnel from diverse cultural, ethnic, religious, and socioeconomic backgrounds. In order to discharge the duties and responsibilities of my position, it was necessary that I deal with individuals from all of these populations in a fair and equitable manner, treating them courteously and respectfully. Used tact and diplomacy to defuse tense and potentially explosive situations; built a quick rapport with people from varied backgrounds, using my strong communication skills and law enforcement experience to handle complex interactions with a wide variety of people.

Education and Training related to this KSA:

Completed one year of an Associate's degree program in Criminal Justice, Oklahoma City Community College, Oklahoma City, OK, 2001-2002; pursuing the completion of this degree as time and my work schedule allow.

Received advanced military training from the U.S. Army which included completion of: U.S. Army Military Police School, Military Police Non-Commissioned Officers Basic Course, Military Police Non-Commissioned Officer Advanced Course.

Finished the Basic Police Officer Training and Baton Instructor Course given at the Department of Veteran's Affairs Law Enforcement Training Center.

Graduated from the State Bureau of Investigation Division of Criminal Investigation Terminal Certification Course.

PRISON SERVICES ASSISTANT DIRECTOR

HAROLD L. DOUGLAS

SSN: 000-00-0000

PRISON SERVICES ASSISTANT DIRECTOR, GS-11 ANNOUNCEMENT #XYZ123

Mandatory Managerial Qualifications:

Qualification (1): Leading Change - The ability to develop and implement an organizational vision which integrates key national and program goals, priorities, values, and other factors. Inherent is the ability to balance change and continuity - to continually strive to improve customer service and program performance within the basic Government framework, to create a work environment that encourages creative thinking, and to maintain focus, intensity, and persistence, even under adversity.

Restructuring Troubled Operations:

While assigned to the Southern District of Alabama, I was selected by the Director to serve as acting U.S. Marshal to the Western District of Louisiana (2003-present). I was tasked to turn around this district, which was in a demoralized state following the dismissal of the previous Marshal. Developed and implemented restructuring plans designed to bring the district back in line with national and program goals, increase staff morale, and restore effectiveness and public trust in the operation. Conducted formal and informal brainstorming sessions with existing personnel to troubleshoot and formulate solutions to specific problems within the organization. Scheduled and coordinated selective retraining of district personnel in order to improve customer service and program performance. Utilized my extensive network of professional contacts to actively recruit new employees, providing strong leadership in key supervisory roles. Within eight months, the district showed marked improvement in all operational areas and morale was improved. Through my initiative, this organization was transformed from a hostile work environment to one which encouraged employees to voice their ideas and take an active role in providing solutions to problems within the district.

In 1999, a Management Team was assembled to completely reorganize the Southern District of Kansas. After determining the minimum qualifications of the ideal candidates, a thorough review of all supervisory personnel throughout the Marshal's Service was conducted. I was selected as one of the four supervisors most qualified to take on the district leadership during this difficult transitional period, and assigned to the Management Team. Prior to the reorganization, this district was noted for its uncooperative attitude. By my willingness to cooperate, can-do attitude, and strong communication skills, I was able to alter our image, both with the public and other agencies. Within a short period of time, we came to be thought of as a professional organization staffed with exceptional personnel who would go to great lengths and provide any and all assistance to outside agencies in order to see that the job is done. Planned and developed modifications and improvements to existing procedures for the coordination and movement of prisoners between agencies. Established effective interagency alliances in order to facilitate the movement of large numbers of prisoners, a special requirement of this district necessitated by the operations of the Vice Presidential Task Force, which made frequent arrests of 25-45 prisoners at a time. Recognized in an official evaluation as "[being] an integral part of the positive changes."

Adaptability to Changing Conditions:
Promoted to Chief Deputy Marshal for the Southern District of Georgia; was then appointed to serve as U.S. Marshal for that district at a time when the Atlanta metropolitan area was supplanting Columbus as the key point of entry for illegal drug smuggling. While supervising as many as 115 deputies, reevaluated organizational priorities and developed a new vision for the district which was consistent with the needs of one of the largest federal judicial districts in the country. In order to handle the increased case load resulting from the enormous number of drug-related arrests and seizures, I coordinated with other federal, local, and state agencies brokering a number of interagency agreements to acquire additional personnel and equipment.

Related Military Experience:
Have demonstrated my ability to manage change as well as balancing change and continuity while serving as a U.S. Marine in a military career that spans nearly three decades. Currently serving as an Intelligence Chief, U.S. Marine Corps Reserves in support of the Marine Force at Camp Casey, Korea, I hold the rank of Master Gunnery Sergeant.

Prior to deployment to Germany, I volunteered to return to active duty and served two tours of duty in the Middle East. Conducted site surveys of all five major Marine Corps camps in order to formulate the Corp's counter-terrorist strategy. Planned and developed an effective barrier plan to protect against terrorist attacks, and was handpicked to serve as assistant to the Provost Marshal of I Marine Expeditionary Force. As Supervisor In Charge of intelligence operations, served as interim supervisor for all intelligence operations until an S-2 officer was assigned to the task force. Provided outstanding leadership and support, a decoy mission designed to convince foreign leaders that the main U.S. attack would come from the south. Recognized in an official evaluation as being "an integral part of our company's success."

Education and Training related to this Qualification:
- Associate of Science degree in Criminal Justice, Jefferson State Community College, Birmingham, AL, 2001.
- Certifying Officers Training Course, Fort Hood, TX, 2001.
- United States Marshal Training #801, Federal Law Enforcement Training Center, Glynco, GA, 1999.
- Chief Deputy Management Training, Xerox Training Center, VA, 1999.
- Supervisory Training, Federal Law Enforcement Training Center, Glynco, GA, 1998-99.
- Joint Combat Operations Training, Combat Maneuver Training Center, Germany 1997.

PRISON SERVICES ASSISTANT DIRECTOR

HAROLD L. DOUGLAS
SSN: 000-00-0000
PRISON SERVICES ASSISTANT DIRECTOR, GS-11 ANNOUNCEMENT #XYZ123

Mandatory Managerial Qualifications:
Qualification (2): Leading People - The ability to design and implement strategies which maximize employee potential and foster high ethical standards in meeting the organization's vision, mission, and goals.

Maximizing Employee Potential:
Currently, while serving as Chief Deputy Marshal (2003-present) for the Southern District of Alabama, I supervise as many as 65 personnel, maximizing employee potential by careful planning of manpower utilization. Coordinate with other federal, state, and local law enforcement agencies to procure additional manpower and equipment for major operations, thus freeing up Marshal Service personnel to perform those tasks which cannot be delegated to outside agencies. Design, implement, and monitor progress of training programs to ensure that every deputy is provided with the tools he or she needs to succeed and excel within the organization. Evaluate the performance of individual deputies and provide positive feedback to encourage excellence. Analyze the needs of each section within the agency, and reassign personnel accordingly, matching the strengths of the employee to the requirements of the department, combining sections or eliminating positions where necessary in order to prevent duplication of effort.

After taking over the Western District of Louisiana as Acting Marshal (2000-03), I revamped the organizational structure of the office, reassigning or transferring existing personnel. Planned and scheduled retraining sessions in an effort to increase efficiency within the district, improve staff morale, and identify potential leaders within the organization to fill supervisory roles vacated during the restructuring of district operations. Monitored performance of each employee in order to provide accountability and recognize excellence. Utilized my extensive network of professional contacts to actively recruit personnel to man key leadership roles, shoring up the organization's command structure during the rebuilding process.

Fostering High Ethical Standards:
During my tenure as Chief Deputy Marshal for the Southern District of Georgia, the sheer volume of currency seized as a result of the increase in drug-related crimes proved to be a powerful temptation to some employees within the organization. In order to curtail theft of cash taken as evidence within the organization, I designed and instituted a system that teamed staff members in such a way that multiple levels within the organization would have to be compromised in order for theft of evidence to take place.

Leadership Within The Community:
Organized and led concerned citizens in my current hometown in efforts to persuade local government officials to take steps that would prevent libraries from shelving materials covered under state and local pornography statutes in circulation areas where children would have access to those materials. As a result of my efforts, a committee has been formed to devise a plan that will prevent children from accessing these materials while still making them available to adults, according to their rights under the First Amendment.

Education and Training related to this Qualification:

- Associate of Science degree in Criminal Justice, Jefferson State Community College, Birmingham, AL, 2001.
- Certifying Officers Training Course, Fort Hood, TX, 2001.
- United States Marshal Training #801, Federal Law Enforcement Training Center, Glynco, GA, 1999.
- Chief Deputy Management Training, Xerox Training Center, VA, 1999.
- Supervisory Training, Federal Law Enforcement Training Center, Glynco, GA, 1998-99.
- Joint Combat Operations Training, Combat Maneuver Training Center, Germany 1997.

PRISON SERVICES ASSISTANT DIRECTOR

HAROLD L. DOUGLAS

SSN: 000-00-0000

PRISON SERVICES ASSISTANT DIRECTOR, GS-11 ANNOUNCEMENT #XYZ123

Mandatory Managerial Qualifications:
Qualification (3): Results Driven - Stresses accountability and continuous improvement. Includes the ability to make timely and effective decisions and produce results through strategic planning and the implementation and evaluation of programs and policies.

Accountability and Continuous Improvement:
As Deputy Chief Marshal for the Southern District of Alabama, my main focus is on improving service and providing accountability while reducing costs. First and foremost, I stress accountability and continuous improvement by setting high standards for my own performance, leading by example. I monitor employee performance through contact with my Supervisory Deputies, and plan and develop training programs to ensure that all Deputies are provided with the knowledge and skills necessary to succeed.

While serving as U.S. Marshal (2003-present) and Chief Deputy U.S. Marshal (2000-03), for the Southern District of Georgia, I fostered continued improvement by eliminating positions that duplicated effort across departmental lines. This freed up a number of personnel who were then retrained and reassigned to positions where the district had previously suffered from a lack of adequate manpower. Thus, the enormous number of cases handled by the Southern District Office was distributed more evenly, leaving each deputy with a more reasonable workload. Additionally, I arranged to utilize outside agencies such as local police where possible, to allow the Marshal Service personnel to focus their efforts on assignments which could not be delegated to outside agencies. As a result, productivity and morale increased, and performance improved throughout the district.

Decision making; strategic planning and the implementation and evaluation of programs:
While serving as U.S. Marshal (2003-present), and Chief Deputy U.S. Marshal (2000-03) for the Southern District of Georgia, the volume of currency our organization seized as a result of the increase in drug-related crimes proved to be a powerful temptation. In order to curtail theft of cash taken as evidence within the organization, I planned and implemented a system that teamed staff members in such a way that multiple levels within the organization would have to be compromised in order for theft of evidence to take place.

In four separate positions, as Supervisory Deputy Marshal for Southern Kansas (1999), Chief Deputy Marshal and U.S. Marshal for Southern Georgia (1999-00), and U.S. Marshal for Western Louisiana (2003-present), I was called upon to play vital supervisory roles in the complete restructuring and reorganization of operations that were demoralized or performing well below expectations. In each case, the overhaul of existing procedures and systems required strategic planning and analysis of areas of strength and weakness in order to develop effective systems, combine departments to increase efficiency, and provide retraining or cross-training to personnel whose positions were no longer viable within the new structure.

In every case, the new systems were implemented with great effect and within a minimal amount of time, all three districts showed marked increases in performance levels while operating in a more efficient and profitable manner. To ensure the success of the restructuring, performance appraisals, employee counseling, and refresher training session were conducted periodically. In addition, my expectations for employee performance were made clear from the outset, so that all personnel were provided with concrete, realistic objectives. Clarifying goals gives the employee a specific target to strive for, and increases their sense of personal accountability, as well as bolstering self-esteem and increasing morale as these objectives are achieved.

Education and Training related to this Qualification:
- Associate of Science degree in Criminal Justice, Jefferson State Community College, Birmingham, AL, 2001.
- Certifying Officers Training Course, Fort Hood, TX, 2001.
- United States Marshal Training #801, Federal Law Enforcement Training Center, Glynco, GA, 1999.
- Chief Deputy Management Training, Xerox Training Center, VA, 1999.
- Supervisory Training, Federal Law Enforcement Training Center, Glynco, GA, 1998-99.
- Joint Combat Operations Training, Combat Maneuver Training Center, Germany 1997.

PROGRAM ANALYST

ALONZO K. ROBERTS
SSN: 000-00-0000
PROGRAM ANALYST, GS-09 ANNOUNCEMENT #XYZ123

KSA (1): Ability to establish and maintain effective working relationships in order to assure coordination with staff members and to carry out liaison functions with parties outside housing operations, state program managers, other DHUD regions or headquarters and private sector contractors.

I apply my ability to establish and maintain effective working relationships in my present job as a Management Services Specialist in the Department of Housing and Urban Development (since 2004). I provide office and administrative support for the New Jersey Regional Office and eleven field- or substations. I work on a regular daily basis with all levels of regional staff, headquarters staff, other Federal agencies, and representatives of private industry in order to coordinate and lead in securing the needed office services and service support for the Regional office.

To insure proper levels of support and maintain effective working relations, I work directly under the supervision of the Section Chief and Financial Management Director while overseeing activities which include: planning, organizing, reviewing, analyzing, and monitoring internal control systems, audit management systems, data needs and administration, and other assigned administrative activities. I provide technical guidance and assistance to team members, resolve problems, and direct the performance of or personally perform complex and difficult assignments in procurement and contract functions; negotiate, administer, and terminate contracts and agreements; provide training in proper contracting methods, procedures, and techniques; provide records management; and oversee office services including mail handling, telecommunications, personal property and equipment accountability.

One of my priorities is in the area of ensuring that cooperation is maintained among all program staffs and outside agencies by resolving problems, settling disputes, discussing contract and procurement requirements, negotiating and interpreting contract terms, and arriving at solutions through compromise. My regular contacts include the Regional and Deputy Administrators, individual program directors, senior agency level officials, representatives of other Federal agencies, private companies, vendors, and other business establishments. As a team member, I work with management, union, and general staff representatives.

Prior to this assignment, I was a Support Services Supervisor from 1998-04 for the Department of Housing and Urban Development. In this capacity I worked in close cooperation with key financial management staff and regional officials in order to provide property management, contracting and procurement, facility maintenance, and equipment repair services for the plus four field and two satellite offices. Provided authoritative advice to key management personnel throughout the region on procurement, contracting, and property management and accomplished all related reporting based on data collection, activity surveys, and inventory analysis.

My ability to establish and maintain cooperative working relations was also displayed as a supervisor for six Administrative Clerks. In this capacity I rated, trained, assigned responsibilities and duties, and made recommendations on disciplinary and promotion actions. I resolved grievances and conducted informal on-the-job training. I gave equal consideration to women and minorities when making supervisory or managerial decisions and recommendations.

Through my thorough knowledge of Federal Procurement Regulations (FPR), I prepared purchase orders and contracts for equipment. Knowledge of the Federal Property Management Regulations (FPMR) was applied to oversee building facilities and office services. Applied knowledge of the organizations, regulations, instructions, and handbooks concerning office and administrative services in order to provide timely and efficient support for program and staff entities.

My personal contacts were numerous and included individuals from throughout the Region, New Jersey offices, other government agencies, and private concerns. The purposes of establishing and maintaining these contacts included gathering information, seeking cooperation, negotiating terms, providing advice and assistance on management matters, and providing supervision and leadership in order to lead team efforts to complete even the most difficult assignments.

In earlier jobs with a General Services Administration (GSA) (1994-98), I established and maintained effective working relationships while advancing from Statistical Clerk, to Services Section Supervisor (Administration), and then to Administrative Assistant. I supervised as many as 25 people and dealt on a daily basis with personnel in a wide variety of other offices through the agency.

Training and education which apply to this KSA element:
Earned a B.A. degree in Business Administration, Rutgers College, Piscataway, NJ 1996; chief courses included Accounting and Finance, Economics, and Management.

Completed training courses which included:

Personnel Management Specialist Training
Telephone Courtesy and Military Correspondence
Supervisory Civil Service Training Courses
Competition in Contracting Act
Government Mailers Seminar
DHUD Basic Management Skills Training Course
Procurement & Contracting Workshop
Labor Relations for Supervisors and Managers
The Government Wide Commercial Credit Card
Supervision and Public Management
Small Purchases/Schedule Contracts
Microsoft Windows 95 Introduction
How to Build a Winning Team
Introduction to Supervision/Supervision & Group Performance
Introduction to the Federal Acquisition Regulations (FAR)
Effectively Handling Adverse & Disciplinary Actions
Equal Employment Opportunity Training, DHUD & Professional

Accident Investigation
Creative Problem Solving
Speeding the Mail Workshop
Introduction to Contracting
Procurement Planning
Travel Regulations Workshop
Total Quality Management

PROGRAM ANALYST

ALONZO K. ROBERTS

SSN: 000-00-0000

PROGRAM ANALYST, GS-09 ANNOUNCEMENT #XYZ123

KSA (2): Ability to understand, evaluate, interpret and apply complex program instructions, procedures, handbooks, and regulations in order to guide and improve operations efforts to support housing development assistance programs.

I apply my ability to understand, evaluate, interpret, and apply instructions and guidance in my present job as a Management Services Specialist in the New Jersey Regional Office of the Department of Housing and Urban Development (since 2004). Because I provide office and administrative support for the New Jersey Regional Office and eleven field- or substations, I work on a regular daily basis with a variety of instructions, SOPs, handbooks, and regulations in order to coordinate and lead in securing the needed office services and service support for the Regional office and find ways to improve operational efforts.

To insure proper levels of support and maintain effective working relations, I work directly under the supervision of the Section Chief and Financial Management Director while overseeing activities which include: planning, organizing, reviewing, analyzing, and monitoring internal control systems, audit management systems, data needs and administration, and other assigned administrative activities. I provide technical guidance and assistance to team members, resolve problems, and direct the performance of or personally perform complex and difficult assignments in procurement and contract functions; negotiate, administer, and terminate contracts and agreements; provide training in proper contracting methods, procedures, and techniques; provide records management; and oversee office services including mail handling, telecommunications, personal property and equipment accountability.

One of my priorities is in procurement and contracting where I negotiate, administer, and terminate contracts and agreements within the guidelines prescribed by law. This includes applying knowledge of guidelines and regulations so that I can determine the method required for each procurement action. I monitor agreements to ensure all terms and conditions are in compliance and that problems are negotiated and resolved.

Some of the vital types of information I must possess in this job are knowledge of all phases of agency and the Federal Administrative Management Process; procedures; acceptable business practices, cost relationships, and market trends; regulations pertaining to space, building facilities, and office services; management controls and practices; audit, audit tracking, and audit resolution; and management control requirements.

I follow guidelines such as DHUD and HDSP-published directives, GSA regulations, Comptroller General decisions, Federal Registers, and statutes. Since these guidelines are not always clear cut, I interpret them by applying sound judgment, ingenuity, and resourcefulness in order to see that they are applied in such a manner as to support programs and achieve results. I provide input into the development or adaptation of guidelines so that the most cost effective and advantageous methods are used.

Prior to this assignment from 1998-04, I was a Support Services Supervisor for the Department of Housing and Urban Development. In this capacity, I worked in close cooperation with key financial management staff and regional officials in order to provide property management, contracting and procurement, facility maintenance, and equipment repair services for the plus four field and two satellite offices. Provided authoritative advice to key management personnel throughout the region on procurement, contracting, and property management and accomplished all related reporting based on data collection, activity surveys, and inventory analysis.

Through my thorough knowledge of Federal Procurement Regulations (FPR), I prepared purchase orders and contracts for equipment. Knowledge of the Federal Property Management Regulations (FPMR) was applied to oversee building facilities and office services. Applied knowledge of DHUD, HDSP, GSA regulations, instructions, and handbooks concerning office and administrative services in order to provide timely and efficient support for program and staff entities. Because these guidelines were not always clear cut, I was called on to provide sound judgment, ingenuity, and resourcefulness in order to interpret and properly apply the appropriate guidelines. Often new guidelines had to be developed or adapted to suit the action being undertaken and problems solved.

In earlier jobs with a General Services Administration (GSA) (1994-98), I applied the ability to understand, evaluate, interpret, and apply procedures and guidelines while advancing from Statistical Clerk, to Services Section Supervisor (Administration), to Administrative Assistant. These jobs all required extensive knowledge and application of existing guidelines and regulations as well as the ability to interpret and analyze them.

Training and education which apply to this KSA element:
Earned a B.A. degree in Business Administration, Rutgers College, Piscataway, NJ 1996; chief courses of study included Accounting and Finance, Economics, and Management.

Completed training courses which included:

Personnel Management Specialist Training
Telephone Courtesy and Military Correspondence
Supervisory Civil Service Training Courses
Competition in Contracting Act
Government Mailers Seminar
DHUD Basic Management Skills Training Course
Procurement & Contracting Workshop
Labor Relations for Supervisors and Managers
The Government Wide Commercial Credit Card
Supervision and Public Management
Small Purchases/Schedule Contracts
Microsoft Windows 95 Introduction
How to Build a Winning Team
Introduction to Supervision/Supervision & Group Performance
Introduction to the Federal Acquisition Regulations (FAR)

Accident Investigation
Creative Problem Solving
Speeding the Mail Workshop
Introduction to Contracting
Procurement Planning
Travel Regulations Workshop
Total Quality Management

PROGRAM ANALYST

ALONZO K. ROBERTS

SSN: 000-00-0000

PROGRAM ANALYST, GS-09 ANNOUNCEMENT #XYZ123

KSA (3): Ability to analyze and present data together with other management information, in a variety of formats in order to assist the Director, to establish priorities, plan and carry out major projects and to formulate work plans and budgets.

My abilities in the areas of analyzing and presenting data, establishing priorities, and formulating plans and budgets is applied in my present job (since 2004) as a Management Services Specialist in the New Jersey Regional Office of the Department Housing and Urban Development. Because I provide office and administrative support for the New Jersey Regional Office and eleven field- or substations, I work under the direct supervision of the section chief on a regular daily basis with all levels of regional staff, headquarters staff, other Federal agencies, and representatives of private industry in order to coordinate and lead in securing the needed office services and service support for the Regional office.

To insure proper levels of support and maintain effective working relations, I oversee activities which include: planning, organizing, reviewing, analyzing, and monitoring internal control systems, audit management systems, data needs and administration, and other assigned administrative activities. I provide technical guidance and assistance to team members, resolve problems, and direct the performance of or personally perform complex and difficult assignments in procurement and contract functions; negotiate, administer, and terminate contracts and agreements; provide training in proper contracting methods, procedures, and techniques; provide records management; and oversee office services including mail handling, telecommunications, personal property and equipment accountability.

Among my priorities are developing plans and courses of action, forecasting and prioritizing requirements, and making recommendations and then implementing effective procedures which will allow for timely and efficient office services. Another priority is assuring resource availability for the staff so that productivity levels remain high. I provide the appropriate support with human and physical resources which will ensure the completion of goals and objectives. I also am responsible for optimizing and accounting for Federal administrative and program funds invested in various regional operations.

Prior to this assignment I was a Support Services Supervisor from 1998-04 for the Department of Housing and Urban Development. In this capacity, I worked in close cooperation with key financial management staff and regional officials in order to provide property management, contracting and procurement, facility maintenance, and equipment repair services for the plus four field and two satellite offices. Provided authoritative advice to key management personnel throughout the region on procurement, contracting, and property management and accomplished all related reporting based on data collection, activity surveys, and inventory analysis.

My knowledge and technical expertise ensured that accurate and timely procurement, contracting, and support services were provided with a direct impact on the Housing

Development Service Program throughout the New Jersey Region. I made decisions and recommendations on regarding the procurement of proper and adequate equipment, supplies, Services, and materials which made a foundation for all agency actions. While developing plans and determining courses of action for projects and functions, I took the initiative to develop new ideas and processes which impacted favorably on the quality of support. I also analyzed and evaluated the implications of changing conditions such as market trends, marketing and business practices to determine what effect they would have on production, pricing, distribution, delivery, and efficiency of services. I applied sound judgment while analyzing conditions and changes in order to select the most appropriate procurement method and cost effective vendor for each requisition.

My knowledge related to this KSA element was displayed in a short-term assignment just prior to the job above. In 1998, I was an Administrative Assistant at a regional General Services Administration office. In this capacity, I monitored the establishment and maintenance of the statistical reporting system and record-keeping systems. I provided leadership for the collection and assembly of data and analyzed the data. I also prepared visual aids such as graphs and charts and coordinated special studies and the preparation and presentation of briefings with forecasts, conclusions, recommendations, and justification.

In earlier jobs with the General Services Administration (1994-98), I applied my analytical and planning skills while advancing from Statistical Clerk, to Services Section Supervisor (Administration), to Administrative Assistant.

Training and education which apply to this KSA element:
Earned a B.A. degree in Business Administration, Rutgers College, Piscataway, NJ 1996; chief courses of study included Accounting and Finance, Economics, and Management.

Completed training courses which included:

Personnel Management Specialist Training
Telephone Courtesy and Military Correspondence
Supervisory Civil Service Training Courses
Competition in Contracting Act
Government Mailers Seminar
DHUD Basic Management Skills Training Course
Procurement & Contracting Workshop
Labor Relations for Supervisors and Managers
The Government Wide Commercial Credit Card
Supervision and Public Management
Small Purchases/Schedule Contracts
Microsoft Windows 95 Introduction
How to Build a Winning Team
Introduction to Supervision/Supervision & Group Performance
Introduction to the Federal Acquisition Regulations (FAR)
Effectively Handling Adverse & Disciplinary Actions
Equal Employment Opportunity Training, DHUD & Professional

Accident Investigation
Creative Problem Solving
Speeding the Mail Workshop
Introduction to Contracting
Procurement Planning
Travel Regulations Workshop
Total Quality Management

PROGRAM DIRECTOR

MARGARET W. EDGE

SSN: 000-00-0000

PROGRAM DIRECTOR, GS-11 ANNOUNCEMENT #XYZ123

KSA (A): Knowledge of Business Management Principles, Practices, Techniques, and Expertise in MWR/CFA Programs.

Highlights of my knowledge in this area: As a military officer, was extensively involved in planning, implementing, marketing, budgeting for, and supervising morale, welfare, and recreation programs. Am very familiar with the process of conducting recurring reviews of internal operating procedures to improve cost effectiveness, streamline organizational structures, and security conformity with sound management principles.

In my current job as a major in the U.S. Army Reserves, (2003-present) conduct annual training at Fort Carson and inspect several COSCOM units to ensure their understanding of and compliance with maintenance, supply, and family care plan programs. Provide specialized expertise related to the development and management of programming and budgeting for Morale, Welfare, and Recreation activities.

While serving as General Manager (Company Commander) of a 180-person company (2000-03), I demonstrated my knowledge of the principles, practices, and techniques involved in the effective management of the morale, welfare, and recreation programs of an organization. I managed human, fiscal, and material resources, providing supervisory oversight to junior managers and other personnel. Directed all personnel actions, including performance evaluations, recommendations for promotions, disciplinary actions, and transfers, as well as handling responsibilities related to housing, physical fitness, training, and safety.

As a Nutrition Instructor and Technical Writer (1998-00), I gained particular insight into the nutritional aspects of morale, welfare, and recreation activities as I used my written and oral communications skills while teaching basic and advanced courses for officer-students and working closely with other specialists to cross train personnel. I developed a wide range of written course materials, lesson plans, etc., and presented this material orally in both classroom and practicum environments. Was cited for "providing clear, complete, technically correct information" in new recipes which were used to totally revise the DOD recipe file. Was described in official performance evaluations as "very astute" with outstanding oral and written communication skills and a degree of dedication to excellence which "far exceeded requirements." Wrote articles which were published in six monthly menus and was cited for my "excellent technical nutrition expertise" which was demonstrated in my articles and while presenting the newly implemented USDA Nutrition Pyramid to food service personnel worldwide.

In prior experience as a Military Officer, was very involved in the programming, budgeting, and management aspects of morale, welfare and recreation activities in every line management and "staff" job which I held in several different companies in the 32nd Support Battalion, Ft. Knox, KY.

As a Logistics Operations Officer (1996-98), managed logistics support for units participating in a major Joint Chief of Staff exercise and deployment to Bosnia. As a subsidiary aspect of my job, was involved in programming for and managing recreation, morale, and welfare activities for the units with which I interfaced. Troubleshot logistics issues related to morale, welfare, and recreation matters as I conducted liaison with task force personnel, the Contracting Office, Budget Office, and Logistics Assistance Office. Selected for a position which would normally have been held by a captain as a first lieutenant, succeeded in a unique environment and was cited for my ability to meet strict time constraints through untiring efforts. Acted as POL Officer during his absence and applied my logistics experience while taking orders, confirming amounts and delivery dates, and ensuring uninterrupted service. Managed Title X funds so that money spent for Bosnia participation was fully documented and while working closely with the project officer, planned an coordinated for more than $133,000 worth of Title X, laundry, and supply funds.

As a Battalion S-4 (1996-98), was involved in programming for and managing recreation, morale, and welfare activities as I served as the principal advisor on supply activities while responsible for internal logistics support in a 650-person battalion. Coordinated arrangements for field services as well as planning and controlling a $460,000 budget for Class II, IV, and VII expenditures; $12.5 worth of organizational equipment, and $685,000 worth of installation property. Described in one OER as "a solid, tough, dependable performer who rose to meet adverse circumstances," ensured that the organization never lacked for supplies or services in one short period which included four field exercises and one session with 1,025 participants.

As a Petroleum Platoon Leader (1996), oversaw training, professional development, performance, and operator maintenance for petroleum, oil, and lubricant support. Through my input into the morale, welfare, and recreation activities, displayed a positive attitude and enthusiastic manner which allowed me to have a "tremendous" impact on the success of this unit. Monitored maintenance status of the unit's fuel tankers, 5-ton tractors, pump, scoop loader, and generator and improved the response time for receiving parts and seeing that they were promptly placed on the vehicle needing service.

As a Supply and Transportation Platoon Leader (1994-96), managed a fleet of 35 cargo and heavy equipment transporters.
- Developed a written skills qualifications practice test which was a major factor in bringing the platoon's average score to 90% which was the highest in the company.

My training and education related to this KSA includes:
Gained professional knowledge of programs related to morale, welfare, and recreation as I completed graduate level work in Human Resources Management, University of Colorado. As a military officer, completed extensive on-the-job training related to morale, welfare, and recreation program planning, programming, budgeting, and management.

Attended numerous training programs for military officers which included the Phase II and Phase I Support Operations Courses, Logistics Executive Development, Quartermaster Officer Advanced and Basic Courses, Transportation and Storage of Hazardous Materials, and the Command and Staff Services School.

PROGRAM DIRECTOR

MARGARET W. EDGE

SSN: 000-00-0000

PROGRAM DIRECTOR, GS-11 ANNOUNCEMENT #XYZ123

KSA (B): Ability to Identify, Analyze, Audit, Evaluate, and Make Decisions in Areas Such as Financial Management, Business Operations, Marketing, Purchasing, and Contracting.

As a major in the U.S. Army Reserves, (2003-present) conduct annual training at Ft. Carson and inspect several COSCOM units to ensure their understanding of and compliance with maintenance, supply, and family care plan programs. In the process of inspecting a wide variety of programs and service operations, I evaluated the prudence of decisions and standard operating procedures in areas such as financial management, business operations, marketing, purchasing, and contracting.

As a member of a Mobile Training Team and SARSS Instructor for Regal Technicians, Inc. (2003-present), I provide administrative and hands-on training at various military installations. In the process of serving as a top-level consultant and "technical expert" on all matters related to training, provide sound advice related to areas including business management, financial management, marketing, purchasing, and contracting. Am presently involved in research, development, and revision of written training materials for MTT (Mobile Training Team) courses. Heavily involved in the design, development, and authoring of instructional materials which include lesson plans, presentation materials, and training databases, as well as comprehensive training materials which include training guides, workbooks, hand outs, completion certificates, and course evaluation forms. Conduct an 80-hour SARSS course by methods which includes 40 hours of formal classroom training, courses, workshops, and seminars and 40 hours of hands-on training in warehouse environments. Provide verbal direction to staff members and prepared written contract proposals. Over the past two years, have taught more than 200 students while serving as a Team Leader.

While serving as Logistics Team Chief and Training Consultant (2000-03), I applied my communication skills as the organization's primary briefer; conducted briefings for visiting VIPs and dignitaries as well as for senior executives. I presented a logistics workshop to 15 units which allowed more than 75 supply specialists to increase their knowledge and enhance their state of readiness. Was described in an annual performance report as "proactive as a teacher and mentor." Prepared and presented a Range Certification course to a finance company and marketed this workshop to the entire readiness group in a formal presentation. Improved the combat readiness of several units by personally training personnel on the Standard Army Training System (SATS) which resulted in enhancing each individual unit's ability to oversee their internal training management.

As a Nutrition Instructor and Technical Writer (1998-00), I used my knowledge of business and management principles while teaching basic and advanced courses for officer-students and working closely with other specialists to cross train personnel. I developed a wide range of written course materials, lesson plans, etc., and presented this material orally in both classroom and practicum environments. Was cited for "providing clear, complete, technically correct information" in new recipes which were used to totally revise the DOD recipe file. Was described in official performance evaluations as "very astute" with outstanding oral and written communication skills and a degree of dedication to excellence which "far exceeded requirements." Wrote articles which were published in six monthly menus and was cited for my "excellent technical nutrition expertise" which was demonstrated in my articles and while presenting the newly implemented USDA Nutrition Pyramid to food service personnel worldwide.

As a Supply and Transportation Platoon Leader (1994-96), managed a fleet of 35 cargo and heavy equipment transporters.

- Developed a written skills qualifications practice test which was a major factor in bringing the platoon's average score to 90% which was the highest in the company.

My training and education related to this KSA includes:

Completed graduate level work in Human Resources Management, University of Colorado.

Attended numerous training programs for military officers which included the Phase II and Phase I Support Operations Courses, Logistics Executive Development, Quartermaster Officer Advanced and Basic Courses, Transportation and Storage of Hazardous Materials, and the Command and Staff Services School.

PROGRAM DIRECTOR
MARGARET W. EDGE
SSN: 000-00-0000
PROGRAM DIRECTOR, GS-11 ANNOUNCEMENT #XYZ123

KSA (C): Knowledge of Civilian Personnel Policies and Procedures.

Overview of my knowledge in this area:
While completing the Inspector General course (2003), I developed extensive knowledge of civilian personnel policies and procedures. This course covered all army rules and regulations, including family support, contracting, and all information related to civilian personnel policies and procedures. For instance, I learned all aspects of Equal Employment Opportunity Commission policies and procedures, as well as proper methods for assisting with and investigating issues related to formal EEOC complaints. Have become knowledgeable of civilian personnel policies and procedures while acting in an Army Reserve position at Ft. Carson, CO (2/03 to present), am a major conducting annual training at Ft. Carson and inspecting COSCOM units to ensure their understanding of and compliance with maintenance, supply, and family care plan programs. Work routinely with civilian personnel officials and have become familiar with policies and procedures related to a wide range of areas including morale, welfare, and recreation fund activities.

As a Logistics Team Chief and Training Consultant (2000-03), I served with the U.S. Army, Second U.S. Army Reserve Component Support, Readiness Group, Ft. Carson, CO. I held dual positions as a supply assistance advisor for approximately 200 National Guard and Reserve units throughout the state and as a training activities developer and advisor. I analyzed organizational and operational deficiencies and developed corrective programs within budgetary guidelines as well as directing training assistance programs, doctrinal objectives, and force modernization issues for 45 advisors in a readiness group with 15,000 soldiers. Managed and allocated fiscal, human, and material resources in support of the organization's training goals and objectives. As supply officer, oversaw the annual operating budget and held responsibility for more than $85,500 worth of equipment. Served as Automated Data Processing Security Officer.

In my civilian job as a Training Specialist (2003-present) with Regal Technicians, Inc., Colorado Springs, CO, I am a member of a Mobile Training Team and SARSSI instructor, provide administrative and hands-on training at various military installations. Am presently involved in research, development, and revision of training courses for MMT (Military Maintenance Technician) training. Responsibilities include designing and developing instructional materials which include lesson plans, presentation materials, and training databases. Also design and develop comprehensive training materials which include training guides, workbooks, hand outs, completion certificates, and course evaluation forms.

Education and Training Related to this KSA:
Completed graduate level work in Human Resources Management, University of Colorado.
Attended numerous training programs for military officers which included the Phase II and Phase I Support Operations Courses, Logistics Executive Development, Quartermaster Officer Advanced and Basic Courses, Transportation and Storage of Hazardous Materials, and the Command and Staff Services School.

KSA (D): Ability to evaluate, execute, consolidate, and implement an operating budget.

Presently in an Army Reserve position at Ft. Carson, CO (2003-present), am a major conducting annual training at Ft. Carson and inspecting COSCOM units to ensure their understanding of and compliance with maintenance, supply, and family programs. As a Logistics Team Chief and Training Consultant (2000-03), I served with the U.S. Army, Second U.S. Army Reserve Component Support, Readiness Group, Ft. Carson, CO. I analyzed organizational and operational deficiencies and developed corrective programs within budgetary guidelines as well as directing training assistance programs, doctrinal objectives, and force modernization issues for 45 advisors in a readiness group with 15,000 soldiers.

As a Logistics Team Chief and Training Consultant (2000-03) I served with the U.S. Army, Second U.S. Army Reserve Component Support, Readiness Group, Ft. Carson, CO. I oversaw a $3,500 annual operating budget and more than $85,500 worth of equipment; was Automated Data Processing Security Officer. Conducted a logistical workshop for 15 units which allowed more than 75 supply specialists to increase their knowledge and enhance their state of readiness.

As a Military Officer (1996-98), served in several different companies in the 32nd Support Battalion, Ft. Knox, KY. and held a variety of positions where I was assigned as a Budget Manager, Supply Officer, and POL Platoon Leader within a mechanized infantry brigade. As Logistics Operations Officer, managed logistics support for units participating in a major Joint Chief of Staff exercise and deployment to Bosnia. Troubleshot logistics issues and conducted liaison with task force personnel, the Contracting Office, Budget Office, and Logistics Assistance Office.

As a Battalion S-4 (1996-98), served as the principal advisor on supply activities while responsible for internal logistics support in a 650-person battalion. Coordinated arrangements for field services as well as planning and controlling a $460,000 budget for Class II, IV, and VII expenditures; $12.5 worth of organizational equipment, and $685,000 worth of installation property.

As Petroleum Platoon Leader (1996), oversaw training, professional development, performance, and operator maintenance for petroleum, oil, and lubricant support. Displayed a positive attitude and enthusiastic manner which allowed me to have a "tremendous" impact on the success of this unit.

Education and Training Related to this KSA:

Completed graduate level work in Human Resources Management, University of Colorado. Attended numerous training programs for military officers which included the Phase II and Phase I Support Operations Courses, Logistics Executive Development, Quartermaster Officer Advanced and Basic Courses, Transportation and Storage of Hazardous Materials, and the Command and Staff Services School.

PROGRAM MANAGER

HAROLD THOMAS LINCOLN

SSN: 000-00-0000

PROGRAM MANAGER, GS-14 ANNOUNCEMENT #XYZ123

KSA #1: Knowledge of federal rules and regulations regarding program planning and budget systems, and requirements of federal, administrative, and appropriations law.

In my current position as Branch Chief, I am responsible for the Region's Budget and, in that capacity, I must be familiar with the U.S. Codes and Office of Management and Budget (OMB) Codes. I have excelled in handling the responsibility of developing the marketing and advertising budget for more than 100 detachments. I provide each detachment with a spending survey to determine what their legitimate needs are, and in formulating their budget I consider each of the following:

production history	budget survey
production potential	expenditure trends
inflation	operating costs in geographical area

I utilize a similar system in determining what is required for the headquarters. The figures are then consolidated and forwarded to my headquarters as a budget request. When the actual budget is received from headquarters, I disseminate to each unit its portion of the budget. On my own initiative, I have developed a computer model assigning each area a weighted factor. The detachments are than issued a portion of the overall budget based on the results of computer run and additional adjustments based on staff input and my leadership in developing complex issues and situations pertaining to the 100 detachments. I am continuously developing and refining procedures to improve the operational planning process as I provide the administrative leadership and coordination critical in the planning and implementation of financial plans and programs.

I utilize spreadsheet management extensively to stay on track with the number of projects with which I am involved. Often I am required to use the techniques of program management due to the length of the program for which I am responsible.

In accordance with Title 31, Section 1301 of the Code, I assure the following:
- That appropriated funds are used only for the purpose for which they were designated
- That expenditures of funds do not exceed the appropriated amount
- That payments are not authorized prior to funds being appropriated

In order to assure quality control and in accordance with Title 31, Section 1514, I developed a system to insure that appropriated fund expenditures were restricted to the amount and period of apportionment. I am required in my current job to utilize fluently the following:
- OMB Circular A-11 – Preparation and submission of estimates when submitting my budget request to higher headquarters
- OMB Circular A-34 while executing my budget during the year

KSA #2: Knowledge of federal extramural resources management regulations and policies.

As Branch Chief, am responsible for the Region's Budget and, in that capacity, I must be familiar with the US Codes and Office of Management and Budget (OMB) Codes. In accordance with Title 31, Section 1301 of the Code, I assure the following:
That appropriated funds are used only for the purpose for which they were designated
That expenditures of funds do not exceed the appropriated amount
That payments are not authorized prior to funds being appropriated

In order to assure quality control and in accordance with Title 31, Section 1514, I developed a system to insure that appropriated fund expenditures were restricted to the amount and period of apportionment. I am required in my current job to utilize fluently the following:

- OMB Circular A-11 – Preparation and submission of estimates when submitting my budget request to higher headquarters
- OMB Circular A-34 while executing my budget during the year

Extensive volunteer involvement which requires my knowledge of regulations:
During the past six years, I have served as a member of the board of directors of the Fort Lewis Federal Credit Union for more than six years. In my current capacity as Treasurer of the Board, I am responsible for making policies and investment recommendations for the $100 million institution. Extensive public relations and communications are also key responsibilities in this job, and I have demonstrated my ability to interact and coordinate with a variety of individuals, including management and staff, in a variety of situations. I attend conferences as delegate for the Credit Union and interact with delegates from hundreds of credit unions and members of the financial community. While frequently traveling to conferences to represent the board, staff and our 36,000 members, I am required to examine the proposed operating budget before it is submitted to the board. I brief the CEO on the procedures used to develop the requests, and each category must be explained in detail and new initiatives and purchases must be justified and able to be defended to the board as a whole. As the treasurer I ensure that the CEO does not exceed the operating budget, and I assure that any additional expenditures must be made with board approval. In the course of performing as Treasurer, I am responsible to assure that the members receive a corresponding benefit for each expense. I must be familiar with the Federal Credit Union Act and Title 12, Section 1861 of the US Code and the Bank Service Act. As a member of the Investment Committee, I have exposure to the following:

- 12 USC 4301, Truth in Savings Act
- 15 USC 1601, Truth in Lending Act
- 15 USC 1671, Consumer Protection Act
- 15 USC 1691, Equal Credit Opportunities Act
- 12 USC 4001, Expedited Funds Availability Act
- 5 USC 8401, Thrift Saving Fund Investment Act

Program Manager, GS-14 Announcement #XYZ123 KSA #2

PROGRAM MANAGER

HAROLD THOMAS LINCOLN

SSN: 000-00-0000

PROGRAM MANAGER, GS-14 ANNOUNCEMENT #XYZ123

KSA #3: Ability to independently analyze complex organizational and resource situations and devise solutions to complex problems.

In my current position as Branch Chief for the Eighth Region (ROTC), U.S. Army Cadet Command, my ability to independently analyze complex organizational and resource situations and devise solutions to complex problems has been tested as I have excelled in handling the responsibility of developing the marketing and advertising budget for more than 100 detachments. I provide each detachment with a spending survey to determine what their legitimate needs are, and in formulating their budget I consider each of the following: production history, production potential, expenditure trends, operating costs in geographical area, inflation, budget survey.

I utilize a similar system in determining what is required for the headquarters. The figures are then consolidated and forwarded to my headquarters as a budget request. When the actual budget is received from headquarters, I disseminate to each unit its portion of the budget. On my own initiative, I have developed a computer model assigning each area a weighted factor. The detachments are than issued a portion of the overall budget based on the results of computer run and additional adjustments based on staff input and my leadership in developing complex issues and situations pertaining to the 100 detachments.

In my job as a Command Sergeant Major, I continuously demonstrated my ability to independently analyze complex organizational and resource situations and devise solutions to complex problems. I was assigned to this job as the Region Sergeant Major of the Eighth Region (ROTC) in 2001 which was responsible for 135 ROTC Detachments in 14 eastern seaboard states and the Virgin Islands. There were numerous situations during this times which tested my analytical and problem-solving abilities. Several funding problems developed during the Advanced Camp for more than 3,000 cadets in 2003. The unit was having trouble determining which funds should be expended for expenses. Travel funds, for example, were being used to pay for cadet laundry. For another example, non-government-affiliated civilians were being invited to camp and allowed to travel on DOD Travel Orders. Several requests for contracts had been returned from the Contracting Office without action because of improper funding or preparation. The commanding general placed me in the resource management office to correct the situation.

- I developed a list of relevant expenditure publications and required the assigned personnel to familiarize themselves with the necessary regulations and publications.
- I also developed check sheets and quick reference guides in order to stay on track.
- I developed proficiency tests to insure personnel were current and instituted measures to insure that no documents left the office without quality assurance.
- I provided instructions on appropriated funds and the correct procedures to process fund expenditures.

My ability to independently analyze and resolve stubborn problems was also demonstrated during my years as a Sergeant Major and Command Sergeant Major. I was hand-picked for a job as Command Sergeant Major in 2000 because a very inefficient and demoralized organization needed a strong leader and resourceful problem solver. I was assigned as Sergeant Major for an 800-person battalion in Ft. Polk, LA, where only about 70% of the soldiers lived in barracks in the battalion area with the rest of the soldiers residing in the local area. The organization had 102 military vehicles with supporting maintenance facilities. One of the first problems I tackled was the fact that the battalion's Personnel Action Center had failed their performance goals for the past several months. The center was rated as 25 of 25! No one was sure even how many soldiers were assigned or present for duty on any given day. Many soldiers had unresolved pay issues for months, and soldiers were departing without receiving awards. The evaluation program was not working, and soldiers were missing out on promotion opportunities because of the late evaluations. After my analysis, I took decisive action.

- I developed Standing Operating Procedures and organized the PAC personnel to correct the deficiencies.
- I developed tracking documents, spreadsheets, and generated workable reports to insure that tasks were performed. I required the PAC officers and team leaders in charge to provide me with periodic updates to insure that actions were being followed up on.
- I developed a priority list to correct the overdue pay inquiries and to complete and forward late evaluation reports.
- I developed a training program to insure that the current PAC personnel and newly assigned personnel were trained to accomplish their mission.

Results: Greatly enhanced operating effectiveness and efficiency

Through my leadership, within 90 days of my arrival, the PAC was exceeding its performance goals. The rating had improved to 3 of 25 and at the 120-day mark, the PAC was rated 1 of 25. The Division Commanding General commended me on the rapid improvement of our rating.

Elimination of a serious maintenance problem:

Another problem which had plagued the organization pertained to preventative maintenance. The battalion vehicle fleet was not rated as combat ready when I arrived. Preventative maintenance was not being performed according to specifications. Records were not being properly kept and replacements parts were not being routinely ordered. The battalion had failed several inspections and the commander and executive officer were in danger of losing their positions. I took immediate action. After surveying the situation for about a week, I was able to determine who was failing to accomplish their tasks. I set up counseling sessions with individuals in assigned areas. I provided each individual with objective standards and also assigned collective goals for groups with overlapping tasks. I adjusted tasks as necessary and changed time lines depending upon mission requirements. I acknowledged personnel who performed well and provided incentives for future performance. Personnel who did not respond were counseled or penalized in proportion to their nonperformance. **Result:** The unit exceeded all standards on each inspection after my arrival. Due to our new maintenance record, the unit was selected to participate in several events representing our division.

PROGRAM MANAGER

HAROLD THOMAS LINCOLN

SSN: 000-00-0000

PROGRAM MANAGER, GS-14 ANNOUNCEMENT #XYZ123

KSA #4: Skill in applying principles and practices of budget formulation and execution.

As the Branch Chief for the Eighth Region (ROTC) U.S. Army Cadet Command, I am responsible for Marketing and Advertising Activities for 140 Senior ROTC Programs on college and university campuses and more than 500 Junior ROTC High School Programs in the 14 Eastern Seaboard States, the Virgin Islands, and Panama. I also advise the Region Commander, five Brigade Commanders, the Professors of Military Science, and the Chief, Operations, Marketing and Public Affairs on Marketing Activities. It is my responsibility to direct the skillful planning and utilization of the Region's $650,000 average yearly budget. I have excelled in applying principles and practices of budget formulation and execution while developing the marketing and advertising budget for more than 100 detachments. I provide each detachment with a spending survey to determine what their legitimate needs are, and in formulating their budget I consider each of the following: production history, budget survey, production potential, expenditure trends, inflation, operating costs in geographical area.

I utilize a similar system in determining what is required for the headquarters. The figures are then consolidated and forwarded to my headquarters as a budget request. When the actual budget is received from headquarters, I disseminate to each unit its portion of the budget. On my own initiative, I have developed a computer model assigning each area a weighted factor. The detachments are then issued a portion of the overall budget based on the results of computer run and additional adjustments based on staff input and my leadership in developing complex issues and situations pertaining to the 100 detachments. I am continuously developing and refining procedures to improve the operational planning process as I provide the administrative leadership and coordination critical in the planning and implementation of financial plans and programs. I utilize spreadsheet management extensively to stay on track with the number of projects with which I am involved.

In my current position, I am responsible for the Region's Budget and, in that capacity, I must be familiar with the US Codes and Office of Management and Budget (OMB) Codes. In accordance with Title 31, Section 1301 of the Code, I assure the following:
- That appropriated funds are used only for the purpose for which they were designated
- That expenditures of funds do not exceed the appropriated amount
- That payments are not authorized prior to funds being appropriated

In order to assure quality control and in accordance with Title 31, Section 1514, I developed a system to insure that appropriated fund expenditures were restricted to the amount and period of apportionment. I am required to utilize fluently the following:
- OMB Circular A-11 when submitting my budget request to higher headquarters
- OMB Circular A-34 while executing my budget during the year

KSA #5: Knowledge of management theories and practices, management analysis principles and techniques.

In my current job as Branch Chief for the Eighth Region (ROTC) U.S. Army Cadet Command, I engage management and staff throughout the region in detailed discussions pertaining to my goal of performing organizational analyses and recommending improved systems, refining our skills in performing program and budget planning, improving our ability to forecast future needs and develop estimates of future resource needs to implement program responsibilities, and determine future resource needs.

In my job as a Command Sergeant Major, I continuously demonstrated my knowledge of management theories and practices as well as management analysis principles and techniques. I was assigned to a job as the Region Sergeant Major of the Eighth Region (ROTC) in 2001 which was responsible for 135 ROTC Detachments in 14 eastern seaboard states and the Virgin Islands. There were numerous situations during this times which tested my knowledge of management theories and practices as I resolved stubborn problems in ways that were consistent with sound management theories and practices. Several funding problems developed during the Advanced Camp for more than 3,000 cadets in 2003. The unit was having trouble determining which funds should be expended for expenses. Travel funds, for example, were being used to pay for cadet laundry. For another example, non-government-affiliated civilians were being invited to camp and allowed to travel on Department of Defense Travel Orders. Several requests for contracts had been returned from the Contracting Office without action because of improper funding or preparation. The commanding general placed me in the resource management office to correct the situation.

- I developed a list of relevant expenditure publications and required the assigned personnel to familiarize themselves with the necessary regulations and publications.
- I also developed check sheets and quick reference guides in order to stay on track.
- I developed proficiency tests to insure those personnel were current. I instituted quality control measures to insure that no documents left the office without quality assurance.
- I provided instructions on appropriated funds and the correct procedures to process fund expenditures.

Under my leadership as Command Sergeant Major, the resource management office successfully let all necessary contracts. It also provided travel orders for more than 7,000 people which consisted of a combination of Active Duty Military, Reserves and National Guards, Cadets, Department of Defense Civilians, University Representatives, and other non-government dignitaries and civilians. In addition, we provided funding for all logistical support for the entire camp, which included lodging, meals, fuel, ammunition, services, vehicle rentals, flying hours costs, uniforms, and heavy equipment. As the Command Sergeant Major I was involved in the acquisition of some major systems such as automation and weapons systems. I was required to be familiar with OMB Circular A-109 Acquisition of Major Systems and OMB Circular A-123 which establishes internal controls.

PUBLIC INFORMATION OFFICER

BENJAMIN FIELDS

SSN: 000-00-0000

PUBLIC INFORMATION OFFICER, GS-09 ANNOUNCEMENT #XYZ123

QUALITY RANKING FACTOR #1: Knowledge of principles, concepts, and accepted practices of either public, business, or judicial administration, such as, budget, procurement, space management, supply management, security, human resources management, and records management.

During my years of U.S. Government service, I have learned the complexity of the principles of public administration at each level — federal, state, county, and municipal. In addition to my work experience at each of these levels, I also attended numerous courses and seminars in which I was updated on purposes, concepts, and changing procedures of public administration including a week-long course on Public Management offered to high-ranking military officers trained for public management positions. Through my work experience and training I have gained a solid appreciation of short-term and long-term goals of public administration and of the practices used to realize these goals. Furthermore, during my service with the U.S. Department of Interior, I was directly involved in the interpretation and execution of federal and state regulations, directives, and policies. Even more specifically during my years at the EOIR, I have learned how the principals of public administration affect the adjudicative function of the immigration judges. The public administration of the court involves a wide range of actions which include, but are not limited to, docket management; the delegation of general office duties (filing; data entry; and a great deal of interaction with the public). I also am involved during the consideration of how to best use available space in order to better serve the public and in the hiring process for additional personnel such as contract interpreters or security personnel required due to the growth in the number of cases on the docket. I periodically communicate with headquarters regarding issues such as docket management and the resolution of technical problems and understand the vital importance of maintaining communication between a local EOIR and headquarters. At Whitworth College, I directed and controlled the budget as well as all administrative support for the photo lab personnel including interviewing and making hiring decisions and controlling procurement of equipment and supplies.

QUALITY RANKING FACTOR #2: Ability to locate and collect information and use qualitative and quantitative analytical techniques to determine a course of action.

In my current position I have many opportunities to locate information and analyze situations in order to identify potential problems and determine the appropriate course of action. There are many issues confronted in the daily activities of the court and just one example of a specific situation which illustrates this skill follows: in 2001 the case load suddenly grew rapidly and I saw the potential for a serious backlog of cases which could not be eliminated by the routine procedures then in place. In response to this problem I implemented the system of "super master calendar hearings" which allowed hundreds of cases to be resolved in a short period of time. This enabled the INS and EOIR systems to eliminate a serious backlog in only one week. This occurred twice and I worked closely with Immigration Judges Harris Bossier, Nicholas Butler and their staff to accomplish this task.

QUALITY RANKING FACTOR #3: Ability to communicate orally in both individual and group settings, in order to provide information, advice and guidance to administrative and program officials; persuade and provide/or obtain information for agency employees on a variety of controversial or complex issues.

As a Court Interpreter, the ability to communicate orally is the most vital and essential tool for my effectiveness. I interpret for and explain immigration laws to aliens in a courtroom environment on a daily basis. I have been certified by the King County Municipal Court, Language Division as a Language Specialist. I interpret and explain courtroom procedures and help in the orientation of aliens, the public, and attorneys to court procedures. I work closely with judges and court personnel to help facilitate the adjudicative functions of the court.

Earlier in my career as an Interpreter/Escort, I interpreted for foreign dignitaries, students, and other official visitors and was chosen on the basis of my fluency in French, German, and Arabic as well as for my degree in International Relations.

Excellent oral communication skills were also essential in teaching positions. As the Director of Public Relations for the Department of the Interior, I taught business relations and effective communication courses. I also offer teaching experience from an earlier position as a photography instructor for Whitworth College, Spokane, WA.

QUALITY RANKING FACTOR #4: Ability to communicate in writing (e.g., writing program-related materials).

As a Public Information Officer, I wrote news releases, monthly newsletters, and articles for the national newspaper "The Chronicle." During my career with the U.S. Government, I have been promoted to higher grades based on several factors, not the least of which is my written communication skills. Additionally, while earning my degree in International Relations, my studies were concentrated in an area which involved extensive research, reading, and writing. I was able to use my work experience while writing detailed reports which fulfilled degree requirements. Wrote "confidential" reports for the Department of the Interior's Language Division.

QUALITY RANKING FACTOR #5: Ability to plan, organize, and direct the work of others in an office environment.

Throughout my career I have been involved in planning, organizing, and directing the work of others in office environments. Through these diverse experiences I have developed the belief that people must work together as a team if there is to be success in achieving goals and objectives. I serve as a role model for other personnel in my current position while applying a proactive approach toward problem solving and while ensuring that assignments are completed on time and to the highest standards. I am currently in a position to observe the EOIR office and its functions and to see the whole picture. This has allowed me to understand the duties of the various personnel in the office and to provide solid leadership.

RADIO NETWORK FIELD OFFICER

ZELDA R. SAMPSON

SSN: 000-00-0000

RADIO NETWORK FIELD OFFICER, GS-07 ANNOUNCEMENT #XYZ123

KSA #1: Knowledge of the capabilities and limitations of radio and radio network equipment.

As a GS-07 Radio Network Field Officer since 11/02 for the National Imagery and Mapping Agency's (NIMA) Communication Division, I routinely conduct studies and surveys which are multiagency and national in scope. I apply my knowledge of the capabilities and limitations of radio and radio network equipment in an environment that maintains continual dialog with network user agency components stationed along one of the four principle borders of the U.S. I ensure that network user needs and training requirements are met and authorize the commitment of communication resources within NIMA and to other federal and non-federal law enforcement agencies. I provide field managers with expert technical advice and assistance on matters related to radio communications support issues. Previously as a Communications Technician (Sector Enforcement Specialist), I utilized my understanding of the capabilities and limitations of the radio network on a daily basis to facilitate communications with and among field officers and agents. I also frequently helped to troubleshoot outages and field communications problems to determine if the problem was with the network or with individual subscriber equipment.

- As a Radio Network Field Officer I frequently define radio communications support requirements for federal, state, and local law enforcement agencies operating on any of the country's borders. My actions and decisions often involve multiple agencies, such as the General Services Administration, Office of Management and Budgets, the Finance Department, and frequently my involvement has had a national impact, as in the case of my technical assistance to the Department of Transportation personnel studying airport communications problems. In each of these situations, I have demonstrated my ability to use a Digital Radio Area Network (DRAN) and other state of the art radio communications technologies to enhance and improve communication capabilities.

- Am involved in the development and utilization of specialized evaluation techniques to monitor performance of systems and equipment at the forefront of radio communications technology.

- Have developed expert knowledge of the total communications program with its 24-hour, seven-day-a-week operations and of the technical aspects of the entire VHF radio network and user equipment. Have applied my overall knowledge to analyze and propose solutions to communications management and field managers and have been involved in numerous major projects that are further detailed in some of the following bullet statements.

Special Projects in which I have demonstrated my knowledge of radio and radio network equipment:

- Because of my communications background and expertise, was appointed to act as the single point of contact for National Imagery and Mapping Agency communications support for "Operation Voyage 2002," the project which is bringing "tall ships" from all over the world together to move from key ports along the east and west coast (Newport News, VA; New Orleans, LA; Fort Lauderdale, FL; Sacramento, CA). My responsibilities involve coordinating radio communications for the event and setting up the radio and computer equipment communications control center. Committee provided the communications support for a high-risk and high-visibility event subject to possible terrorism.

- Played a vital role in a complex project, which consolidated seven regional communications centers (sectors) into a centralized National Investigative Training Center (NITC) located in New Orleans, LA. Oversaw the initial 25-person staff, which grew to 45 members as other sectors closed down and their staff members were integrated. Initiated and developed the procedures for shutting down the New Orleans, Dallas, and Memphis sectors including establishing the time tables and explaining shutdown procedures to top-level management personnel. Coordinated the telephone and radio circuit turnovers for the VHF network and assisted in the design of the sector operations floor in the permanent center.

Related training:

Procedural Review and Management Control Training, 2004
NIMA First-line Supervisor Refresher Course, 2002
Management Training Workshop, 2001
Interpersonal Relations and Negotiation Skills Training, 2001
Mid-level Management, 2001   Sector Enforcement Specialist Class, 2000
Train the Trainer for the RC, 2000   (Class Coordinator), 2000
COMSEC Training, 1999   NIMA Instructor Training, 1999

RADIO NETWORK FIELD OFFICER

ZELDA R. SAMPSON

SSN: 000-00-0000

RADIO NETWORK FIELD OFFICER, GS-07 ANNOUNCEMENT #XYZ123

KSA #2: Ability to present information in writing.

My written communication skills are applied on a regular basis in my present assignment as a GS-07 Radio Network Field Officer since 11/02. On a regular basis, I produce memos to high level NIMA management personnel; letters to high-level outside federal, state, or local agencies and military officials; standard operating procedures; NIMA directives; training manuals; and reports to higher level managers.

A focal point of this job is directing a wide range of technical studies to include planning and directing reviews to determine the capabilities and limitations of radio and radio network equipment belonging to NIMA. Evaluate study findings in terms of their relationship to other efforts planned or in progress and submit written proposals to Center management on hardware, software, and systems modifications as appropriate and in order to meet the ever-changing requirements of the network user community.

- Prepare numerous written reports and critiques while serving as the single point of contact for National Imagery and Mapping Agency communications support for "Operation Voyage 2002," the project which is bringing "tall ships" from all over the world together to move from key ports along the east and west coast (Newport News, VA; New Orleans, LA; Fort Lauderdale, FL; Sacramento, CA). My responsibilities involve coordinating radio communications for the event and setting up the radio and computer equipment in a Communications Control Center environment. I produce written and oral briefings and provide weekly status reports to NIMA management. Committee members include high level officials from the Chicago Police Department, U.S. Marines, National Guards, and the Central Intelligence Agency.
- Have developed expert knowledge of the total communications program of National Imagery and Mapping Agency with its 24-hour, seven-day-a-week operations and of the technical aspects of the entire VHF radio network and user equipment and participated in projects during which communications management and field managers received analytical written reports and studies that I prepared following the successful conclusion of such projects as the following: (1) Managed a 2002 Northwest communications study which resulted in the reprogramming of approximately 150 pieces of equipment. Faced with a lack of proper communications in the area, the Finance Department authorized a project to correct the problems. I oversaw the training of 98 NIMA officers and outside law enforcement personnel after analyzing the network, making a written proposal to add and delete some sites, and change frequencies on some sites. Coordinated the team that completed the reprogramming and training and achieved a 100% improvement in radio communications capabilities. (2) Directed a more recent 2003 project in the Chicago metropolitan area, which began with the same complaint but involved 250 NIMA officers, 250 pieces of radio equipment, and the training of 250 special agents.
- Became part of a specially selected team that began meetings in April 2002 with high-level technical officials of the National Imagery and Mapping Agency. The new system at O'Hare International Airport was the primary source of open joint discussions on the facility and management concepts. Created extensive written paperwork related to these talks which facilitated the sharing of problem solving

concepts, the use and deployment of new technologies, planning and migration of new digital systems, and the proposal of design plans for evolving airport coverage scenarios using new and existing technologies as well as written briefing papers.

- Was selected for additional duty assignment as the National Systems Manager (NSM) for the main computer system used by National Imagery and Mapping Agency. Developed and implemented new profile codes to be used on a national level and a special query to be used by sector enforcement specialists, which saved time and allowed data to be more productively manipulated. I also produced written manuals and standard operating procedures.
- Coordinated four communication systems requirements at preclearance stations in Peoria, Bloomington, Aurora, and Chicago, Illinois. Began the project by interpreting and maintaining frequent contact with high-ranking government officials in order to facilitate frequency authorization and permission for work to be done. I prepared correspondence and written reports as needed.

I applied my written communication skills daily as a GS-07 Communications Branch Chief from 1999-02, when I supervised and managed a staff of 10 while overseeing day-to-day and program operations and dealing effectively with frequent and ongoing staff shortages in a 24-hour, seven-day-a-week command center. Specially selected to oversee, develop, and manage projects which called for expertise in formulating technology and utilizing the latest technological advances in communications and computer systems, provided thorough written reports following the successful completion of each project.

Highlights of studies and projects during which I prepared extensive written communication:
- Was chosen as one of a team of three assigned as Investigation Representatives tasked with developing and implementing a management training workshop. This program was a part of the Illinois Regional Commissioner's "Innovation Project" and resulted in providing more than 150 supervisors in the area with the proper training. The course, for which I wrote the course syllabus, handouts, and manuals, was then implemented by the National Investigative Training Center and used nationwide.
- Served on a team, which developed a two-week Sector Enforcement Specialists class where I prepared course outlines, agendas, manual, and handouts. I then returned to the center to reevaluate and fine tune the course of instruction.
- Was a major player in the development and implementation of the standard operating procedures used to run this center with its 24-hour, seven-day-a-week operating schedule.

Related training:
NSM Training, 2004
Procedural Review and Management Control Training, 2004
NIMA First-line Supervisor Refresher Course, 2002
Train the Trainer for the RC, 2002
Interpersonal Relations and Negotiation Skills Training, 2001
Mid-level Management, 2001
Management Training Workshop, 2001
Sector Enforcement Specialist Class, Class Coordinator, 2000
COMSEC Training, 2000
NIMA Instructor Training, 1999

RADIO NETWORK FIELD OFFICER

ZELDA R. SAMPSON

SSN: 000-00-0000

RADIO NETWORK FIELD OFFICER, GS-07 ANNOUNCEMENT #XYZ123

KSA #3: Demonstrated ability to utilize commercial off-the-shelf software.

I demonstrate my ability to utilize commercial off-the-shelf software on a daily basis in my present assignment as a Radio Network Field Officer (since 11/02). To carry out my responsibilities, I use Microsoft Windows ME and XE, Microsoft Office software, and Microsoft Word. I also extensively use the Micron SE software to access the National Imagery and Mapping Agency mainframe computer.

- Frequently utilize commercial off-the-shelf software including the Microsoft suite as I work to define radio communications support requirements for federal, state, and local law enforcement agencies operating on any of the country's borders. These actions involve multiple agencies as well as having a national impact. Pursue the goal of meeting requirements and resolving communications problems through the applications of digital, and other state of the art radio communications technologies. Oversee the field testing of prototype hardware and software, both commercial and NIMA specific. Am involved in the development and utilization of specialized evaluation techniques to monitor performance of systems and equipment at the forefront of radio communications technology.

- Use commercial off-the-shelf software as I direct a wide range of technical studies to include planning and directing reviews to determine the capabilities and limitations of radio and radio network equipment not belonging to NIMA. Use PowerPoint to prepare and give presentations. Determine the efficiency of existing hardware and software and ascertain user acceptance of newly deployed technologies. Submit proposals to center management on hardware, software, and systems modifications as appropriate and in order to meet the ever-changing requirements of the network user community.

My ability and knowledge in the area of utilizing off-the-shelf software was also demonstrated in an earlier job as Chief, Communications Branch (1999-02). I supervised and managed a staff of 10 while overseeing day-to-day and program operations and dealing effectively with frequent and ongoing staff shortages in a 24-hour, seven-day-a-week command center. During my time in this job, I was specially selected to oversee, develop, and manage projects which called for expertise in formulating technology and utilizing the latest technological advances in communications and computer systems and which included the following projects:

- Sought out and evaluated the utility of commercial software with an eye toward anything that would make the jobs of the Sector Enforcement Specialist easier and more efficient.

Related training:
NSM Training, 2004
Procedural Review and Management Control Training, 2004
NIMA First-line Supervisor Refresher Course, 2002
Train the Trainer for the RC, 2002
Mid-level Management, 2001
Management Training Workshop, 2001

ZELDA R. SAMPSON
SSN: 000-00-0000

RADIO NETWORK FIELD OFFICER, GS-07 ANNOUNCEMENT #XYZ123

KSA #4: Demonstrated ability to direct and incorporate the actions of specialists supporting a national DRAN based radio communications program.

Details of experience related to this KSA as Chief, Communications Branch:
As Chief, Communications Branch (1999-02), I supervised and managed a staff of 10 while overseeing day-to-day and program operations in a 24-hour, seven-day-a-week command center. Frequently served as Acting Communications Manager overseeing a staff of 25 Sector Enforcement Specialists, Electronic Technicians, and Covert Electronics Technicians supporting national and national DRAN based radio communications programs.

- **Projects related to DRAN:** Directed and coordinated four major radio initiatives in Peoria, Bloomington, Aurora Preclearance Stations located in Illinois. I was instrumental in facilitating an DRAN network configured for the inspectors to operate in a voice privacy environment utilizing Digital Radio Area Networks (DRAN). This involved frequency coordination with the government and the Finance Department Frequency Management staff. It involved training all of the NIMA Inspectors involved in the NIMA VHF DRAN program. This was the first time that a preclearance station in Illinois was able to operate their radio network in a Data Encryption Standard (DES) utilizing DRAN. Also coordinated four communications systems requirements at preclearance stations in Peoria, Bloomington, Aurora, and Chicago, Illinois. Began the project by interpreting and maintaining frequent contact with high-ranking government officials in order to facilitate frequency authorization and permission for work to be done correctly. Was the first person to introduce a DRAN network in this Northwestern Region.

- **Other special projects involving DRAN:** Directed four major radio projects which involved redesigning the VHF radio network and programming various types of VHF radio equipment. Was also instrumental in the planning of specifications of DRAN including building specific units and mapping of the radios to facilitate Digital Radio Area Network (DRAN). This project involved training the officers on the operation of the radio equipment and DRAN. Also directed a 2003 project in the Chicago metropolitan area which began with the same complaint but involved 250 NIMA officers, 250 pieces of radio equipment, and the training of 250 special agents in the use of a DRAN radio network.

- **Network analysis related to DRAN:** Analyzed the O'Hare International Airport communications system after complaints were received that personnel could not communicate while on airport grounds. Analyzed the network, completed radio checks, met with key personnel, and made recommendations which resulted in sites being added and 150 officers receiving retraining. The sites that will be added will enhance this DRAN network. Worked with top FAA officials because the new site (opening in 2004) is located at the FAA tower.

Related training:
Procedural Review and Management Control Training, 2004
NIMA First-line Supervisor Refresher Course, 2002
Train the Trainer for the RC, 2002

RESPIRATORY THERAPIST

CAITLIN M. RICHARDSON

SSN: 000-00-0000

RESPIRATORY THERAPIST, GS-06/07 ANNOUNCEMENT #XYZ123

Respiratory Therapist, GS-06/07 Announcement #XYZ123 KSA #1

KSA #1: Knowledge of a variety of respiratory therapy procedures and techniques including the functioning characteristics of complex respiratory equipment.

In my current job as **a Registered Respiratory Therapist for Macomb Medical Center in Santa Rosa, CA (2003-present),** I am involved in all aspects of respiratory patient care as well as overseeing the managerial and administrative duties of the operating room, intensive care unit, emergency department, telemetry, general floor care, and maternity ward. Through my expertise and extensive knowledge of hospital procedures, hospital equipment, and direct patient care, I am responsible for the care, administration, sterilization, maintenance, and utilization of the following equipment and procedures:

Check your spelling!

cardiopulmonary resuscitation	electrocardiography
therapeutic gas administration	intubations (endotracheal)
cooximeter and ABG machine	extubations
arterial sticks (radial, brachial and femoral)	pulmonary function testing
mechanical ventilation (adult and neonatal)	transporting critical patients
physiologic and hemodynamic monitoring	arterial blood gas machines
assist during bronchoscopies and thoracentesis	ECG machines
aerosol, MDI, and humidity therapy	

Check the spelling of all names of products etc.!

In my current position, I am involved in a wide range of personnel and patient issues including the training and supervision of respiratory students and new employees, scheduling and processing outpatients, maintaining patient records and departmental files, accounts receivable, bookkeeping, and transporting critical patients. I demonstrate my adaptability and versatility while handling various departmental duties on a weekly rotational basis in the emergency room (ER), intensive care unit (ICU), operating room (OR), maternity ward, telemetry, and general floor care.

I operate and maintain the following ventilators: Servo 900 B & C, Puritan Bennett 7200, Adult Star, Sechrist, and Respironics BIPAP; utilize the following ABG machines: ABL 330 and ABL 5; and have experience with the Marquette Mac 15 EKG machine.

Education and training related to this KSA:

- Received Associate in Science degree in Respiratory Therapy from Devereaux Community College, Santa Rosa, CA, 1999.
- Received N.A.L.S. Certification, June 1998; valid through June 2004.
- Received B.L.S. Certification, November 1999; valid through November 2005.
- Board Registered Respiratory Therapist since July 1999.
- Board Certified Respiratory Therapist since June 1999.
- Possess extensive knowledge and expertise in maintenance and quality control; am extremely proficient in hospital and personal computers and software programs.
- B.S. in Health Administration, Devereaux Community College, Santa Rosa, CA.

KSA #2: Knowledge of anatomy and physiology including an in-depth understanding of the structure and function of the lungs and bronchi as related to gas exchange and ventilation, in order to administer special ventilatory techniques.

Respiratory Therapist, GS-06/07
Announcement #XYZ123
KSA #2

In my current job as **a Registered Respiratory Therapist for Macomb Medical Center in Santa Rosa, California (2003-present),** I am involved in all aspects of respiratory patient care as well as overseeing the managerial and administrative duties of the operating room, intensive care unit, emergency department, telemetry, general floor care, and maternity ward. I possess extensive knowledge and expertise in hospital procedures, hospital equipment, and direct patient care.

Through my expertise and extensive clinical experience, education, and training in hospital procedures, equipment, and direct patient care, I have gained valuable knowledge related to human anatomy involving the respiratory system, ventilation, oxygenation, and other bodily functions.

Patients requiring respiratory care usually suffer from other physical ailments or impairments and require special consideration. As a respiratory specialist with diagnostic capabilities who has earned the trust and respect of doctors, nurses, and supervisors, I am able to determine patient needs and offer recommendations on treatment options and appropriate medications.

In my current position, I am involved in a wide range of personnel and patient issues including the training and supervision of respiratory students and new employees, scheduling and processing out-patients, maintaining patient records and departmental files, accounts receivable, bookkeeping, and transporting critical patients. I demonstrate my adaptability and versatility while handling various departmental duties on a weekly rotational basis in the emergency room (ER), intensive care unit (ICU), operating room (OR), maternity ward, telemetry, and general floor care.

Education and training related to this KSA:
Received Associate in Science degree in Respiratory Therapy from Devereaux Community College, Santa Rosa, CA, 1999.
Received N.A.L.S. Certification, June 2000; valid through June 2004.
Received B.L.S. Certification, November 1998; valid through November 2005.
Board Registered Respiratory Therapist since July 1999.
Board Certified Respiratory Therapist since June 1999.
Possess extensive knowledge and expertise in maintenance and quality control; am extremely proficient in hospital and personal computers and software programs.
Earning B.S. degree in Health Administration with extensive coursework in computers, Devereaux Community College, Santa Rosa, CA

RESPIRATORY THERAPIST

CAITLIN M. RICHARDSON

SSN: 000-00-0000

RESPIRATORY THERAPIST, GS-06/07 ANNOUNCEMENT #XYZ123

KSA #3: Knowledge of respiratory pharmacology in order to identify complications and interactions of drugs.

In my current job as **a Registered Respiratory Therapist for Macomb Medical Center in Santa Rosa, California (2003-present),** I am involved in all aspects of respiratory patient care as well as overseeing the managerial and administrative duties of the operating room, intensive care unit, emergency department, telemetry, general floor care, and maternity ward. I possess extensive knowledge and expertise in hospital procedures, hospital equipment, and direct patient care.

Through my extensive knowledge, education, and training in pharmacokinetics and pharmacodynamics, I routinely recommend various medications as well as determine proper medication dosages. Additionally, I am entrusted and respected for my judgment in recommending, ordering, and administering a multitude of respiratory medications. As part of my job description, I am required to monitor all medicated patients for desired treatment results and any adverse reactions. Following are a few of the common respiratory medications I am familiar with:

inhalation drugs for bronchodilation	proventil
bronchoconstriction	racemic epinephrine
mucolytics	mucomyst
wetting agents	saline

Various forms of administration with the above medications are as follows: MDI, nebulizer, IPPB, or via endotracheal tubes. When prescribing and administering medications, special consideration, care, and sensitivity should be given to children and to the elderly. Possible side effects of respiratory drugs may include increased heart rate, nausea, vomiting, and bronchospasms. In my current position, I am involved in a wide range of personnel and patient issues including the training and supervision of respiratory students and new employees, scheduling and processing out-patients, maintaining patient records and departmental files, accounts receivable, bookkeeping, and transporting critical patients. I demonstrate my adaptability and versatility while handling various departmental duties on a weekly rotational basis in the emergency room (ER), intensive care unit (ICU), operating room (OR), maternity ward, telemetry, and general floor care.

Education and Training related to this KSA:

Associate in Science degree in Respiratory Therapy, 1999.
Received N.A.L.S. Certification, June 2000; valid through June 2004.
Received B.L.S. Certification, November 1998; valid through November 2005.
Board Registered Respiratory Therapist since July 1999.
Board Certified Respiratory Therapist since June 1999.
Possess extensive knowledge and expertise in maintenance and quality control; am extremely proficient in hospital and personal computers and software programs.
Earning B.S. degree in Health Administration with extensive coursework in computers, Devereaux Community College, Santa Rosa, CA.

SECRETARY/PERSONAL ASSISTANT

RICHARD ANDREWS

SSN: 000-00-0000

SECRETARY/ PERSONAL ASSISTANT, GS-07 ANNOUNCEMENT #XYZ123

KSA #1: Knowledge of the functions and organizational structures of a major military headquarters.

In my current position at one of the largest U.S. military bases in the world, I have developed extensive knowledge of the functions and organizational structure of a major headquarters, and have become increasingly knowledgeable of the hierarchy involved in order to accomplish the essential functions of my job within that structure.

Experience with the Special Operations Battle Lab Concept Directorate (SOBL-CD): Especially in my present job as secretary and personal assistant to the Director of Special Operations for the Department of Defense (2003-present), I have become very familiar with the functions and organizational structure of a major headquarters. I interact with individuals at all organizational levels of this major headquarters.

Interactions with officials throughout the organizational structure of SOBL-CD: Perform extensive liaison on a daily basis between the Directorate and officials of the U. S. Special Operations Command (USSOCOM), USASOC, TRADOC, the Combined Arms Centers (CACs), XVIII Airborne Corps, and the Advisory Group, which consists of personnel from the North Atlantic Treaty Organization (NATO), National Reconnaissance Office (NRO), Office of Inspector General (DoDIG), and all branches of the Armed Forces including the National Guard. In addition, I coordinate daily with the chiefs of subordinate divisions and other personnel both within the Directorate and within the Department of Defense. Coordinates the Director's schedule to coincide with the Commanding General's and Assistant Commandant's calendars, when necessary.

Screen all incoming telephone calls and correspondence, directing requests for information to the appropriate individuals within the organization.

Knowledge of the structure and purpose of SOBL-CD: The Directorate is composed of several divisions, consisting of staff from civilian grades GS-03 through GS-12 and military personnel from MSG through COL. I maintain a solid working knowledge of the SOBL-CD mission in order to provide constructive feedback and recommendations to the director on administrative and clerical processes and procedures that could better accomplish the mission. The director is chairman of several special boards which involves preparing formal in-process reviews (IPRs), officers efficiency reports, decision and discussion papers, contracts, staff studies, and formal reports to higher headquarters. The SOBL-CD is responsible for future training operations, formulation, direction, and planning.

SECRETARY/PERSONAL ASSISTANT

RICHARD ANDREWS

SSN: 000-00-0000

SECRETARY/ PERSONAL ASSISTANT, GS-07 ANNOUNCEMENT #XYZ123

KSA #2: Ability to communicate with high level civilian and governmental officials.

In my current position as secretary and personal assistant to the Director of Special Operations for the Department of Defense (2003-present), I demonstrate my ability to communicate effectively with high level civilian and military officials on a daily basis. I interact with civilian personnel as high as GS-12 and military personnel at all levels, arranging meetings and briefings between the Director and various high-ranking officers throughout the installation, including the Commanding General and the Assistant Commandant.

Within the Directorate, I have daily interaction with military and civilian personnel at all levels of rank. I also interact with the Director on a daily basis, making recommendations on administrative and clerical processes and procedures; and to suggest new policies or procedures to better accomplish the mission. While screening all incoming calls and correspondence, I determine the nature of the call and then direct it to the appropriate person within the organization.

As Support Coordinator for the Branch Assistance Division of the Fort Polk Readiness Group, I worked under the general supervision of the Chief of Combat Arms and Combat Support Division. Planned and coordinated a number of program responsibilities, interacting with officials at all levels of civilian and military service on a daily basis.

Prepared and presented verbal briefings to Colonels from National Guard and Reserve Component units. Reviewed work load reports and procedures to ensure work load and manpower utilization were reported correctly, discussing discrepancies and recommended corrective action to the Team Chiefs. Communicated with officials within command channels and between other agencies, to conduct briefings and discuss recommendations to resolve problems and requests for assistance. Contacted the S-3 and DOIM when the computer terminal was down or not working properly, and scheduled a service call.

Earlier as Secretary for the Director of ADDS Test Division, I communicated with high level civilian and military officials while arranging official and social meetings and briefing, issuing telephone invitations and interacting with various officials to coordinate with the Director and resolve any scheduling conflicts.

RICHARD ANDREWS

SSN: 000-00-0000

SECRETARY/ PERSONAL ASSISTANT, GS-07 ANNOUNCEMENT #XYZ123

KSA #3: Ability to communicate in writing.

In my present position as secretary and personal assistant to the Director of Special Operations for Department of Defense (2003-present), I use word processors and other computer software to prepare a variety of narrative and tabular material according to prepared formats, form letters, standard paragraphs, and mail lists. Provide writing assistance during the production and distribution of periodic performance evaluations, narratives for awards and medals, and memorandums. Proofread officer and enlisted efficiency reports and civilian performance appraisals for personnel under director's supervision. Provide support documents, ensuring that appropriate guidelines are followed and that efficiency reports and performance appraisals are completed on time.

Review documents prepared for signature of the director to include memorandum, nonmilitary letters, staff studies, etc., for conformance with regulatory guidance, grammar, format, and special policies of the directorate. Return these items to the originator for correction when not in conformance with known policies, or when correspondence regulations have not been followed. Compose personal, official, and other materials, assuring compliance with correspondence rules and regulations guidance and known viewpoints of director. Prepare a variety of narrative and tabular materials (e.g., correspondence, reports, and speeches), correcting errors in grammar, spelling, and punctuation. Refer to dictionaries, style manuals, and established typing/correspondence policies of the organization to ensure accuracy and precision of language as well as adherence to established formats.

In a previous position as Support Coordinator for the Branch Assistance Division of the Fort Polk Readiness Group, independently prepared administrative correspondence and recurring special summary reports, ensuring that grammar, spelling, and punctuation were correct. Refer to dictionaries, style manuals, and established typing/correspondence policies of the organization to ensure accuracy and precision of language as well as adherence to established formats. Extracted pertinent information and consolidated manpower data, using this material to compose and prepare written reports to my supervisor for submission to higher headquarters.

Provided writing assistance during the composition and production of periodic performance evaluations, narratives for awards and medals, and memorandums. Proofread officer and enlisted efficiency reports and civilian performance appraisals for personnel under director's supervision. Provide support documents, ensuring that appropriate guidelines are followed and that efficiency reports and performance appraisals are completed on time.

PARAMEDIC

FRANKLIN MICHAEL ROBERTS

SSN: 000-00-0000

PARAMEDIC, GS-09 ANNOUNCEMENT #XYZ123

KSA #1: Knowledge of Ambulance Readiness Procedures.

I have 20 years' experience in Emergency Services. Vehicle, equipment, and supply check have always been a daily responsibility in every position I held. My first responsibility on shift each day is vehicle, equipment, and supply check. Vehicle check includes preoperation checks and first line maintenance. Checking fluid levels, oil, radiator, transmission, power steering, windshield washer, fuel, and batteries, and replacing as necessary. Checking safety and emergency lights for proper function, checking tires for tire pressure, alternator, fuel, speedometer, etc. It has also been my responsibility to notify the chain of command of any condition that would render the vehicle inoperative of limit the crew from performing its duties. As shift leader and senior paramedic on shift, it has been my responsibility to take a vehicle off line if it cannot be operated safely.

Reveal situations that show off your knowledge.

- Equipment and supply checks: Monitor defibrillator, suction, splints, backboards, cervical collar oxygen regulators ETC; all must be checked, tested and maintained in working order.
- Supplies must be checked each shift and replaced as needed. Vehicle equipment and supplies must be restocked quickly and prepared for next call.
- The most important factor in readiness is personnel. Qualified people who are responsible for maintaining vehicles, equipment, and supplies. Personnel must also maintain knowledge, skills, and abilities with training, continuing education, and peer review.

My experience in EMS has prepared me for the role of supervisor. I have created vehicle equipment and supply checks for the EMS service, I consistently received high marks in this area of evaluation, and I received **Employee of the Month**, (an award determined by the votes of fellow employees). I also received many awards of appreciation for community services. I am certified by the American Heart Association in Pediatric Advance Life Support, Advance Cardiac Life Support Instructor, and Basic Cardiac Life Support Instructor Trainer. I am also certified by the American Red Cross as a Basic Cardiac Life Support Instructor and First Aid Instructor. The national AHA Emergency Cardiac Care Subcommittee has established a "Chain of Survival," designed to ensure the greatest chance of survival in an emergency.

Early Access: As a leader in this area it is my responsibility to strengthen the chain because a chain is only as strong as its weakest link. Early Access can be materialized by proper advertising and a reliable 911 system. 911 should be displayed on all emergency vehicles.

Early CPR: Early CPR can only be accomplished by a community wide public education program. Every EMS professional should be an expert in CPR, and experts should teach others.

Early Defibrillation: Early Defibrillation is now part of the basic CPR course. We should work towards the goal of putting Automatic External Defibrillators in the hands of every first responder.

Early Advance Cardiac Life Support: Early Advance Cardiac Life Support can only be accomplished by an efficient Emergency Medical Services.

KSA #2: Skill in providing advanced life saving medical treatment in emergency situations.

Paramedic, GS-09
Announcement #XYZ123
KSA #2

I have an Associate's degree in emergency medicine, which includes advance cardiology, pharmacology, as well as pathophysiology and management of medical emergencies. I have also remained certified in Advanced Cardiac Life Support, an advanced cardiac course for critical care providers, intensive care, emergency department and prehospital emergency care personnel. ACLS is the standard of care for cardiac emergencies. This course includes: 1) cardiac anatomy and physiology from chemical and cell level to pump action and resuscitation procedures, electrical conduction system and coronary circulation as well as pulmonary circulation and systemic circulation, 2) cardiac pharmacology which includes indications, contraindications, precautions, dosage, and mechanism of action for the following drugs: Oxygen, Epinephrine, Atropine, Lidocaine, Procainamide, Bretylium, Varapamil, Sodium Bicarbonate, Morphine, Calcium chloride, Norepinephrine, Dopamine, Dobutamine, Isoproterenol, Amrinone, Digitalis, Sodium nitroprusside, Nitroglycerin, Propanolol, Metroprolol, Furosemide, Adenosine, and Magnesium, 3) Cardiac dysrhythmis interpretation and treatment for the following: Sinus rhythm, Sinus bradycardia, Sinus Tachycardia, Sinus Arrhythmia, premature atrial complexes, premature junctional complexes, premature ventricle complexes, atrial tachycardia, Junctional tachycardia, Supraventricular tachycardia, Ventricular tachycardia, Atrial flutter, atrial fibrillation, first degree block, second degree block, and third degree block.

Check on proper names.

Other critical care courses I am certified for include: Pediatric Advanced Cardiac Life Support (PALS), and Emergency Medical Services for Children (EMSC). I became certified in ACLS in 1998, and I have repeated the course 5 times, becoming more proficient each time, and in 2002 I became an ACLS instructor. I have taught the latest changes in ACLS and Emergency Cardiac Care. I am also a Basic Cardiac Life Support Instructor Trainer, and I train instructors to teach CPR. Basic Life Support is a most important skill, and I believe EMS personnel should be responsible for teaching the public, as an informed public can make a difference. To insure the greatest opportunity for survival, CPR must be initiated as soon as possible by a bystander, as this can keep the patient viable until advanced care is available.

I have over 6 years of experience as an advanced life support provider: 2 years with Craven County EMS as an EMT-Intermediate, 1 year with Tobias County EMS and almost 4 years with the Washington, DC Ambulance Section. I taught advanced life procedures and ACLS for 2 years at Ft. Belvoir. I have worked on several cardiac arrest patients, and I have seen a patient who had been pulseless, unable to breathe on his own, later walk out of the hospital and go on to lead a productive life.

SUPPLY SPECIALIST

CURTIS L. STRICKLAND

SSN: 000-00-0000

SUPPLY SPECIALIST, GS-06/07 ANNOUNCEMENT #XYZ123

Supply Specialist, GS-06/07 Announcement #XYZ123 Task A

TASK A. Performs SARSS-1 catalog research and file management functions.

In my present position as General Supply Specialist (since 5/2002) for a major civilian contracting firm, I am the interface between the ULLS-A/G (Unit Level Logistics System Air/Ground) and the SARSS-1 system for my unit and am the "resident expert" in solving problems between the systems.

- Establish and maintain an accurate, detailed, and current log sheet for all SARSS-generated Supply Status Reports (SSRs)
- Ensure that logsheets for SARSS-generated SSRs include all of the following information:
- SSR voucher number
- Determination of whether or not causative research is required (Yes/No)
- Number of line items listed on the SSR
- Total and adjusted gains to date
- Total and adjusted losses to date
- Total and adjusted dolar value to date
- Date submitted for review or approval and date returned
- Establish, update, and maintain and SSR supsense file for all SSRs currently in progress, adding all documentation to the file as research is conducted.
- Ensure that the access roster to the SSR suspense file is strictly maintained to maximize document control.

While serving as an Operations NCO (1996-2002) at MMC level, functioned as Training NCO. Conducted both hands-on and formal classroom instruction on the operation of the SARSS-1 system, which encompassed input-output, daily/monthly transactions, document history inquiries, and current trends and problems with the system.

Education and training:
Bachelor of Arts in Business Administration, Morgan State University, Baltimore, MD, 2002. Completed extensive training which included course work completed at the U.S. Army Quartermaster School:
Commissary Management
Senior Supply/Services Sergeant
Supply NCO Advanced Course
DSU/GSU Mechanized Stock Control
Division Logistics Systems
Unit and Organizational Supply Basic Course
Basic Supply NCO Course
Aircraft Repair Parts Specialist
Stock Control and Accounting Specialist
Additional course work included NCO Logistics Program, TRANE/Bryant Decentralized Automated Service Support System, and the U.S. Army Basic Leadership Course.

CURTIS L. STRICKLAND

SUPPLY SPECIALIST, GS-06/07 ANNOUNCEMENT #XYZ123

TASK B. Provide technical advice on SARSS-1 procedures in compliance with regulatory requirements.

Supply Specialist, GS-06/07 Announcement #XYZ123 Task B

In my present position as General Supply Specialist (since 5/2002) for a major civilian contracting firm, I am the interface between the ULLS-A/G (Unit Level Logistics System Air/Ground) and the SARSS-1 system for my unit and am the "resident expert" in solving problems between the systems.

- Establish and maintain an accurate, detailed, and current log sheet for all SARSS-generated Supply Status Reports (SSRs)
- Ensure that logsheets for SARSS-generated SSRs include all of the following information:
- SSR voucher number
- Determination of whether or not causative research is required (Yes/No)
- Number of line items listed on the SSR
- Total and adjusted gains to date
- Total and adjusted losses to date
- Total and adjusted dolar value to date
- Date submitted for review or approval and date returned
- Establish, update, and maintain and SSR supsense file for all SSRs currently in progress, adding all documentation to the file as research is conducted.
- Ensure that the access roster to the SSR suspense file is strictly maintained to maximize document control.

While serving as an Operations NCO (1996-2002) at MMC level, functioned as Training NCO. Conducted both hands-on and formal classroom instruction on the operation of the SARSS-1 system, which encompassed input-output, daily/monthly transactions, document history inquiries, and current trends and problems with the system.

Education and training:
Bachelor of Arts in Business Administration, Morgan State University, Baltimore, MD, 2002. Completed extensive training which included course work completed at the U.S. Army Quartermaster School:
Commissary Management
Senior Supply/Services Sergeant
Supply NCO Advanced Course
DSU/GSU Mechanized Stock Control
Division Logistics Systems
Unit and Organizational Supply Basic Course
Basic Supply NCO Course
Aircraft Repair Parts Specialist
Stock Control and Accounting Specialist
Additional course work included NCO Logistics Program, TRANE/Bryant Decentralized Automated Service Support System, and the U.S. Army Basic Leadership Course.

SUPPLY SUPERVISOR

KENNETH S. MOSLEY

SSN: 000-00-0000

SUPPLY SUPERVISOR, GS-07/11 ANNOUNCEMENT #XYZ123

KSA #1: Knowledge of Impact of DLA Logistical Support to Military Services Readiness.

With more than 18 years in the military, I have extensive knowledge of the importance of effective logistical support operations to the readiness of military services. DLA Logistics Support Programs are responsible for providing military operations with the materiel necessary for them to function at a high state of readiness. I have held logistics management positions where I oversaw logistics support for day-to-day operations as well as for troop movements and deployments, and I was often handpicked as a consultant for special projects.

In my current position as a Supervisory General Supply Specialist since 06/01, I apply my knowledge of the impact of DLA logistical support while managing, directing, and implementing supply and services functions to military organizations throughout the U.S. and the Middle East. Supervising 95 members of a multinational workforce, I manage activities which include subsistence requisitioning, transportation, storage, accountability, and the preparation of materials for storage, transportation, and utilization. In addition to planning and directing various financial management and operational programs for the Supply and Services Division, I provide logistical support diverse facilities. These include the Central Issue Facility, laundry, Installation Property Book Office, Self Service Supply Center, graves registration, retail fuel operations, and organizational property book operations.

While serving as Supply/Maintenance Management Officer for the 14th Support Battalion in 1997, I was entrusted with a project for which I planned, organized, and directed the closeout of an Army Area Supply Depot for Class II, III (P), VII, and IX supplies during a down-sizing. **A main objective was to complete the downsizing without compromising the level of service or the combat readiness of customer organizations.** To accomplish this I transferred all on-hand stock to another supply point and set up a Central Receiving Point which in still in operation. I developed the internal and external Standard Operating Procedures as well as the structure for the transportation network which supported the operation. Prepared and presented briefings to general-level officers and gained their direct approval for my plan of action. **Despite the complexity of the project, supply support continued without interruption, combat readiness was not compromised, and more than 25 positions were phased out at a savings of $1.3 million annually.**

As a Supervisory Inventory Management Specialist, from 04/00 until 11/01, I directed day-to-day operations in a Commodity Management Branch that supported military operations throughout the region. I supervised 20 Item Managers to ensure that they maintained, adjusted, and established requisition objectives, retention levels, maintenance work requests, and the proper disposition of serviceable and unserviceable assets.

Due to my extensive knowledge of logistical support, I was hand-picked as a Branch Chief for a Material Management Center in Bosnia. While supervising 20 employees, I directed and approved local purchase activities for procurement of perishable and semi-perishable food products in support of the U.S. military presence in Bosnia. I was selected for this position on the basis of my reputation for expertise in analyzing, managing, coordinating, and procuring any type of product including subsistence. I was selected because of my thorough understanding of supply management logistical support functions for what was essentially a top-level consulting/staff position as a Storage Specialist in a Defense Logistics Agency Stockpile Depot (8/94 to 5/95). I analyzed the effectiveness of existing supply, procurement, transportation, cataloguing, provisioning, storage, and distribution procedures. Conducted formal and informal management studies to evaluate overall performance of systems and to identify improvements.

While serving as Support Supply Technician and Accountable Officer, I oversaw logistics management, supervision, and coordination for all sections of the largest non-divisional Class II, III, IV, and VII supply point in Bosnia. In an operation which exceeded $75 million annually in supplies, I oversaw activities ranging from personnel supervision, to procurement, to the management of the receipt, storage, and issuance of supplies to supported customers. I obtained required supplies through standard military procedures as well as from local sources.

Education and Training Related to this KSA:
In addition to earning my Bachelor of Arts degree from Eastern Michigan University in Ypsilanti (2002) and an Associate of Arts degree from Henry Ford Community College (7/01), have also attended the following colleges and universities: Brigham Young University, Laie, Hawaii, 1999, nine semester hours; McNeese State University, Lake Charles, LA, 1997, nine semester hours; Military training programs I completed included the following:

> the Contracting Officer Representative Course and a Management and Leadership workshop, US Army Quartermaster School
> Introduction to Management in Logistics and Introduction to Defense Financial Management correspondence courses
> Tactical Army Combat Service Support computer System/Standard Army Retail Supply System-1 (TACCS/SARSS-1) Supervisors Workshops
> Logistics Applications Automated Marking and Symbols (LOGMARS)
> Decentralized Automated Service Support Systems (DAS-3)
> Direct Support Unit Standard Supply System (DS-4) Management Course
> Division Logistics Property Book Management Course

SUPPLY SUPERVISOR

KENNETH S. MOSLEY

SSN: 000-00-0000

SUPPLY SUPERVISOR, GS-07/11 ANNOUNCEMENT #XYZ123

KSA #2: Knowledge of Supply Management Logistical Support Functions such as Supply, Procurement, Transportation, Cataloguing, Provisioning, Storage, and Distribution.

In my current position as a Supervisory General Supply Specialist since 6/01, I apply my knowledge of supply management logistical support functions while managing, directing, and implementing supply and services functions throughout the U.S. and the Middle East. With approximately 95 members of a multinational workforce under my supervision, I manage a wide range of activities which include subsistence requisitioning, transportation, storage, accountability, and the preparation of materials for storage, transportation, and utilization. While planning and directing financial management and operational programs for the Supply and Services Division, I oversee logistical support functions such as supply, procurement, transportation, cataloguing, provisioning, storage, and distribution. I oversee these activities in areas as diverse as the Central Issue Facility, laundry, Installation Property Book Office, Self Service Supply Center, graves registration, retail fuel operations, and organizational property book operations.

From 04/00 until 11/01 as a Supervisory Inventory Management Specialist, directed day-to-day operations in a Commodity Management Branch. Supervised 20 Item Managers and applied my knowledge while seeing that they maintained, adjusted, and established requisition objectives, retention levels, maintenance work requests, and the proper disposition of serviceable and unserviceable assets.

On the basis of my knowledge of logistical support functions, I was hand-picked as a Branch Chief for a Material Management Center in Bosnia, supervising as many as 20 employees while directing and approving local purchase activities related to procuring perishable and semi-perishable food products. I was selected because of my reputation for expertise in analyzing, managing, coordinating, and procuring any type of product including subsistence. I continuously directed, coordinated, and evaluated the findings of management studies which had been designed to evaluate performance and identify system improvements.

Due to my extensive knowledge of supply management logistical support functions, I was selected for what was essentially a top-level consulting/staff position as a Storage Specialist in a Defense Logistics Agency Stockpile Depot (8/94 to 5/95). I analyzed the effectiveness of existing supply, procurement, transportation, cataloguing, provisioning, storage, and distribution procedures, conducting formal and informal management studies to evaluate overall performance of systems and to identify improvements. By troubleshooting problems with existing systems and suggesting solutions I was able to increase the level and quality of assistance available to customers and effect more efficient service delivery.

On another occasion, from April 1991-November 1992 I took over as Supply Management Officer at a time when the operation was plagued with chronic backlogs of maintenance jobs, with some jobs more than 90 days late. The backlogs, as well as serious malfunctions and shortages in the supply system which caused stockouts and downtime, were having a strong negative impact on military services readiness and causing extreme customer dissatisfaction. I planned and directed assigned missions of Area V retail supply, supervising and guiding the work of 125 warehouse personnel, including eight supply managers and four maintenance managers. To deal with this situation, I analyzed supply pipeline problems, production schedules, shop stock levels, and the excess repair parts program in order to develop more effective methods of managing these areas. Prioritized various projects, including requirements determination, maintenance operations, forecasting, procurement, and financial management. Delegated tasks to the supervisor who was most capable of quickly and effectively dealing with a given situation. Maintained open lines of communication between my office and personnel at all levels. Provided "leadership by example" and conducted myself in a reasonable and consistent manner, ensuring that all employees were treated fairly by all levels of management. Gained the trust and respect of warehouse, maintenance and support personnel. I improved the profitability of Area V retail supply activities while reducing stockouts and inventory carrying costs, as well as increasing customer satisfaction and service delivery. By cutting costs while increasing overall efficiency, was able to obtain the maximum benefit from available human, physical, and financial resources.

Education and Training Related to this KSA:
In addition to earning my Bachelor of Arts degree from Eastern Michigan University in Ypsilanti (2002) and an Associate of Arts degree from Henry Ford Community College (7/01), have also attended the following colleges and universities: Brigham Young University, Laie, Hawaii, 1999, nine semester hours; McNeese State University, Lake Charles, LA, 1997, nine semester hours; Military training programs I completed included the following:

  the Contracting Officer Representative Course and a Management and Leadership
  workshop, US Army Quartermaster School
  Introduction to Management in Logistics and Introduction to Defense Financial
  Management correspondence courses Tactical Army Combat Service Support
  computer System/Standard Army Retail
  Supply System-1 (TACCS/SARSS-1) Supervisors Workshops
  Logistics Applications Automated Marking and Symbols (LOGMARS)
  Decentralized Automated Service Support Systems (DAS-3)
  Direct Support Unit Standard Supply System (DS-4) Management Course
  Division Logistics Property Book Management Course

SUPPLY SUPERVISOR

KENNETH S. MOSLEY

SSN: 000-00-0000

SUPPLY SUPERVISOR, GS-07/11 ANNOUNCEMENT #XYZ123

KSA #3: Knowledge of DoD Major Supply Program Goals, Objectives, Work Processes, and Administrative Operations.

Throughout my extensive career in military and civilian logistics support, I was frequently placed in "hot-seat" management jobs in charge of logistics management and was often handpicked to act as a consultant for special projects. In these roles, I have consistently demonstrated my knowledge of DoD major supply program goals, and objectives, as well as of work processes and administrative operations.

From February 2001 to August 2001, I was asked to assume leadership of the Armament & Combat Vehicle Division for the Middle Eastern Materiel Management Center at a time when this center was experiencing low morale, lagging productivity, and unacceptable customer support levels. I was selected for this position because of my reputation as an effective leader and innovative problem-solver. As Chief of the Armament and Combat Vehicle Division, (GS-10), I established free and open lines of communication among Management Center command staff, local Bosnian National employees, and U.S. military personnel. While emphasizing a Total Quality Approach to management, I established a dialog which enabled me to develop a team approach to problem analysis and problem solving. Through retraining of existing staff; providing fair, consistent supervision; and the implementation of a viable awards program, I improved productivity throughout the organization. I designed and implemented procedures to reward to excellent performers while offering firm but tactful counseling for marginal performance. Utilized group activities such as Division meetings, Division picnics, and other in-house promotions to foster a team atmosphere and strengthened the bond between co-workers. Within a few weeks, I had quickly gained the respect of Division personnel and improved the morale and productivity of Management Center employees. Productivity nearly doubled, customer satisfaction soared, and the general attitude of the Center's staff reflected a confident, competent, and professional work force. The 13 Bosnian managers, master sergeant, and two Bosnian junior employees I managed significantly improved their ability to efficiently handle the requisitioning, redistribution, and excess turn-in of assets valued at more than $425,000.

On another occasion, from April 1991 - November 1992, took over as Supply Management Officer at a time when the operation was plagued with chronic backlogs of maintenance jobs, with some jobs more than 90 days late, as well as serious malfunctions and shortages in the supply system causing stockouts, downtime, and extreme customer dissatisfaction. As Supply Management Officer, planned and directed assigned missions of Area V retail supply, supervising and guiding the work of 125 warehouse personnel, including eight supply managers and four maintenance managers. Analyzed supply pipeline problems, production schedules, shop stock levels, and excess repair parts program in order to develop more effective methods of managing these areas. Prioritized various projects, including requirements determination, maintenance operations, forecasting, procurement, and financial management. Delegated tasks to the supervisor who was most capable of quickly and effectively dealing with a given situation. Maintained open lines of communication between my office and personnel at all levels. Gained the trust and respect of warehouse, maintenance and support personnel. Improved the profitability of Area V retail supply activities while reducing stockouts, decreasing inventory carrying costs, and boosting customer satisfaction. Reduced costs while increasing overall efficiency, obtaining the maximum benefit from available human, physical, and financial resources.

As a Supply/Maintenance Management Officer for the 14th Support Battalion, I was asked to plan, organize, and direct the close-out of an Army Area Supply Depot for Class II, III (P), IV, VII, and IX supplies in a Theater downsizing initiative, without compromising the service to or Combat Readiness of existing customers. To comply with Theater downsizing initiatives, planned and executed the closure of a Major Supply Point while assuring uninterrupted service to all customers. Planned and directed all aspects of the transfer of all on-hand stocks to another Army Supply Point and set up a Central Receiving Point that is still in operation. Developed internal and external Standing Operating Procedures and organized the structure of the transportation network to support the operations in an armistice and combat environment. Planned, organized, and directed briefings for General Level Officers on my planning matrix for the project and gained direct approval to execute this plan. Assured careful planning and implementation of procedures used to transport HAZMAT materials. Resolved numerous problems and overcame multiple complexities in directing this major project under tight deadlines in such a way that Combat Readiness was not compromised. Over 25 manned positions were phased out, resulting in a $1.3 million savings per year, without negatively impacting the level of service provided to the Customers or degrading their Combat Readiness. Millions of dollars in assets were transferred safely, a new service center was opened, and an inefficient site was closed with no loss of customer service.

Education and Training Related to this KSA:

In addition to earning my Bachelor of Arts degree from Eastern Michigan University in Ypsilanti (2002) and an Associate of Arts degree from Henry Ford Community College (7/01), have also attended the following colleges and universities: Brigham Young University, Laie, Hawaii, 1999, nine semester hours; McNeese State University, Lake Charles, LA, 1997, nine semester hours; Military training programs I completed included the following:

 the Contracting Officer Representative Course and a Management and Leadership workshop, US Army Quartermaster School
 Introduction to Management in Logistics and Introduction to Defense Financial Management correspondence courses
 Tactical Army Combat Service Support computer System/Standard Army Retail Supply System-1 (TACCS/SARSS-1) Supervisors Workshops
 Logistics Applications Automated Marking and Symbols (LOGMARS)
 Decentralized Automated Service Support Systems (DAS-3)
 Direct Support Unit Standard Supply System (DS-4) Management Course
 Division Logistics Property Book Management Course

SYSTEMS ANALYST

MICHAEL DENNIS

SSN: 000-00-0000

SYSTEMS ANALYST, GS-09 ANNOUNCEMENT #XYZ123

KSA 1: ABILITY AND WILLINGNESS TO ACCEPT RESPONSIBILITY AND MAKE DECISIONS. Describe experiences (work, school or others) in which you have volunteered or been required to accept responsibility and/or make decisions either independently or with minimal supervision.

It is my style to make decisions carefully, after extensive analysis and thorough investigation. After graduating from the University of Delaware, I decided to relocate, and I carefully embarked upon the process of deciding which company I wanted to work for. After extensive analysis, I decided that Amtrak was the best employer in Baltimore, MD and I performed the networking which led to my employment in 2001 as an Electronic Commerce Analyst and Systems Analyst. In the same fashion, I have decided to seek employment with Department of the Interior.

Throughout my tenure at AMTRAK, I have become known for my eager acceptance of additional responsibilities and I have consistently volunteered for involvement in as many projects as I could. Although I enjoyed the "textbook training" I received in college, I feel there is no better teacher than hands-on experience, and I have valued my ability to increase my knowledge through hands-on problem solving experience which I have gained because I have volunteered for additional projects and responsibilities during one of the busiest times in the company's history. In my current position, I shoulder a large amount of responsibility and yet work with little to no supervision. I am proud of the fact that I was selected as Amtrak's "Employee of the Year", and this recognition was due in part to my ability and willingness to accept responsibility and make decisions.

A situation which illustrates my willingness to accept responsibility as well as my ability to make decisions is a current project for which I volunteered which involves the responsibility for automating incidental billing for the AMTRAK North-Atlantic Region. This is a high-profile assignment with vast implications and, if executed well, the bottom line will save AMTRAK considerable operating expenses and produce increased revenue. As the sole implementer of this project for the North-Atlantic Region, I have become one of the most requested customer service providers available for any issues that may arise, and I am frequently in a position in which I must make logical and common-sense decisions which balance customer needs with company requirements. I am entrusted with complete decision-making authority and am essentially in a policymaking role since so many of my decisions pertain to issues which are in "uncharted territory." An example of such an issue concerned a large timber customer. This customer was the recipient of poor service and was not receiving empty railcars. This was causing the customer to switch more and more of its business to the trucking industry. On my own initiative, I investigated the reason for the declining service and I discovered a forecasting issue which the customer was not aware of.

Education and Training related to this KSA:
Bachelor of Science degree in Business Administration, Newark, DE, 1999.
Received Advanced Management-Level training and ATK Electronic Operation training from Amtrak Rail Services, 2001.

KSA 2: ABILITY TO READ AND INTERPRET WRITTEN INSTRUCTIONS, POLICIES AND PROCEDURES.

KSA 2: ABILITY TO READ AND INTERPRET WRITTEN INSTRUCTIONS, POLICIES AND PROCEDURES. Describe situations in which you have had to read and interpret different types of written material (instructions, policies and/or procedures). Be specific about instances where such instructions were not detailed, specific enough or were confusing. What steps did you take to clarify and execute those instructions in order to obtain desired results?

I have earned a Bachelor of Science degree in Business Administration with a concentration in Management which required me to refine to a very high level my ability to read and interpret written instructions, policies, and procedures. In the process of creating written products and analyzing case studies, I refined my analytical skills and written communication skills to a high level.

The major part of my current job as a Systems Analyst involves working with problem resolution and customer satisfaction concerns. On most occasions, I am alerted to problems and issues via direct e-mailings to me or through help desk tickets which I retrieve off an electronic database. Therefore, my ability to read and interpret written instructions, policies, and procedures is critical to my success on a daily basis. By the time I assume responsibility for an issue, several people have handled the original communication, and numerous people have failed to find a solution. This can lead to key bits of information having been eliminated or reworded due to various interpretations and suggestions by various parties down the line. Many times, the underlying issue is quite vague and I am left having to start fresh from the beginning. It is my responsibility to clarify the exact issue and formulate a resolution plan. I often have to perform extensive investigative work in order to trace the problem to its root symptoms and earliest manifestations.

A recent example which illustrates my ability in this area concerns an e-mail that I received from upper management. The issue concerned poor bill of lading data that a customer was submitting. Not being a subject matter expert in this area, I was confused as to what the immediate issue was and what exactly I was looking for. The written communication was confusing and lacking in specifics. My first step was to seek out a known expert in this area. Upon receiving clarification, I was able to see the underlying concern. I was then able to recommend and implement changes in this customer's bill of lading patterns. Upon apprising the customer of the situation, he understood that his bills of lading needed to be generated using my suggested format, and I took the time to train the customer in the proper paperwork procedures so that written communication would be clear and obtain the desirable results in a timely fashion. All future bills have successfully interfaced in our computer systems.

Education and Training related to this KSA:
Bachelor of Science degree in Business Administration, Newark, DE, 1999.
Received Advanced Management-Level training and ATK Electronic Operation training from Amtrak Rail Services, 2001.

SYSTEMS ANALYST

MICHAEL DENNIS

SSN: 000-00-0000

SYSTEMS ANALYST, GS-09 ANNOUNCEMENT #XYZ123

KSA 3. ABILITY TO INTERPRET AND FOLLOW ORAL INSTRUCTIONS.

Describe instances (work, school, or other) where you had to follow oral instructions. Be specific about experiences where such instructions were not detailed, not specific enough, or were confusing. What steps did you take to clarify and execute those instructions in order to obtain desired results?

Both in college and at work, I have had numerous opportunities to refine my ability to interpret and follow oral instructions while also achieving much success due to my skill in these areas. At the University of Delaware, where I majored in Business Administration, large lecture-style classes allowed me to enhance my listening skills, and I refined my ability to focus attentively on key issues while listening carefully in order to cull the important information. Subsequently in my first job as a Systems Analyst and Electronic Commerce Analyst with AMTRAK Technology, I have utilized my ability to interpret and follow oral instructions while providing superior customer service, taking the initiative to reduce operating expenses, and converting new corporate customers to new systems. I have applied my ability to interpret and follow oral instructions while participating in the development of functional and technical design documents and developing/presenting product presentations to customers. In planning and facilitating numerous team meetings, I have applied my strong skills related to interpreting and following oral instructions.

Early in my career at AMTRAK, I volunteered to take a new job assignment which presented me with an opportunity to utilize my oral communication skills in order to benefit my employer. The assignment required me to maintain several Intranet databases and mainframe computer systems, and the training required me to sit with the soon-to-be-departing co-worker and listen as she explained the job process. There was no written documentation on the process; she had been performing the job for several years and, although the process had become routine to her, she provided sparse and incomplete details of how the process worked. Therefore, I received rather incomplete training. This became clear when I actually assumed full responsibility for the task. With incomplete written notes that I had taken while processing her oral communication, I decided quickly that I needed to seek expert guidance in order to clarify the process. I sought out the administrators of the databases to identify what exact steps were necessary to complete my new job task. After approaching the process in this investigative and analytical fashion, I was able to discover the insights and details I needed in order to see how the process worked as a whole. After I gained a comprehensive understanding of the process, I was then able to work at an even higher level of activity in which I combined my initiative and creativity with my refined understanding of the process. I successfully implemented a change that significantly reduced the processing time and, with a quicker processing time, my department was able to function in a more effective and efficient manner.

Education and Training related to this KSA:
Bachelor of Science degree in Business Administration, Newark, DE, 1999.
Received Advanced Management-Level training and ATK Electronic Operation training from Amtrak Rail Services, 2001.

KSA 4: ABILITY TO WRITE LOGICALLY - SEQUENCED REPORTS. Describe experiences (work, school, or other) where you were required to research, prepare, and write logically sequenced reports. Specify positions you have held (volunteer, paid, self-employed) where your writing skills proved to be a factor in your success (i.e. writing for student/commercial newspaper, etc.).

Throughout my academic career, I was required to provide written reports and documentation. In college, many classes required me to write case studies. To complete these studies, it was required that I do much research and preparation in order to reach an effective conclusion. Since I obtained a Bachelor of Science degree with a concentration in Business Management from the University of Delaware, I spent significant portions of my time as a college student writing logically sequenced reports, researching problems, and authoring papers presenting issues, conclusions, and recommendations.

During college, I took a senior-level management class which required me to develop extensive written materials. I was required to analyze American Airlines position in the commercial aviation industry and make suggestions which would strengthen the company's market position. After reading and research, I conducted a thorough investigation that utilized several different resources. I then culled all of the pertinent information and assessed the most pertinent issues and variables. I then developed conclusions and generated suggestions which would be in the best economic and marketing interests of American Airlines. My efforts resulted in not only an 'A' for the project, but also an 'A' in the class.

In my current position as a Systems Analyst at AMTRAK Technology, I routinely write logically sequenced reports and provide written documentation of any tasks that I perform. I have also played a key role in the development of functional and technical design documents. Many of the reports I complete on a routine basis include step-by-step "what if..." and "if/then..." flowcharts. It is necessary that these documents be written in a clear and concise manner as these are used in the training sessions for any new employees in my department. Another documentation task I perform routinely is to provide monthly progress reports to customers. These reports document all railroad activity pertaining to a particular site for a given month, and they help to provide the customer with a written document which details the resolution of a problem from start to finish. As these reports are presented to the customer, as well as upper management, they must be concise, factual, and to the point. I have frequently been commended for my excellent written communication skills including my ability to communicate technical and complex issues in a clear, straightforward fashion which can be utilized for management decision making.

Education and Training related to this KSA:
Bachelor of Science degree in Business Administration, Newark, DE, 1999.
Received Advanced Management-Level training and ATK Electronic Operation training from Amtrak Rail Services, 2001.

TRAINING INSTRUCTOR

JESSE BLAKE
SSN: 000-00-0000
TRAINING INSTRUCTOR, GS-09 ANNOUNCEMENT #XYZ123

KSA #1: Ability to Communicate in Writing.

In my present job as an Instructor, Staff Group Leader Intern since 10/03, I apply my communication skills while performing all duties of a military instructor including, but not limited to, serving as a mentor and facilitator for a student staff group. One of my main responsibilities is in the area of developing and implementing training plans which includes developing, creating, and preparing written materials as well as multimedia and slide presentations using Microsoft Office applications, including Word, PowerPoint, and Excel. In addition, I interpret and apply Department of the Army (DA) curriculum guidelines, integrate this additional material into the lesson plans and other written course materials that I develop. Also conduct assessments of full group and small group performance within all measured proficiencies, preparing a variety of written reports documenting my findings and delineating areas where improvements are needed.

As a Senior Simulations Coach/Assistant Operations Officer from 8/00 to 10/03, I planned, prepared, and conducted computer simulation staff training exercises for reserve, active duty, and National Guard commands, producing a wide range of written course materials. Planned, wrote, coordinated, and executed exercises, preparing written training materials and supplementary documentation used to train assigned personnel and client unit personnel in computer simulations.

As a Senior Instructor, SIM Coach, and Assistant Operations Officer from 5/98 to 8/00, performed instructional and administrative duties for a 425-person Battle Command Staff Simulation Brigade.

As Chief, Lessons Learned Division from 7/95 to 5/98, reviewed and analyzed doctrinal issues as they pertained to tactics and fielding of new equipment.

As a Small Group Instructor, from 7/92 to 7/95, developed written lesson plans and other materials, prepared for and taught classes, evaluated and counseled students, and participated in all phases of their training.

Throughout my extensive career as a military officer, I have demonstrated my exceptional written communication skills while preparing a wide variety of written reports and other materials, such as Officer and Non-Commissioned Officer Evaluation Reports, recommendations for awards, and other narrative material.

Education and training related to this KSA:
My formal education includes:
M.A. Middle Ages Education, Kentucky State University, 2002.
M.P.A., Public Administration, Morehead State University, 1999.
B.A., Political Science and History, Johnson C. Smith University, 1997.
I completed extensive training with the U.S. Army which included:
Total Army Instructor Training, 1996.

KSA#2: Ability to Communicate Orally.

In my present job as an Instructor, Staff Group Leader Intern since 10/03 I apply my verbal communication skills while performing the duties of a military instructor including, but not limited to, serving as a mentor and facilitator for a student staff group. One of my main responsibilities is in the area of developing and implementing training plans, I present course materials orally in lecture format, through question-and-answer sessions, and through role playing. Also conduct assessments of full group and small group performance within all measured proficiencies. As an instructor in a professional educational program for military executives, I communicate daily with students, other instructors, and staff personnel.

As a Senior Simulations Coach/Assistant Operations Officer from 08/00 to 10/03, I planned and conducted computer simulation staff training exercises for reserve, active duty, and National Guard commands. Conducted daily instruction sessions for assigned personnel and client unit personnel, training them using both prepared materials and computer simulations such as Corps Battle Simulations (CBS), Brigade/Battalion Simulations (BBS), and Spectrum. The latter is a computer simulation which develops both military and civilian staff members in disaster relief and humanitarian support.

As a Senior Instructor, SIM Coach, and Assistant Operations Officer from 5/98 to 8/00, performed administrative and instructional duties for a 425-person Battle Command Staff Simulation Brigade. Exercised my oral communication skills while conducting counseling sessions with individual students as well as during tutoring sessions and other additional one-on-one instruction for students who were having difficulties with the course materials.

As a Small Group Instructor, from 7/95 to 5/98, led and trained a small group of from 15 to 25 new second lieutenants who were students in the Officer Basic Course at the Army's Quartermaster School. Oversaw all aspects of their combined training, leadership development, physical conditioning, and welfare. Taught numerous classes, providing students with counseling and evaluation related to both personal and professional matters, and participated in all phases of their training. Was cited in an official evaluation for being able to step in and begin the effective training of two small groups. As an Air Defense Artillery Combat Trainer from 7/92 to 7/95, observed, analyzed, and trained all maneuver units in the continental United States in the application of current air defense doctrinal procedures to increase preparation for actual combat through coaching which provided realistic battlefield effects/simulations and in-depth debriefing seminars.

Education and training related to this KSA:
My formal education includes:
M.A. Middle Ages Education, Kentucky State University, 2002.
M.P.A., Public Administration, Morehead State University, 1999.
B.A., Political Science and History, Johnson C. Smith University, 1997.

Many people feel that their "dream job" would be a job working for the U.S. Postal Service. If you wish to apply for employment with the U.S. Postal Service, the forms 171 or 612 or the federal resume are, as of this date, the basic application with which you would apply for work. Getting a full-time job in the postal service right "off the bat" can be very difficult. Part-Time Flex (PTF) and Rural Carrier positions are the majority of the jobs available. The Veterans Administration and the local Employment Security Commission handle the "casual" or part-time positions, so they are your best points of initial contact. On rare occasions, where a job is hard to fill, a full-time postal service job will be posted in the newspaper.

If you are trying to get your foot in the door at the Post Office, you would be well advised to consider applying for any type of part-time or casual position, even if they are not what you are ideally looking for. As in most organizations, it is easier to move around and transfer into a better job once you are "in the system." Although there are few full-time jobs available to outsiders, once you get inside the postal service, there are many openings that become available. Once you are inside the system, you apply for other positions with the form 991, which is shown on the next two pages.

You might be interested to learn what happens once you submit your 171 or 612 in hopes of being tapped for a postal service position. Human Resources at a central location will screen all the 171s (or 991s, if you're already in the system), and up to five people will be chosen to interview for the position. A three-person board of local postal personnel will actually do the interviewing; one of the interviewers will be from Human Resources and the other two will be people who are knowledgeable of the position being filled. Bear in mind that there can be very long lead times throughout this whole process. But let's assume that you are one of those selected for the interview. After the interview, the board will make a decision on whom to hire, and you will receive a phone call if you are selected. If you are not selected, you will learn by mail. Background checks and physical exams requested will be paid for by the USPS.

If you are lucky enough to get an interview, you need to understand that a post office interview is like any other interview. You are trying to sell yourself! Since it may have been a long time (months probably) between submitting your paperwork and interviewing for the job, it's wise to prepare for the interview by reading the KSAs you submitted. Sample KSAs are also shown in this section. The U.S. Postal Service may request that you demonstrate your knowledge, skills, or abilities by presenting your information within a precise framework referred to as "STAR." STAR stands for Situation, Task, Action, and Result, and you are asked to describe a situation or event in which you did, said, produced, or accomplished something which illustrated your level of proficiency related to that KSA. Postal Service KSAs based on the STAR format can be shorter than KSAs for other federal service jobs. Often a single incident will reveal your competence in a certain area. Remember here to be very detailed, and try to make sure that you clearly show the result you were able to achieve by your involvement in the situation or event you are describing. In KSAs for non-postal service jobs, you often need to "translate" jargon into language that can be understood by others. For example, military professionals need to make sure that their experience is "translated" into terminology that civilians can understand. In the case of postal service KSAs, however, you are often writing about very technical matters for an audience that is very familiar with the "language" of the postal service, so you can feel comfortable using technical terminology and acronyms.

POSTAL KSAS

KAREN SWAIN

SSN: 000-00-0000

ISS/REC SUPERVISOR · ANNOUNCEMENT #XYZ123

**ISS/REC Supervisor
Announcement #XYZ123
Management KSA #1**

KSA #1: Knowledge of data entry operations, including an understanding of production, quality control methods, and procedures

The two situations described below illustrate my knowledge as well as my ability to expertly apply my knowledge in this area.

While supervising on the ISS operation at the Boston P & DC, I detected that the Return to Sender mail was being incorrectly keyed. I notified the MDO that the mail was being misdirected because the REC keyers could not see the RTS stamp. I furthermore contacted the MDO at the REC and informed her that all of the images should be keyed as RTS until further notice. I also notified the ET to disconnect the ISS from the REC in order to prevent current mail from being combined with the RTS mail. **Result: This action on my part prevented loop and misdirected mail of the Return to Sender.**

During my detail as acting supervisor at the BREC, I reviewed the accuracy rates of all employees assigned to my pay location. I began daily edits for players who were below the 98% accuracy requirement. I also talked with each employee, addressing their errors. During these discussions, I discovered that many of the keyers were unclear on the coding rules. I took the time to explain the rules and made sure they understood what they were supposed to do. **Result: At the end of my assignment, there was a major improvement in the quality of those employees' performance, and this action on my part further resulted in providing the BREC with highly valuable keyers who were subsequently considered expert at their jobs.**

KSA #2: Ability to quickly and efficiently respond to fluctuations in work load requirements and utilize employees and equipment accordingly

There are three situations which demonstrate my ability to quickly and efficiently respond to fluctuations in work load requirements and utilize human and physical resources appropriately.

There were occasions when the Cambridge P & DC experienced power outages preventing images from transferring to the Boston REC. On one such occasion, I had approximately 80 keyers under my supervision and a rapidly decreasing mail volume from Cambridge due to the disconnection. Since we support three (3) other plants, I contacted each and advised them of our situation with the Cambridge plant. I requested that they send all the mail they had in their facility to be processed by the ISS. I had all available consoles switched from Cambridge to accommodate the other three (3) plants. **Result: This action allowed early clearance for the three plants. Upon reconnection to Cambridge, I was able to place all keyers on Cambridge consoles and this action on my part prevented a plant failure.**

While working as the ISS Supervisor at the Boston plant, I was notified that we would be receiving mail from the Cambridge plant to process. I reassigned employees at the other operations to relieve those operating the ISSs during lunch and breaks to ensure a continuous operation. I also contacted the Boston REC and requested maximum number of keyers to contend with the extra mail volume. **Result: This action allowed us to process all the mail in our operation and prevented plant failure.**

While assigned as a 204-B at the Boston REC, I was monitoring the Westchester plant status reports when I noticed that we had a very low volume of images to process. The plant's projections reflected a high volume of mail to be processed and identified the need for the maximum number of keyers to be assigned to our consoles. I informed the plant of the situation and requested that they turn off the RCR, thereby permitting a quicker transfer of images. **Result: This action on my part allowed us to process all the images and meet the plant's clearance time.**

POSTAL KSAS

KAREN SWAIN

SSN: 000-00-0000

ISS/REC SUPERVISOR · ANNOUNCEMENT #XYZ123

KSA #3: Ability to forecast mail volume and work force requirements

The three situations described briefly below illustrate my ability to predict future mail volume and human resources needs.

While working as the ISS Supervisor at the Cape Cod plant, I was notified that we would be receiving mail from the Westchester plant to process. I reassigned employees at the other operations to relieve those operating the ISSs during lunch and breaks to ensure a continuous operation. I also contacted the Cape Cod REC and requested maximum number of keyers to contend with the extra mail volume. **Result: This action allowed us to process all the mail in our operation and prevented plant failure.**

There were occasions when the Cambridge P & DC experienced power outages preventing images from transferring to the Boston REC. On one such occasion, I had approximately 80 keyers under my supervision and a rapidly decreasing mail volume from Cambridge due to the disconnection. Since we support three (3) other plants, I contacted each and advised them of our situation with the Cambridge plant. I requested that they send all the mail they had in their facility to be processed by the ISS. I had all available consoles switched from Cambridge to accommodate the other three (3) plants. **Result: This action allowed early clearance for the three plants. Upon reconnection to Cambridge, I was able to place all keyers on Cambridge consoles and this action on my part prevented a plant failure.**

While assigned as a 204-B at the Cape Cod REC, I was monitoring the Westchester plant status reports when I noticed that we had a very low volume of images to process. The plant's projections reflected a high volume of mail to be processed and identified the need for the maximum number of keyers to be assigned to our consoles. I informed the plant of the situation and requested that they turn off the RCR, thereby permitting a quicker transfer of images. **Result: This action on my part allowed us to process all the images and meet the plant's clearance time.**

KSA #4: Ability to prepare, maintain, and interpret reports related to productivity, work hours, mail volume, operating budget, injuries and accidents, and time and attendance

**ISS/REC Supervisor
Announcement #XYZ123
Management KSA #4**

The three situations described below illustrate my ability pertaining to this requirement/factor.

While working as the ISS Supervisor at the Boston plant, I was notified that we would be receiving mail from the Westchester plant to process. I reassigned employees at the other operations to relieve those operating the ISSs during lunch and breaks to ensure a continuous operation. I also contacted the Boston REC and requested maximum number of keyers to contend with the extra mail volume. **Result: This action allowed us to process all the mail in our operation and prevented plant failure.**

While assigned as a 204-B at the Boston REC, I was monitoring the Cambridge plant status reports when I noticed that we had a very low volume of images to process. The plant's projections reflected a high volume of mail to be processed and identified the need for the maximum number of keyers to be assigned to our consoles. I informed the plant of the situation and requested that they turn off the RCR, thereby permitting a quicker transfer of images. **Result: This action on my part allowed us to process all the images and meet the plant's clearance time.**

There were occasions when the Cape Cod P & DC experienced power outages preventing images from transferring to the Boston REC. On one such occasion, I had approximately 80 keyers under my supervision and a rapidly decreasing mail volume from Cape Cod due to the disconnection. Since we support three (3) other plants, I contacted each and advised them of our situation with the Cape Cod plant. I requested that they send all the mail they had in their facility to be processed by the ISS. I had all available consoles switched from Cape Cod to accommodate the other three (3) plants. **Result: This action allowed early clearance for the three plants. Upon reconnection to Cape Cod, I was able to place all keyers on Cape Cod consoles and this action on my part prevented a plant failure.**

POSTAL KSAS

KAREN SWAIN
SSN: 000-00-0000
ISS/REC SUPERVISOR · ANNOUNCEMENT #XYZ123

**ISS/REC Supervisor
Announcement #XYZ123
Management KSA #5**

KSA #5: Ability to manage the work of others to meet productivity, safety, and quality goals, including scheduling, coordinating, monitoring, and evaluating the work

The four situations below illustrate my ability pertaining to this requirement/factor.

During my detail as acting supervisor at the Boston REC, I reviewed the accuracy rates of all employees assigned to my pay location. I began daily edits for players who were below the 98% accuracy requirement. I also talked with each employee, addressing their errors. During these discussions, I discovered that many of the keyers were unclear on the coding rules. I took the time to explain the rules and made sure they understood what they were supposed to do. **Result: At the end of my assignment, there was a major improvement in the quality of those employees' performance, and this action on my part further resulted in providing the BREC with highly valuable keyers who were subsequently considered expert at their jobs.**

During my tour at the BREC, I received a request for more keyers for the Cambridge plant in order to compensate for the arrival of late mail to be processed by the ISS. I consulted with the Boston plant and, due to their low volume of mail, I was able to provide Cambridge with more keyers. **Result: The increase in keyers to the Cambridge plant allowed us to process the mail in a timely manner.**

While in a supervisory position at the BREC, I was responsible for employee performance evaluations in my assigned pay location. For the majority of my tour, there was one other supervisor and myself monitoring the work floor. In order for us to perform our evaluations, we would rotate in order to supervise productivity and meet with our employees. **Result: By working together, this allowed us to complete our job requirements in a timely manner with the added result that morale and productivity increased because of employees' perception that we were listening to them and concerned with establishing and maintaining harmonious work relationships.**

During my employment as the Training Instructor for Boeing Support Systems, I was responsible for the supervision and instruction of prospective Data Conversion Operators. With individuals working at their own pace, I was required to work one-on-one in their training to ensure their understanding of the coding rules. **Result: As a result, the last 190 employees hired by Boeing were under my instruction, and many hold positions now with the U.S. Postal Service at the Boston REC.**

KSA #6: Ability to establish and maintain effective team and individual work relationships with employees, other managers, and union representatives

The four situations below illustrate my ability pertaining to this requirement/factor.

During my detail as acting supervisor at the Boston REC, I reviewed the accuracy rates of all employees assigned to my pay location. I began daily edits for players who were below the 98% accuracy requirement. I also talked with each employee, addressing their errors. During these discussions, I discovered that many of the keyers were unclear on the coding rules. I took the time to explain the rules and made sure they understood what they were supposed to do. **Result: At the end of my assignment, there was a major improvement in the quality of those employees' performance, and this action on my part further resulted in providing the BREC with highly valuable keyers who were subsequently considered expert at their jobs.**

While in a supervisory position at the BREC, I was responsible for employee performance evaluations in my assigned pay location. For the majority of my tour, there was one other supervisor and myself monitoring the work floor. In order for us to perform our evaluations, we would rotate in order to supervise productivity and meet with our employees. **Result: By working together, this allowed us to complete our job requirements in a timely manner with the added result that morale and productivity increased because of employees' perception that we were listening to them and concerned with establishing and maintaining harmonious work relationships.**

While supervising at the Boston REC, I was often responsible for establishing the master edits to be utilized in monitoring employee performance. On one such occasion, employees argued that an image did not appear in its entirety on their monitors. Upon hearing their dissatisfaction with the edit, I requested the "ET" to bring the image up on these monitors and adjust the screen in all directions to give the keyers every possible view. **Result: After seeing that the image was clearly visible, the employees were satisfied with the edit results, and this situation resulted in a more harmonious working environment.**

During my employment as the Training Instructor for Boeing Support Systems, I was responsible for the supervision and instruction of prospective Data Conversion Operators. With individuals working at their own pace, I was required to work one-on-one in their training to ensure their understanding of the coding rules. **Result: As a result, the last 190 employees hired by Boeing were under my instruction, and many hold positions now with the U.S. Postal Service at the Boston REC.**

POSTAL KSAS

KAREN SWAIN

SSN: 000-00-0000

ISS/REC SUPERVISOR · ANNOUNCEMENT #XYZ123

**ISS/REC Supervisor
Announcement #XYZ123
Management KSA #7**

KSA #7: Ability to implement and monitor building, equipment, and systems maintenance activities and programs

The two situations below illustrate my ability pertaining to this requirement/factor.

While supervising at the Boston REC, I was often responsible for establishing the master edits to be utilized in monitoring employee performance. On one such occasion, employees argued that an image did not appear in its entirety on their monitors. Upon hearing their dissatisfaction with the edit, I requested the "ET" to bring the image up on these monitors and adjust the screen in all directions to give the keyers every possible view. **Result: After seeing that the image was clearly visible, the employees were satisfied with the edit results, and this situation resulted in a more harmonious working environment.**

While assigned as a 204-B at the Boston REC, I was monitoring the Cambridge plant status reports when I noticed that we had a very low volume of images to process. The plant's projections reflected a high volume of mail to be processed and identified the need for the maximum number of keyers to be assigned to our consoles. I informed the plant of the situation and requested that they turn off the RCR, thereby permitting a quicker transfer of images. **Result: This action on my part allowed us to process all the images and meet the plant's clearance time.**

KSA #8: Ability to communicate effectively in order to train and give guidance to employees

The three situations below illustrate my ability pertaining to this requirement/factor.

During my employment as the Training Instructor for Boeing Support Systems, I was responsible for the supervision and instruction of prospective Data Conversion Operators. With individuals working at their own pace, I was required to work one-on-one in their training to ensure their understanding of the coding rules. **Result: As a result, the last 190 employees hired by Boeing were under my instruction, and many hold positions now with the U.S. Postal Service at the Boston REC.**

During my detail as acting supervisor at the BREC, I reviewed the accuracy rates of all employees assigned to my pay location. I began daily edits for players who were below the 98% accuracy requirement. I also talked with each employee, addressing their errors. During these discussions, I discovered that many of the keyers were unclear on the coding rules. I took the time to explain the rules and made sure they understood what they were supposed to do. **Result: At the end of my assignment, there was a major improvement in the quality of those employees' performance, and this action on my part further resulted in providing the BREC with highly valuable keyers who were subsequently considered expert at their jobs.**

While in a supervisory position at the BREC, I was responsible for employee performance evaluations in my assigned pay location. For the majority of my tour, there was one other supervisor and myself monitoring the work floor. In order for us to perform our evaluations, we would rotate in order to supervise productivity and meet with our employees. **Result: By working together, this allowed us to complete our job requirements in a timely manner with the added result that morale and productivity increased because of employees' perception that we were listening to them and concerned with establishing and maintaining harmonious work relationships.**

POSTAL KSAS: SUPERVISOR

NESTOR HERNANDEZ

SSN: 000-00-0000

Supervisory KSA #1

KSA #1: ORAL COMMUNICATIONS: Ability to communicate information, instructions, or ideas orally in a clear and concise manner in individual or group situations

Situation #1: In April 1997, in my capacity as Platform Supervisor, I observed that platform clerks were not following the posted work schedule. We were short manpower in the bullpen which delayed the unloading of incoming mail trucks.

Action: I used my oral communication skills to locate a platform clerk who was not following the posted schedule and who was not in his assigned position. I utilized tact, instructional techniques, and motivational skills to inform and persuade this worker about the importance of his precisely following the work schedule.

Result: As a result of my oral communication effectiveness:
- The trucks were able to be unloaded on schedule, and
- The worker gained a new appreciation of how much he was needed in the position for which he was assigned. I was proud that I was able to achieve this result while actually improving worker morale and making the worker aware of his importance to the overall mission.

Situation #2: With the implementation of the RBCS mail flow, it became imperative that we increase the percentage of mail canceled everyday to forty percent. It then became my job to inform and motivate my crew to achieve the desired cancellations rate by 1800.

Action: To accomplish this mission, I held a service talk and informed my crew of the new goals and explained to them the new methodology that would be used to get the job done. I stressed the importance of gathering all raw mail from behind each star route as it arrives rather than staging the containers. I also identified the mail in a central location. After the talk and the change in the way of identifying staging the raw mail, my crew achieved the 40 percent cancellations rate for two consecutive weeks.

Result: After the initial two weeks of the new cancellation program, there was some fluctuating in the obtainment of the forty percent goal due to experimentation with manpower needs. However, the foundation was set to achieve the goal on a consistent basis which is now the situation.

KSA #2: LEADERSHIP: Ability to direct or coordinate individual or group action in order to accomplish a task or goal

Situation #1: In February 1999, in my capacity as Manual Operation Supervisor, I was responsible for staffing all floor functions, which included the box section, letter case, city bump table, damaged mail, priority, outgoing and secondary letters, and SCF. This involved the assignment of tasks to 20 individuals. On February 15, 1999, a key employee involved in customer service called in sick, thereby causing serious strain on the SCF operation with the potential of causing numerous customer problems.

Action: I realized that there was no one trained to perform the job of the individual on sick leave. Therefore, utilizing my leadership and decision-making abilities, I developed a plan to assure productivity. I identified a clerk who was, in my opinion, rapidly trainable. I immediately gave this clerk a "crash course" in the handling of large parcels and completing paperwork, and I utilized my leadership ability to provide this individual with the confidence to do this job for which he had no prior training.

Result: All parcels were posted with no diminishing of customer service or customer satisfaction.

Situation #2: While detailed to the Supervisor of Distribution Operations position from June 15, 1998 to September 5, 1998, we were having trouble making timely dispatches from all machines.

Action: I examined possible causes of the problem and devised a new methodology on how to solve the problem. I ensured that prior to each dispatch, the sweeper would pull the dispatch ten minutes before and stage it for the expediter.

Result: Consequently, dispatch discipline improved and overnight ODIS scores for our neighboring MSC improved.

Supervisory KSA #3

KSA #3: HUMAN RELATIONS: Ability to interact tactfully and relate well with others

Situation #1: In January 1999, in my capacity as Manual Operation Supervisor, I experienced a situation which tested my human relations skills. An employee whom I supervise approached me with a complaint that he was not called in to arrive two hours early for overtime, although his fellow workers had been called. This employee emphasized that this had happened several times previously. The employee was highly agitated and distressed.

Action: I immediately decided to assign a Shop Steward to hear his grievance. The Shop Steward and employee had a discussion which lasted approximately 15 minutes, after which I was called into the office to join the Shop Steward and the employee. When I was asked by the Shop Steward to recommend a course of action, I offered to let the employee work an extra two hours of overtime at the end of his tour on that day and come in two hours early the next day.

Result: The employee was satisfied with the solution I recommended, and he also seemed very pleased with the fact that we took prompt action to listen to his complaint. Therefore, this matter was resolved in a manner which maximized human relations effectiveness within the post office.

Situation #2: While detailed to the Supervisor of Distribution Operations position on the platform, I was confronted with a situation when an important task came up and a spontaneous job reassignment had to be made to cover the emergency. I reassigned an employee to solve the problem; however, I failed to notify his group leader that I had reassigned him. As a result, the group leader became upset and accused the subordinate that I reassigned of being malevolent. I immediately became aware that I had made a mistake by not informing the reassigned employee's group leader of his new status.

Action: I immediately pulled both employees to the side and apologized for not using the chain of command before making the reassignment. As a result of our conversation, it became apparent that this was a common occurrence that had caused problems in the past.

Result: The result of the meeting was that a new awareness was created concerning the importance of using the chain of command in making personnel changes and a better working environment was created.

NESTOR HERNANDEZ

SSN: 000-00-0000

KSA #4: PROBLEM ANALYSIS: Ability to analyze problems, work performance, suggestions, and complaints by listening, observing, gathering, organizing, and interpreting information

Situation #1: In October 1999, in my capacity as Manual Operation Supervisor, I observed a problem which could have caused serious detriment to productivity. Specifically, outgoing and surface mail were being left behind on the SCF cases. I further observed that a lot of mail was Atlanta-postmarked for that day.

Action: I immediately organized personnel to pull down the surface and outgoing mail and take it back to the outgoing operation to be finalized for dispatch. This was accomplished without detriment to any other internal activities.

Result: All Atlanta-postmarked mail was finalized and dispatched on time, thereby assuring outstanding customer service.

Situation #2: On a reoccurring basis, we were finishing our 892 program well after our scheduled cutoff time.

Action: The first thing I did was to analyze the mail flow to see what was causing the problem. My investigation showed that the late allocation of keyers by the Rec Site after 2250 was creating an avalanche of excessive 892 mail that could not be processed timely before cutoff time on one DBCS. I decided that in order to meet cutoff time, I needed to start another DBCS at 2100. This adjustment allowed us to clear our volume by 2230. It did, however, create more tied-out bundles for the airlift sacks due to the fact that full trays were not created on second DBCS by the end of distribution. It did ensure, however, that all overnight surface mail was finalized by cutoff time.

Result: The final outcome of the decision was to have 892 mail distributed and ready for dispatch in a timely manner and enhanced service standards not only for overnight delivery but also for two-day and three-day delivery.

POSTAL KSAS: SUPERVISOR

NESTOR HERNANDEZ

SSN: 000-00-0000

KSA #5: DECISION MAKING: Ability to develop plans, evaluate their anticipated effectiveness, make decisions, and take appropriate action

Situation #1: In July 1998, in my capacity as Manual Operation Supervisor, I observed that a large volume of mail was being sent to the Manual Cases from Automation at the end of each tour. This practice had caused our efficiency rate to plummet to an all-time-low of 83%!

Action: I tracked the mail and found that three-day states mail was weighed to the outgoing operation. The mail was then counted as a Plan Failure and delayed volume and recorded on the DMCR. After determining that these flawed procedures were causing the problem, I made prudent decisions to remedy the inefficiency. Specifically, I decided that immediate and intensive retraining or workers in the proper procedures was in order. I trained several manual runners in operations such as weight scales and opening unit codes. This retraining was accomplished carefully over a two-week period.

Result: The manual runners were trained to recognize their own mail and place mail pieces in the correct operation, thereby reducing Plan Failures and the delayed volume. The result was that efficiency soared to an acceptable 92% and increased gradually thereafter until achieving a 98% efficiency rate.

Situation #2: We were experiencing difficulties with not clearing the 971 mail in a timely manner and I had to come up with a plan or identify how we could clear 971 OG more efficiently.

Action: At 5 P.M. I started up outgoing and by doing so, it allowed the (LSM) letter sorting machine to get rejects earlier while also allowing me to clear my 971 operation earlier. In addition 892 outgoing operation also was able to receive their mail in a timely fashion.

Result: As a result of this procedure we have been meeting our clearance time and two-day state mail and surface dispatch has vastly improved.

KSA #6: WRITTEN COMMUNICATIONS: Ability to write letters, simple reports, and employee evaluations clearly and effectively and to complete standardized reporting forms accurately

Situation #1: In my capacity as Supervisor, I am responsible for preparing employee evaluations. This is a tool utilized to ascertain if the employee is compatible with postal standards. On one occasion I prepared a written employee evaluation which identified numerous deficiencies and errors in the employee's work habits, including such things as a lack of focus on key tasks which resulted in unacceptable efficiency.

Action: I prepared an employee evaluation and provided oral feedback in a counseling session. At first the employee was distressed to see his faults identified specifically and in writing. However, I emphasized that his flaws could be improved and made recommendations for his improved efficiency.

Result: This employee, with my help and leadership, learned the scheme in half the time and became one of our main keyers for local mail. This result occurred because I prepared precise, detailed, and constructive written communication which helped transform this employee from a marginal to an excellent and highly motivated worker.

Supervisory KSA #7

KSA #7: MATHEMATICAL COMPUTATIONS: Ability to perform addition, subtraction, multiplication, and division with whole numbers, fractions, and decimals

Situation #1: End-of-run reports have to be turned in each day to in-plant support. These reports have to contain accurate counts of Express Mail pieces, Parcel Post, and mail left on the floor. In my capacity as Platform Supervisor in May, 1997, I observed an employee who was dispatching mail without taking count of the city parcel post mail. At the end of this particular day, therefore, I had no mathematical calculations to turn in.

Action: I immediately trained this employee in performing correct addition computations.

Result: As a result, I obtained computations so that I could perform the necessary advanced mathematical computations including subtraction, multiplication, and division in order to prepare end-of-run reports.

Situation #2: A part of my duties when supervising the ISS System is to keep a continuous count of my own time, the image generation rate of mail I am running, the amount of images on hand, and the keying rate of the DCOs at the Rec Center.

Action: In order to do this, I constantly have to calculate percentages and convert my findings into projections that allow me to process the mail by clearance time. To do this I keep a count of my script and meter volume and then multiply these different volumes by the image that will be generated. I then add this estimate to the images already in the system. Once I obtain this figure, I multiply the keying rate of DCOs by the number of Keyers I have allocated. By doing this, I get an idea of how long it will take me to process my on-hand volume and how much volume I will need to divert to downstream operations in order to meet my clearance time. By using this procedure, I have been able to project my processing window accurately on a consistent basis. This has facilitated our ability to clear our mail in a timely fashion. For example: When I took over the buffer on the ISSs from Tour II, I had 38,348 images with 42 DCOs keying at 894 images per hour. In the next hour, if they maintained their keying rate I could process 37,548 images per hour stage. In front of ISS was approximately 500 feet or approximately 125,000 pieces of script mail. Using a 65% image generation rate I calculated that I could generate an additional 81,250 pieces of mail by adding the buffer count to the projected images.

Result: I came up with a total of 119,598 images, and I had three hours and eleven minutes run time. I added another twenty minutes run time to compensate for breaks by the DCOs; that gave me a total of 3 hours and thirty minutes run time. Therefore, I could run to 1830 with on-hand volume without having to divert to MPLSM.

NESTOR HERNANDEZ

SSN: 000-00-0000

KSA #8: SAFETY: Knowledge of safety procedures needed to ensure that safe working conditions are maintained. Included is knowledge of the procedures and techniques established to avoid injuries. Also included is knowledge of normal accident prevention measures and emergency procedures

Supervisory KSA #8

Situation #1: In August 1998, accidents were on the increase, primarily with regard to APCs and BMCs. The injuries sustained caused more than seven days absence for one individual as well as numerous lost days for other individuals.

Action: I identified that the safety problems were occurring because employees were not operating the equipment properly. I immediately instituted refresher safety classes for employees. I determined that there was a need for employees to learn proper techniques of safely operating heavy equipment. I and other supervisors took turns teaching those safety classes each month.

Result: There was an immediate decrease in the number of safety accidents and incidents, and there was a cost savings because of fewer man-hours lost due to injuries. Employees became skilled in identifying damaged equipment and quickly removing the dangerous equipment from the floor, thereby anticipating potential safety problems.

Situation #2: Within a short period of time, we had a rash of accidents concerning the proper usage of all-purpose containers. All of the accidents revolved around the proper securing of the top shelf and the proper closing and securing of the top gate.

Action: On my own initiative I held a safety briefing on the proper usage of all-purpose containers. I explained the importance of securing the top shelf in the "up" position by making sure that all restraints were used and properly seated to prevent the shelf from accidentally falling. I also stressed the point that the top gate should be securely seated and checked before moving. I added that if any of the safety devices were defective, that the container would be tagged orange and put out of circulation until it was properly fixed by maintenance.

Result: By monitoring the usage of all-purpose containers and making on-the-spot corrections when they were discovered to be mishandled, I was able to eliminate all-purpose container accidents under my supervision.

ABOUT THE EDITOR

Anne McKinney holds an MBA from the Harvard Business School and a BA in English from the University of North Carolina at Chapel Hill. A noted public speaker, writer, and teacher, she is the senior editor for PREP's business and career imprint, which bears her name. Early titles in the Anne McKinney Career Series (now called the Real-Resumes Series) published by PREP include: *Resumes and Cover Letters That Have Worked, Resumes and Cover Letters That Have Worked for Military Professionals, Government Job Applications and Federal Resumes, Cover Letters That Blow Doors Open,* and *Letters for Special Situations.* Her career titles and how-to resume-and-cover-letter books are based on the expertise she has acquired in 20 years of working with job hunters. Her valuable career insights have appeared in publications of the "Wall Street Journal" and other prominent newspapers and magazines.

PREP Publishing Order Form

You may purchase any of our titles from your favorite bookseller! Or send a check or money order or your credit card number for the total amount*, plus $4.00 postage and handling, to PREP, 1110 1/2 Hay Street, Fayetteville, NC 28305. You may also order our titles on our website at www.prep-pub.com and feel free to e-mail us at preppub@aol.com or call 910-483-6611 with your questions or concerns.

Name: _____

Phone #:_____

Address: _____

E-mail address:_____

Payment Type: ☐ Check/Money Order   ☐ Visa   ☐ MasterCard

Credit Card Number: _____ Expiration Date: _____

Put a check beside the items you are ordering:

☐ Free—Packet describing PREP's professional writing and editing services

☐ $16.95—REAL-RESUMES FOR RESTAURANT, FOOD SERVICE & HOTEL JOBS. Anne McKinney, Editor

☐ $16.95—REAL-RESUMES FOR MEDIA, NEWSPAPER, BROADCASTING & PUBLIC AFFAIRS JOBS. Anne McKinney, Editor

☐ $16.95—REAL-RESUMES FOR RETAILING, MODELING, FASHION & BEAUTY JOBS. Anne McKinney, Editor

☐ $16.95—REAL-RESUMES FOR HUMAN RESOURCES & PERSONNEL JOBS. Anne McKinney, Editor

☐ $16.95—REAL-RESUMES FOR MANUFACTURING JOBS. Anne McKinney, Editor

☐ $16.95—REAL-RESUMES FOR AVIATION & TRAVEL JOBS. Anne McKinney, Editor

☐ $16.95—REAL-RESUMES FOR POLICE, LAW ENFORCEMENT & SECURITY JOBS. Anne McKinney, Editor

☐ $16.95—REAL-RESUMES FOR SOCIAL WORK & COUNSELING JOBS. Anne McKinney, Editor

☐ $16.95—REAL-RESUMES FOR CONSTRUCTION JOBS. Anne McKinney, Editor

☐ $16.95—REAL-RESUMES FOR FINANCIAL JOBS. Anne McKinney, Editor

☐ $16.95—REAL-RESUMES FOR COMPUTER JOBS. Anne McKinney, Editor

☐ $16.95—REAL-RESUMES FOR MEDICAL JOBS. Anne McKinney, Editor

☐ $16.95—REAL-RESUMES FOR TEACHERS. Anne McKinney, Editor

☐ $16.95—REAL-RESUMES FOR CAREER CHANGERS. Anne McKinney, Editor

☐ $16.95—REAL-RESUMES FOR STUDENTS. Anne McKinney, Editor

☐ $16.95—REAL-RESUMES FOR SALES. Anne McKinney, Editor

☐ $16.95—REAL ESSAYS FOR COLLEGE AND GRAD SCHOOL. Anne McKinney, Editor

☐ $25.00—RESUMES AND COVER LETTERS THAT HAVE WORKED. McKinney. Editor

☐ $25.00—RESUMES AND COVER LETTERS THAT HAVE WORKED FOR MILITARY PROFESSIONALS. McKinney, Ed.

☐ $25.00—RESUMES AND COVER LETTERS FOR MANAGERS. McKinney, Editor

☐ $25.00—GOVERNMENT JOB APPLICATIONS AND FEDERAL RESUMES: Federal Resumes, KSAs, Forms 171 and 612, and Postal Applications. McKinney, Editor

☐ $25.00—COVER LETTERS THAT BLOW DOORS OPEN. McKinney, Editor

☐ $25.00—LETTERS FOR SPECIAL SITUATIONS. McKinney, Editor

☐ $16.95—REAL-RESUMES FOR NURSING JOBS. McKinney, Editor

☐ $16.95—REAL-RESUMES FOR AUTO INDUSTRY JOBS. Patty Sleem

☐ $24.95—REAL KSAS--KNOWLEDGE, SKILLS & ABILITIES--FOR GOVERNMENT JOBS. McKinney, Editor

☐ $24.95—REAL RESUMIX AND OTHER RESUMES FOR FEDERAL GOVERNMENT JOBS. McKinney, Editor

☐ $24.95—REAL BUSINESS PLANS AND MARKETING TOOLS ... Samples to use in starting, growing, marketing, and selling your business

_____ **TOTAL ORDERED**

_____**(add $4.00 for shipping and handling)**

_____**TOTAL INCLUDING SHIPPING**

PREP offers volume discounts on large orders. Call us at (910) 483-6611 for more information.

THE MISSION OF PREP PUBLISHING IS TO PUBLISH
BOOKS AND OTHER PRODUCTS WHICH ENRICH
PEOPLE'S LIVES AND HELP THEM OPTIMIZE THE
HUMAN EXPERIENCE. OUR STRONGEST LINES ARE
OUR JUDEO-CHRISTIAN ETHICS SERIES AND OUR
REAL-RESUMES SERIES.

Would you like to explore the possibility of having PREP's writing
team create a resume for you similar to the ones in this book?

For a brief free consultation, call 910-483-6611
or send $4.00 to receive our Job Change Packet to
PREP, 1110 1/2 Hay Street, Fayetteville, NC 28305. Visit our
website to find valuable career resources: www.prep-pub.com!

QUESTIONS OR COMMENTS? E-MAIL US AT PREPPUB@AOL.COM